EUI – Series C – 5.1
Rudolf Wildenmann (Gen. Ed.)
The Future of Party Government
Vol. 1: Castles/Wildenmann (Eds.), Visions and Realities
of Party Government

European University Institute
Institut Universitaire Européen
Europäisches Hochschulinstitut
Istituto Universitario Europeo

Series C

Political and Social Sciences
Sciences Politiques et Sociales
Politik- und Sozialwissenschaften
Scienze Politiche e Sociali

5.1

Badia Fiesolana — Firenze

The Future of Party Government

A Series under the General Editorship of
Rudolf Wildenmann

Volume 1

Visions and Realities of Party Government

edited by
Francis G. Castles and Rudolf Wildenmann

1986

Walter de Gruyter · Berlin · New York

Library of Congress Cataloging-in-Publication Data

The Future of party government.
(Series C--Political and social sciences = Sciences politiques et sociales ; 5)
"A series under the general editorship of Rudolf Wildenmann."
Includes index (v. 1).
Contents: v. 1. Visions and realities of party government / edited by Francis G. Castles and Rudolf Wildenmann.
1. Political parties--Europe--Addresses, essays, lectures. 2. Europe--Politics and government--1945– --Addresses, essays, lectures. I. Wildenmann, Rudolf. II. Series: Series C--Political and social sciences ; 5.
JN94.A979F88 1986 324.24 86-2030
ISBN 0-89925-162-5 (v. 1)

CIP-Kurztitelaufnahme der Deutschen Bibliothek

The future of party government : a ser. under the general editorship of Rudolf Wildenmann. – Berlin ; New York : de Gruyter
(European University Institute : Ser. C, Political and social sciences ; 5)
NE: Wildenmann, Rudolf [Hrsg.]; Istituto Universitario Europeo ⟨Fiesole⟩: European University Institute / C
Vol. 1. Visions and realities of party government. – 1986

Visions and realities of party government / ed. by Francis G. Castles and Rudolf Wildenmann. – Berlin ; New York : de Gruyter, 1986.
(The future of party government ; Vol. 1) (European University Institute : Ser. C, Political and social sciences ; 5)
ISBN 3-11-010651-5
NE: Castles, Francis G. [Hrsg.]; Istituto Universitario Europeo ⟨Fiesole⟩: European University Institute / C

Dust Cover Design: Rudolf Hübler, Berlin. – Setting and Printing: Arthur Collignon GmbH, Berlin. – Binding: Verlagsbuchbinderei Dieter Mikolai, Berlin.
Printed in Germany.

Preface

This is the first volume to appear from a major research project on *The Future of Party Government* directed by Professsor Rudolf Wildenmann and supported by the European University Institute (EUI). The primary objectives of the project as a whole were an analysis of the problems confronted by party government — the predominant institutional form of contemporary democratic government — in the modern state and an assessment of the probable and possible developmental tendencies of that institutional form.

The scope of such an endeavour is quite enormous, requiring, as it does, a review of contemporary social and political theory, the development of new concepts and the analysis of existing ones, a study of contemporary government in a large number of countries and an attempt, through comparative analysis, to locate patterns of similarity and difference in respect of such matters as structural development, political behaviour, policy-making and the emergence and possible resolution of the problems of modern industrial societies. It may be objected that the scope is too great and it verges on arrogance to bring so much within the compass of a single research project. But our justification is that these issues — and, most precisely, the linkages between them — are crucial to an understanding of the strengths and frailties of democratic government. It may be arrogant to attempt such a study; it is an abdication of scholarly and democratic responsibility not to do so!

Nevertheless, even with the very large group of European and American scholars who have participated in various aspects of this project in the period 1980-84, it was necessary to attempt to keep things within a reasonable compass. Thus, for instance, our discussion of democratic theory is specifically related to the problems of contemporary democratic states and we have not attempted to enter into any debate concerning normative goals or the history of ideas. Similarly, rather than develop any comprehensive social theory, we have located our analysis in an exposition of the difficulties faced by governments in the modern state. Further, we have been most fortunate in being in a position to build our analysis on a firm foundation of previous scholarship on a variety of aspects of the party government problematic provided by other recent research projects. These include a number of studies sponsored by the European Consortium for Political Research on "Recent Changes in Party Systems" (directed by Hans

Daalder, Mogens Pedersen and Rudolf Wildenmann), "Centre-periphery Problems" (Stein Rokkan and Derek Urwin), "Local Government" (Ken Newton), "Government Overload" (Richard Rose) and "Party Differences and Public Policy" (Francis G. Castles), as well as other studies on "European Elections" (Karlheinz Reif) and on elites in the Federal Republic of Germany (Rudolf Wildenmann, Max Kaase and Ursula Lange-Hoffman).

Many of the findings of the project on *The Future of Party Government* have already been published in journal articles or as working papers.

The first two major volumes of research appear in the form of this volume on "Visions and Realities" and a volume soon to be published, which brings together a number of country studies, examining the nature of party government in a number of modern states, including France, Britain, the United States, Germany, Italy, the Scandinavian countries and Switzerland. These two volumes are specifically interlinked, insofar as the hypotheses advanced and the concepts developed in the first volume are investigated, developed and refined in the individual country studies of the second volume. Subsequent volumes are likely to investigate a number of issues concerning political mobilisation and political legitimacy, which emerge from the research as being of primary importance in understanding problems of contemporary democratic government. Other projected volumes include one on contemporary approaches to the analysis of public policy, emphasising those problems which arise in times of crisis and dilemmas of welfare and warfare, and another on the relationship between political elites and masses. A further study will focus on the way in which European integration has influenced the nature of party government and the nature of the emergent relationships between the EC and the national governments. A final volume called "Learning Democracy" will deal with basic cleavage problems in modern society, evaluating existing approaches to the problems of "interests", mapping out the basic needs and attributing them to the various parties in different countries, whilst also trying to simulate possible scenarios of the development of party government with the major variables identified, thus contributing to the general "relative" theory of democratic government.

The guiding principles of the EUI are rightly insistent that major research projects of this kind should include substantial involvement by doctoral students. In furtherance of this idea more than ten individual dissertations on various themes connected with the project are currently under preparation by research students at the Institute.

This first volume on "Visions and Realities" attempts to encompass several objectives. First Rudolf Wildenmann's essay on "The Problematic of Party Government" sets out the programmatic agenda for the project as a whole: what are the problems faced by democratic party government in the late twentieth century and how may they best be resolved? The first step in that process is to clarify the whole host of concepts that surround the notions of democratic party government (see essay by Dick Katz) and political problem-solving (Gunnar Sjöblom). A further step is to identify the linkages between party government and its capacity to resolve problems with the major institutional features of political organisation in modern societies. Here, we single out for particular analysis the impact of electoral and constitutional structures on the effectiveness of party government (Gianfranco Pasquino) and the problem of whether the bureaucratic structure of contemporary states is any longer controllable by the democratic parties (Giorgio Freddi). Finally, we turn to the emergence, maintenance and possible disappearance of democratic party governments. Giuseppe di Palma examines a variety of scenarios by which party government has arisen in the post Second World War period and identifies their strengths and weaknesses, and Gordon Smith, in a concluding essay, looks to the future to establish the parameters within which we may legitimately speculate concerning the developmental tendencies of party government.

The scholars connected with the project wish to thank the European University Institute and its governing bodies, especially the Academic Council and the Research Council, for the encouragement and support given to the project. Not only did the EUI provide the necessary funds for the project for three years, but it also proved to be a most appropriate place to carry out such a project, both in its institutional concept as a research institute and for the charming and intellectually stimulating atmosphere at the Badia Fiesolana, San Domenico, Firenze.

The Director of the project owes very special gratitude to the two Presidents of the EUI who were in office during the lifetime of the project. In the first year Max Kohnstamm with his immense experience in European affairs, his dedication to humanity, democracy and peace, his common sense and his loyalty to the Institute and its members, after some hesitation regarding the scope of the project, initiated the pilot phase and thereafter often demonstrated his faith in the research group. After the change in the presidency, Werner Maihofer put his full weight behind the project. Being a philosopher of law – most particularly, a philosopher of liberal democracy – he immediately realised the intrinsic value of the project and rendered most valuable advice and help. Also having had vast experience in government, he contributed in his own very special and personal way to the understanding of the problems of the research itself. Almost two decades of cooperation between Werner Maihofer and Rudolf Wildenmann since the time of the student unrest in the sixties (in fact a turning point for contemporary political and democratic values) proved to be a strong intellectual and emotional basis for a concern for the future of democratic government.

The research group also appreciates the assistance of ZUMA (Centre for Surveys, Methods and Analysis at Mannheim) in developing methodological tools and processing data and especially the help of Manfred Küchler, the then Acting Director of ZUMA.

We wish to record our special thanks to Luciano Bardi who made a very major contribution by facilitating the academic coordination of the project.

We also give our thanks for the professional administrative support we received from staff at the EUI, especially from the Publications Officer, Brigitte Schwab, and would express our gratitude to Rosmarie Wildenmann, who contributed very much to the final reading of the manuscripts and the proofs and who also prepared the index. Last but not least we owe much gratitude to our two secretaries: Maureen Lechleitner in the Department of Political Science and Elizabeth Webb, the project secretary. Their contribution was far beyond the call of normal duty. Not only did they cope in a dedicated and cheerful way with a never-ending flow of manuscripts from all quarters of the globe, but they also managed to resolve the many problems of the numerous scholars visiting the Badia during the life of the project.

The Director of the project gives his thanks to all the members of the research group who gave so freely of their time, experience and scholarship in pursuit of the development of this joint research endeavour. On behalf of all the contributors, he wishes to express his sincere thanks to Francis G. Castles for his enormous intellectual input and his painstaking efforts as the editor of this first volume. He also wishes to record his personal thanks to Francis G. Castles who transformed his German English into the idiomatic original English of his thoughts.

Francis G. Castles
Rudolf Wildenmann

Table of Contents

Chapter I

The Problematic of Party Government

RUDOLF WILDENMANN

Contents

I. The Problem

"The party state — and is there any alternative?" ("*Parteienstaat — oder was sonst?*") was the title Wilhelm Grewe gave his article, very influential in Germany in the fifties (Grewe, 1951). In it, he argues that the epoch of "democracy of the notables" is past and offers a programmatic presentation of the view that not only must democracy be representative, but governments must, like parliaments, derive from political parties. Rather similar ideas were expressed in other quarters; for example by Gerhard Leibholz, who became one the most eminent theorists of the party state concept, and through the Party Commission of the Federal Ministry of the Interior directed by Wilhelm Scheuner. To Grewe, the "integration of the state" could not be sought in a reassertion of the "Reich idea", the revival of the specifically German, romantic idealist ideology which Hugo Preuss had attempted to achieve in his draft constitution for the Weimar Republic, but must come through the dominant political activity of the parties: *sine parte nulla salus*.

By the time that Grewe's article was written, in fact, not only had parties been reorganised or refounded in the Federal Republic — following authorisation procedures by the American, British and French military governments – but a new party system had emerged with three distinct political groupings: the Christian Democratic Union (CDU) and its Bavarian counterpart (CSU), the Social Democrats (SPD) and the (Liberal) FDP (cf. Wildenmann, 1954). In reality, Germany in the period from 1949 to 1957 saw the emergence of a system of party government and Grewe, Leibholz, Scheuner and others were acknowledging the normative force for German constitutional law of this *de facto* development. Yet what the Federal Republic was doing, in its own particular way, was but a reiteration of developments that had already occurred in other European nations or was, at least, occurring simultaneously. In Western Europe after the Second World War, two-party, multi-party and many-party systems became the rule – and still are. The British system of government, The "Westminster Model" was seen by many as the model of "party government", and its advocates in the British military administration in Germany had successfully propagandised its virtues. The French Fourth Republic continued – with only a few alterations in the rules of the political game – the tradition of party parliamentarianism begun in the Third Republic. In the Benelux countries, Scandinavia and Ireland, multi-party systems formed the central core of the "ruling organisation". In Italy after 1943 there had been constituted, following more than twenty years of Fascism, a new multi-party system. Austria, following a phase of "black-red" coalition (i. e. joint government by the ÖVP and SPÖ), developed by the mid-sixties a type of party government which is not only formally similar to that of the Federal Republic, but also similar in having three distinct party groupings.

More significant than the fact that most Western European countries had developed articulated party systems in the years after the Second World War was the fact that *party government* had itself become the norm – i. e. party had become the preeminent institution of political rule – although the extent of "partyness of government", to use Richard Katz's term, differed markedly from country to country (see Katz, 1982; also below, Chapter II). The trend was to continue with Spain and Portugal abandoning authoritarian for party government in the seventies. Paradoxically, de Gaulle's attempt through the restructuring of the Fifth Republic to end the "rule of the parties" led to the transformation of French party parliamentarianism into an unambiguous party government (cf. Reif, 1983). Among the industrialised democracies, only two countries stand out as exceptions: Switzerland and the United States. The quasi "directorially" governed democracy of Switzerland, with its strong plebiscitary institutions and its specific federalism, does not meet the criteria for party government set out by Katz (see pp. 43–44 infra). In the USA, the two-party system which developed after the Jacksonian era – especially in respect of presidential elections – dominates the scene, and it does fulfil one important criterion insofar as the most important posts in the bureaucratic hierarchy are filled by party members or supporters of the incoming President.

However, the specific political coordination organised along party lines and through democratic parliamentary institutions, along lines familiar in Britain, Austria, the Federal Republic or France, is clearly missing in the USA. Governing by changing majorities is the rule in both the USA and Switzerland; nevertheless, the American President with his kitchen cabinet recruited along party lines, for the most part, exercises a central role.

In contemporary industrial societies, democracy is generally conceived of as party government, whatever other structural constitutive elements may influence or bring about political opinion formation. In such societies, it is to the parties' leading staff organisations that the central role of coordination and aggregation of interests, mediation of social values and political decision-making devolves, and this is clearly the more so for the parties in government. Moreover, this pivotal role is intensified both because of the sharp rise in governments' power to dispose of the national product and to allocate and transfer resources through budgets and because of the extension of politics into virtually every sphere of modern life, not excepting the Church and cultural institutions. Thus, the future of democracy has become closely bound up with the future of party government.

However, in the meantime, party government has become burdened with many new problems over and above the general problems inherent in government as such. A distinct section of the younger generation — and, indeed, some of their elders — dispute both its legitimacy and its ability competently to resolve what they consider to be the most vital issues of our times. The precise nature of the relationship between party government and other important societal organisations has been the subject of much speculation, not all of it comforting; as, for instance, the suggestion that neo-corporatist forms of decision-making, involving the collusion of parties and major organised societal interests, are subversive of democratic participation (cf. Schmitter, 1982). Moreover, the nature of information processes in countries with party government are becoming progressively more complex and difficult (see Wildenmann, 1983). Newly developed communications structures pose conundrums: do they make it more likely that political actors will be able to use their greater control of information to manipulate the populace, or can they, by providing greater openness and a wider breadth of offerings, give greater scope for critical reasoning in the formation of political opinion? Indeed, even greater availability of information at a popular level might not be an unmixed blessing, if problems of selecting information and 'overload' led to a mass retreat into apathy!

Finally, many important political decisions have been shifted out of the realm of government proper. Thus, monetary policy becomes chiefly the concern of central banks, fundamental evaluative decisions fall within the domain of constitutional courts and even the implementation of policy ceases to be exclusively a matter for government agencies, but becomes to varying degrees a matter for quasi-governmental bodies and for self-regulation within and between major organised collectivities. The diversification and differentiation of executives and legislatures into specialised institutions and the consequent "mixed" implementation of political decisions give governmental systems a new quality. Very often coordination of goals, purposes or measures is lacking under such circumstances, which in turn increases the general uncertainty of political decisions and may lead to policies with effects diametrically opposed to those intended. Certainly, the contemporary literature on policy formulation is replete with examples of phenomena of this kind.

Thus, we are confronted with a fundamental problem. The party government idea is the major component of our conception of functioning democracy and the party government model is in diverse forms the common core of political organisation in modern industrial societies. Yet, in its contemporary workings, party government is beset by difficulties; whilst seemingly ubiquitous, it may perhaps have a greater burden of responsibility than a real ability to shape or change matters. Certainly, the degree to which the domain of party government has been and is being eroded as a consequence of the problems sketched above and the extent to which parties may have ceased to be the influential organs for the coordination and definition of issues requires much further empirical study. The project on *The Future of Party Government*, of which this book is but the first part, is premised in the view that the discussion and explanation of these issues requires both historical and systematic treatment. The broken relationship between normative theories of democracy (see Maihofer, 1983) and the realities revealed by the sociology of governmental power — a clear instance of the schizophrenia of political understanding — further makes it essential to take a concrete rather than an abstract approach, since social, economic, technical, scientific and cultural developments, each moving in different directions and at different speeds, interact to create situations, the understanding and explanation of which create specific intellectual problems. Hence democracy as such, and especially contemporary party government, can only be analysed by means of theories of sufficient complexity to capture the reality of such situations.

II. The Roots of Party Government

The primary objective of this introductory essay is to explore the main outlines of the problematic of party government, many aspects of which will be taken up in much greater detail in the analytical and country-by-country volumes which constitute the body of the research project on the *The Future of Party Government*. In particular, we shall here have something to say about the historical development of the party government form of democratic organisation, the conditions under which it is maintained and the kinds of conflict which characterise it. Further, we shall examine some of the major dimensions of the problems that confront contemporary party government – most notably, recruitment and selection problems, the development of the mass media and growing international penetration. We then turn our attention to the future prospects of party government and advance a number of criteria by which further development may be judged.

In proceeding to examine the historical development of party government, an essential first step is to clarify somewhat both the concept of the modern "state" and that of "party government" itself. Max Weber's classical definition of the modern state identifies a number of important elements which he combines into an ideal type; that is, inductively derived generalisations from the past – frozen history, as it were. By "state" (*Herrschaftsverband*) he denotes a "ruling organisation" characterised by a legal order – a distinct national system of laws and jurisprudence. The defining criteria of administration in the modern state are generality, equality of treatment, hierarchical structure, specialisation of function and a more or less intensive confidentiality. The ruling organisation controls the currency, the taxation system, public order, public works and the social services (in contemporary terms, the welfare state). Most important of all, however, in Weber's view, the ruling organisation of the modern state has a monopoly of the exercise of force, and it is this monopoly, in particular, which creates its need for legitimacy. Heuristically, this definition of the "state" is still extremely valuable and contemporary discussions of the concept start from Weber not merely out of deference to the history of ideas. Nevertheless, it is important to stress that, in its general as well as in its particular national manifestations, the empirical reality of the modern state manifests great deviations from and complex intertwinings of the various features located by Weber in his ideal type, which was itself more than somewhat influenced by the Prussian-German context in which it was created.

From our standpoint, Weber's analysis of the structure of the ruling organisation of the modern state neglects certain aspects crucial to an understanding of party government, particularly in a contemporary context. Most important, his concept of state does not differentiate between democratic (i. e. rational) ruling organisations and those based on charismatic or traditional legitimation, and the definition does not cover what Weber described as "organisations of violence" (a term he used of the CPSU of his own times). Moreover, understandably enough in the context of a conceptualisation drawn at the time of the ending of the First World War, a variety of international developments influencing the nature and functioning of the contemporary state are not foreshadowed. We shall return to this question of the international context of the modern state, since the contemporary problem of party government is very much a function of these developments of the post Second World War era.

Party government is the crucial agency of institutional legitimisation in democratic ruling organisations, distinguishing the democratic modern state from other types. It arises, despite all its varied manifestations in the different European countries, from a number of fundamental and similar developments since the French Revolution, the constitutional watershed of modern times. More than the American Revolution which preceded it, it sets the contemporary value horizon of European politics with its highly charged concepts of "liberty, equality, fraternity" and its demand for control of the rulers by the ruled. It was from the French Revolution that there developed those energies which have since made democracy as a social belief the dominant theme of subsequent political developments and political revolutions in a process of internalisation of values which has been universal in extent. At the same time, the idea of popular government formulated in the United States of 1776 has been taken up institutionally and constitutionally, finding its typical expression in the division of powers.

It is from this latter development that parliaments, chambers, or whatever the assemblies of popular representatives may be called in various languages, emerge. In Britain, the "Cabinet" separated out as a government, deriving its legitimation no longer from the King but rather from the elected parliament. Switzerland, Germany, Austria and the United States, each in its own way and time, developed federal structures as a special variant of the division of powers, and one contrasting strongly with the centralism of France or Britain. The next great step came with the rise of organised mass parties and the prolonged struggle for universal suffrage, both a consequence of the emergence of political organisations of the working class. The workers' organisations confronted the socially rooted "conservative" forces and forced them in turn to found political parties (for a paradigmatic example relating to Swedish developments, see Nedelmann, 1975). In essence, the formation of these party systems along religious or industrial lines of conflict was substantially complete by the nineteen twenties (see Lipset & Rokkan, 1967).

An understanding of these diverse developments affecting the realms of values, constitutional and organisational forms, and of their complex interpenetration in the fabric of the modern state, is crucial for an analysis of the problems of government today. Democratic values may be realised in very different ways, and may even be transformed into their opposite; indeed, the democratic belief very often serves as a form of camouflage for organisations dedicated to the purpose of violence. Fascism, Nazism, Peronism, etc. are but the most flagrant examples of what one might describe as the alibi function of social beliefs. Similarly, the division of powers does not necessarily simultaneously imply democratic government, but is (or was) compatible with a variety of forms of authoritarianism. Federal structures follow rules of their own, and party systems do not necessarily result in party government. For analytical purposes, it is essential to treat each individual element separately, but the crucial feature of party government is the binding together through parties of all these elements. Depending on how the parties permeate and dominate parliaments and other state institutions, on the way in which the ruling party (or coalition) obtains its legitimacy and its room for manoeuvre, and on the extent to which party leaderships have developed into a body that co-ordinates or mediates virtually all aspects of policy, the problems of democracy will themselves be different. Certainly, the German advocates of the "party state" had not imagined that the party organisations — formally acknowledged by the constitution, but formed outside the constitutional institutions proper — would develop into the real centre of power.

III. Conditions

Party government is fully developed where not only do parties compete for the electors' votes, but also where elections decide the next government in a virtually plebiscitary manner. The question of whether there is any real chance of a possible change of government thereby becomes the decisive criterion of popular government. In theory, the possibility of a change may always be assumed, but, in practice, the probability varies quite markedly. The possibility of change depends on: (1) the social basis of the parties competing for office, (2) the manner in which the electoral system converts votes into parliamentary mandates (cf. Wildenmann *et al.*, 1965) and thereby affects the formation of majorities, (3) the mode of institutional regulation of the competition for power (e. g. rules governing party finance — cf. Schleth, 1973 and Wildenmann, 1967) and its effect on voter mobilisation, (4) the nature of information processes, (5) the nature and extent of emotional and structural linkages between the electorate and parties, (6) the manner in which society is politically and socially structured, (7) the differential distribution of political experiences and attitudes as between different groups or layers of society and as between political activists and others, and (8) the manner and the rules by which the circulation of political positional elites takes place and the processes and institutions (e. g. media) through which reputational elites are redefined.

The interaction of these conditions makes for the diversity of forms of party government manifested in contemporary Western Europe. Italy has in the DC (Christian Democrats) a (crumbling?) "hegemonic" party (Sartori, 1976). In Sweden, the position of the Social Democrats is no less hegemonic — having been in government uninterruptedly for more than forty years and resuming office once more in 1982 after a gap of only six years. In Belgium, the Flemings are structurally in a minority amongst the positional elites and in the population, and the country has until recently been ruled exclusively by a Francophile positional elite. In the German Federal

Republic, the CDU/CSU's electoral chances (based on a level of voter support of 44-49%) are structurally greater than those of the SPD (38-45% of the vote), but — up to now — still leaving the FDP as the decisive factor determining coalition possibilities. In Britain, where in the post-war era parties have tended to alternate in office and there is generally a reasonable chance of a change of government at any given election, the legitimacy of governments elected in this way is meeting with increasing criticism, not only from liberal intellectuals (cf. Finer, 1980), but also from increasingly large groups of the voting population. The problem of representational legitimacy is particularly acute at the present time, when the opposition to the Conservatives is split into two camps with almost no possibility, under the existing relative majority system of election, of winning a parliamentary majority. Yet again, the existence of relatively large Communist parties in France and Italy creates special difficulties for party government in those countries. Examples can be multiplied almost endlessly to demonstrate the diverse manner in which conditions interact to produce specific manifestations of party government and create particular impediments to party government also functioning as fully democratic government.

There is a widespread view that competition by parties (or by "elites") for governmental status — by contrast with authoritarian, totalitarian or praetorian regimes — not merely permits a multiplicity of opinions, but allows the formation of, and gives recognition to, an organised opposition, which is an essential element of democracy as such. Moreover, government action itself is considerably, and as it were dialectically, influenced by the consequent openness of political goals and the discussion of specific measures so generated. It is certainly true that competition for government office and the connected principle of majority decision do count as essential and fundamental attributes of democracy (although not all theorists see them as sufficient conditions), but that does not exclude the possibility, to use a metaphor, that the feuding "party barons" of government and opposition may conduct their battles on the backs of the "peasant" electorate; that what we are dealing with is a kind of party feudalism, the structure of which is stabilised by the chances of mobilisation and manipulation in contemporary society. Even the degree of effectiveness of the opposition as a component of democracy in each case (i. e. the extent to which the opposition actually limits government action), is dependent on the nature of social and institutional conditions, as well as on historically and constitutionally shaped structures, all of which vary from country to country. Permanent minority status for groups or groups organised in parties is by no means rare. Moreover, election promises and government action quite frequently differ markedly, since the issues that inform electoral campaigning tend to be defined by the chances of winning and are remote from the issues actually faced after an election. In sum, it is often the case that under the conditions of actual party government, verbal protestations of democracy are considerably at variance with the actual nature of the ruling organisation of the modern state. Here there is much scope for social and political criticism and for the empirical study of problems of party government.

The confrontation of the real conditions of rule with the elementary norm of democratic theory, that any particular government can be voted out, does not however exhaust the problem. Empirical observations in Britain, France or the Federal Republic – that is, even in countries with highly developed party government, and without even considering the presidential form in the United States – raise the issue of whether party government may not be developing in the direction of some quasi-charismatic legitimation of the ruling organisation. The suggestion is not that all top political actors must possess such charisma or preserve it after an election, but rather that we are witnessing a move towards a charismatic party collectivism, in which the popular charisma of individual leaders does constitute a definite resource in winning the political game. In Britain, commentary and debate on this theme has been current since the fifties, with a particular focus on the power of, and the constraints surrounding, the Prime Minister. In the Federal Republic, whilst a conception of "Chancellor democracy" is quite apparent in the conduct of the voters, such a structural development was not foreseen by the founding fathers of the constitution and was not inherent in the design of the constitutional machinery, however much a "strong democratic government" may have been wanted as an "answer to National Socialism" (A. Arndt, in the Parliamentary Council). In France, there has always been a real tendency towards a charismatic breakthrough to Bonapartism, but the institution of the Fifth Republic has had the somewhat paradoxical consequence of (unintentionally) creating the conditions for party government, whilst creating in the President a permanent quasi-charismatic focus of legitimation. In an historical garb, that changes from place to place, and in a relatively short-lived manner, the various political actors at the summit of politics are adulated, whether they be called J. F. Kennedy, Reagan, Thatcher, De Gaulle, Mitterand, Adenauer, Helmut Schmidt or Helmut Kohl. However, the persons of the powerful, typecast and hyped-up as they are by the media of mass communication, become more important in the eyes of the voters than the offices that are supposed to be entrusted to them for a period; hence the orientation to office ceases to be embedded in structural exigencies and becomes instead a matter of subjective qualities. Fine distinctions are important here: the distinction between an emotional, but at bottom rational recognition of leadership qualities, and the emotional symbolisation of individuals onto whom the wishes of the people or part of the people are projected; the difference between the readiness to trust oneself to an accepted party leadership, whilst maintaining the ability to criticise, and a mass trust in the image of appearances; the difference between respect for a person on the basis of experience and a mass enthusiasm. These differences, however, categorically determine the content of the ruling organisation concerned.

The tendency to quasi-charismatic collectivism brings the issue of the legitimacy of party government into sharp focus. If democracy is understood in Schumpeter's or Down's sense as a competitive struggle by leadership groups for the temporary support of the voters, then one might well conclude that democracy existed so long as an essentially bipolar competition of leadership groups with reasonably equal chances of governing was guaranteed by institutional and organisational means (i. e. where the electoral system leads to the formation of a majority on the basis of an open society without any lasting political and social minorities). But the main problem with such an assumption is not so much the failure of this type of ruling organisation to match up the realities of democratic practice – an objection frequently encountered in the literature on "formal democracy" – but rather that such an open, informed and reasonable society is a marginal case. In reality, it cannot be achieved even with a majoritarian electoral system unless other conditions are such as to undermine hegemonic positions. Further, access to the party leadership groups tends to bring about a very one-sided selection of personnel in virtue of the *libido dominandi* (the lust for power). This issue of the constraints on leadership is closely tied to twentieth century assumptions about the limitless "manipulability" of politics by political actors in the modern state. Certainly, the probability of unconstrained manipulation is a function of the actual working of constitutions, the extent to which democratic values are internalised in society, how the media works and the nature of oppositional forces. Also, any judgement of the degree to which "lust for power" and "manipulability" are dominant depends on a careful differentiation between leaders' "aspirations for power" and their "aspirations for policy". Nevertheless, there are abundant examples of political leaders who have complied with the constraints before they achieved powerful positions, but once having done so, tried to ignore them to the greatest extent possible.

Issues of the match between democratic theory and practice are not the only ones to raise question-marks about the nature of contemporary quasi-charismatic party government. The giganticism of big party political organisations, as they have developed, especially since the Second World War, raises problems of its own. Furthermore, not only are there manifest problems concerning the legitimacy of this form of government, but there are also serious questions that can be and have been raised about its *effectiveness,* i. e. its capacity to cope with problems. These problems of legitimacy and effectiveness are closely interlinked, and a discussion and analysis of their nature forms much of the substance of this first volume on *The Future of Party Government.*

IV. The Importance of Conflict Areas

Party government is a phenomenon of industrial societies. Even if one does not assume, as in Marxist theory, that the ruling organisation of modern states is merely the "superstructure" of a capitalist society, but rather takes the view that party government is an autonomous institutional development, partly independent in its decision-making structures, it remains the case that there is a real correspondence with other structural developments in society. Its value conceptions correspond to democratic standards or relate to them, even where, as we have seen, legal norms take on the character of an alibi function. Its existence presupposes a high degree of demographic, technological, scientific and economic development, without which it would not in any sense be conceivable. The view that certain levels of economic development must be attained as a precondition of democratic development is not one that can be rejected out of hand (cf. Muller, 1979). Furthermore, party government is closely bound up with the development of legal rules that set boundaries of differing effectiveness to the scope for political action and which may be used by the ruled as instruments for exercising sanctions against the political misconduct of leaders. However, it should be noted, that not all groups in a society are in an equally good position to use these; there is evidence that the asymmetry of access to politics is appearing in a new form in contemporary states, with the state-employed classes having privileged access (see Kaase, 1981). Moreover, there has never been any lack of imagination on the part of politicians in getting rid of uncomfortable legal rules or getting around them; machiavellianism is less a matter of "morals" than of real constraints (the more so since the literature has not, whether in Kant, Durkheim, Piaget or Kohlberg, unambiguously identified either the origins or nature of moral concepts, and, indeed, this can hardly be clarified without taking into account the effectiveness of institutions).

The received wisdom concerning the predominant lines of conflict in industrial societies – and hence of the determination of party political preference and affiliation – is that class and religiosity constitute the primary dimensions. This basic picture of conflict between industrialists (managers) and workers, and between those with and without religious ties, does retain some crude explanatory power. With the exception of voters with a Protestant ethical affiliation, voters with church ties, especially Catholics, are extremely likely to be "conservative in values", while those without religious ties or lay people tend towards a more "progressive" stance. Workers have a leftist orientation and entrepreneurs a rightist one. However, this basic model of conflict and political orientation in industrial societies, always much more applicable in Europe than in the United States, is today generally breaking down and must be discarded in any detailed empirical analysis. New patterns are emerging, determined in a complex manner by degree of organisation, degree of the individual means of subsistence (wealth) or collective welfare and by the profound primary political experiences of individuals. Above all, however, it is the very organisation of the party system in each country which has become the primary factor influencing the distribution of political orientations.

There is, moreover, a reciprocal interaction here, with the distribution of political orientations itself conditioning the freedom of action of party governments and their affiliated organisations. A bimodal distribution where, say, a few votes may bring about a shift in the positionally relevant allocation of parliamentary seats, favours the effectiveness of government action, since it is most likely to correspond with the conditions of party government. On the other hand, it has the disadvantage of a tendency to rigid party organisation and discipline and frequently to a larger discrepancy between electoral promises and subsequent government action. The marginal votes may well correspond to the ideal typical image of "middle" voter (of bourgeois provenance), as in the case of the Federal Republic, or, just as likely, be based on the extreme position or lack of political knowledge of the particular marginal voter. Obviously, as was noted previously, the nature of the electoral system is also a crucial factor here.

A multimodal distribution of orientations has a more or less opposite effect, with a centrifugal tendency to rigid and extreme conditions, as in Italy. Its most important drawback is the hiatus between electoral choice and government formation. The ultimate outcome of an election (assuming that it is possible to form a coalition at all), namely the formation of a government, cannot be predicted and is beyond the control of the electorate. Capacity for consensus can hardly be expected under such circumstances, unless in the cynical form that the voters are at one in their indifference to which party groupings eventually coalesce to form the government. On the other hand, the electoral system underlying this distribution may be perceived in public debate to be basically "fair", and, certainly, in terms of equal access to structural minorities, the unlimited proportional representation system is "fair" in giving minorities a possibility of articulating their views, if not always giving them a chance to govern.

The problem areas that politics in an industrial society has particularly to deal with and that confront contemporary party governments are the specific cleavages of such a society. In accordance with schema devised by Karl Deutsch, Bruno Fritsch and this author, eight fundamental areas of this kind can be identified, each of which has a corresponding source of social and political differentiation. They are:

(1) The reproduction of economic capital including productivity increases, which is the source of industrial conflict.
(2) The promotion of scientific and technical potential, which is the source of differentiation in terms of influence and status.

(3) The degree of mobility, both horizontal and vertical, in a society, which is the source of differential chances of personal development.
(4) The degree of mutual solidarity – including the "agreement between generations" as to horizontal social redistribution – which is the source of differential protection against the social risks faced by individuals and families.
(5) The relationship between man and environment, the source of possible destruction or despoilation of man's existential conditions.
(6) The creation and maintenance of the conditions of creativity, which is the source of cultural distinctions between individuals.
(7) The rule of law in domestic affairs, creating "security" of private and community life.
(8) International security through peaceful and institutionalised conflict resolution.

In other words, economic, research, infrastructure, social, environmental, educational policies, lawful regulations of domestic conflict and international peaceful conflict resolution are the central tasks and central issues of contemporary government. Each of these areas has its own regularities, complexities and "speed" of development. In all these fields not only are concrete problems likely to arise as a consequence of social and economic change, but also specific social expectations develop with which governments have to cope.

Thus the welfare state demands – discounting more direct subventions in infrastructure and personnel – a redistribution of the social product which amounts to some 20% of GNP (see Flora, 1981) on average in the European states (with a range from 15-30%). This redistribution involves two crross-cutting flows: from one group of society to another and a horizontal distribution of an insurance kind. The welfare state has by its creation and extension created a massive rise in expectations of government action, just because its programmes cater to the most basic existential conditions of the citizen, by providing care in the form of sickness, old age and survivors' pensions, unemployment and accident insurance and guarantees for family maintenance. But to the degree that the programmes of the welfare state actually increase the demand for the extension of the welfare state, these demands may well be in partial contradiction to the economic productivity conditions from the yield of which they must be ultimately financed.

Infrastructural expenditure in the contemporary state serves not only to finance luxury goods. The road network, for instance, guarantees individual mobility, which in turn is a precondition of the mobility of labour. Environment policy is not merely a symbol of, and a response to, the fundamentalist attitudes of the younger generation, but is a necessity for the preservation of reasonable conditions of existence for the great majority, leaving aside all considerations of romanticism. The new technologies signal a massive transformation of social communication; developing them in a context of freedom involves very special problems of social consensus and liberty. Scientific progress is not only Janus-faced in offering the potential for both progress and destruction, but also presupposes vast financial resources and at the same time an educational policy geared to continuous long-term change. Demographic developments — virtual zero population growth in the advanced states and a changing dependency ratio (i. e. a continuous decline in the percentage of the economically active) — pose very major dilemmas, the solution of which seem scarcely resolvable without further (possibly, environmentally damaging) economic growth.

As these examples show, the problems faced by contemporary governments are closely interrelated, and their solution requires new social, economic and political ideas and codes of conduct. In other words, the legitimacy of democracies is dependent upon the effectiveness of government action, and this is in turn reciprocally linked to the nature of the government, its manner of governing, and the consensus it enjoys.

V. Recruitment and Selection Problems

The issue of governmental effectiveness is not merely a question of "overload", that rising expectations and needs in society outstrip the resources available (cf. Rose, 1980). It is primarily a matter of whether party government is able to produce from within itself the people that need to be selected for official tasks and has the capacity to create a structure of communication and coordination that will mediate consensually between government action and society.

It is doubtful in the extreme whether personnel selection through party channels can fully match these challenges under contemporary conditions. The present system calls first of all for the freeing of those occupying specialised posts from all others tasks. Indeed, there no longer seems to be a place for "honourables" and thereby for a wide range of talents. In the Federal Republic, the trend towards a "parliament of bureaucrats" was already clear in 1953 (see Wildenmann, 1953). Central government tasks were, however, during that period of "high achievement motivation", and because of the pressure of immediate problems (unemployment, integration of refugees, treaties with the West, European development and co-determination) often entrusted to people who did not come from party careers. Even in the SPD, the organisational solidarity of which is proverbial, the then chairman, Kurt Schumacher, asked that candidates for public office be chosen not on the basis of party seniority, but on the basis of ability. He himself in the period after 1946 took care to encourage young blood, which was subsequently, in leadership positions, to determine the fate of the party over a long period. Such a careful approach to the leadership succession – the encouragement and bringing on of talent – has however, with notable or even outstanding exceptions, gone out of fashion. The appearance of the parties is primarily characterised by people belonging to the state-supported classes with specific professional training and roles, and, most particularly, by teachers.

A French study (Cayrol, 1983) demonstrates the extraordinary change in the composition of the French parties in the last thirty years. It is no longer lawyers, managers or the liberal professions that constitute the majority of representatives, but teachers paid by the state. The same tendency is apparent across Europe, and even the directly elected European Parliament is part of the same trend. To use Max Weber's categories, the politicians no longer live for politics, but from politics, which alone provides (or seems to provide) them with enhanced opportunities for success and social prestige. These then are professional politicians, who ensure themselves against the risks once inherent in party political activity by a reliance on guaranteed state funds. Those best able to do this are teachers of all kinds, especially given the "overproduction" in the educational establishment, which has also been a singular feature of the previous thirty years. Party government is based on a political class *sui generis*, freed from the compulsions of other professions, practised in making use of formal or informal behavior in the pursuit of political career, adroit in the arts of manipulation, subject only to the "rules" of struggle for position and interchangeable among different offices rather in the way that the procurators of ancient Rome were rotated from province to province.

The cultural peculiarities of individual countries may somewhat modify or disguise this fundamental tendency. Without literary or artistic competence, higher offices may scarcely be obtainable in France; the French national claim to speak for a universal human dignity is still kept alive. In Britain, a public school or Oxbridge background, with its accumulation of knowledge concerning the ability and particularly the "character" of candidates, is still a guide to personnel selection, especially in the Conservative Party. And, it may even be surmised that the rise of the British SDP may have such "elitist" structural causes. In Italy, even the petty officials of parties of the Left in municipal or regional office still make a show of the forms and elegance of cultivated manners. The Federal Republic may be the sole major country in which the levelling out of educational, and hence social, classes together with the collapse of the traditional educational ethos shows the more starkly monotonal structure of the "political class". Certainly, in Germany, the discrepancy in the selection procedure between the political and other social elites is particularly clear, and the opportunity for cultural elites to take public office is much circumscribed (effectively restricted to natural scientists, technicians, economists and, most prominently, lawyers). For the rest of the intellectual and cultural elite, serious political activity is but a playground for licenced "court jesters".

Harking back to Mosca, one is tempted to suggest that the new "ruling class" is recruited out of the state-employed sector, and that the formula of its rule can be deduced from a kind of feudalism revisited, mainly that of state guaranteed income and pension provisions. For them, the state has become the "object" of education, of role significance, of income and of status allocation, as well as being the source of social meaning and legitimation. Among the developments that have led to this special type of party government, the penetration of parties by those belonging to the state-paid class has the predominant place. Other social groupings with clearly different conditions of existence, such as entrepreneurs, workers or even artists, have rather become objects of politics and have partly lost their character as subjects; despite all the class and status differences between such groups, this is the characteristic of their common fate.

VI. Media and Information Problems

The exceptions to this new political class stratification, which is becoming increasingly characteristic of contemporary party governments, are the journalistic actors of the mass media – or at least they may be exceptions! While such slogans as "the power of the media" or "control of the media" may be based on some element of truth, such as the increasing perception by journalists of their role as "co-politicians without a seat" (Carlo Schmid in a discussion), they, unfortunately, obscure reality more than they reveal it.

Two restrictive developments reduce the autonomous participation of the media in political decision making processes and their role of "agenda setting" – the latter, often much over-emphasised in the literature. On the one hand, technical constraints have brought into being huge publishing concerns, which no longer leave their "products" up to the free play of opinion, but trim them to fit a given audience according to the tenets of tested commercial success. The media are constantly attempting to divine the fears, resentments or submerged desires of their audience and to bring them to market (cf. Reismann) in a manner reminiscent of the attempts of party propagandists to market their idols. This is less true of such quality daily papers as "The Times", the "Süddeutsche Zeitung", "Le Monde", "Corriere della Sera" or the "Neue Zürcher Zeitung"; but it is very much so of the visual media, especially the TV monopolies, and of the weekly or monthly magazine productions. The trend to "mass communication as systems control" (Schatz-Bergeld, 1970) cannot be overlooked; and part of the struggle over the new media technologies, such as cable and optical fibre communications, reflects the efforts of these major commercial concerns to get their hands on these media also. Opinions and news selection are no longer a result of systematic effort to provide an opportunity for open opinion formation, but are deformed and "commodified" into "products". An emotionally loaded polarisation of public debate, including a ruinous competition for goals, persons and voters, is hardly avoidable.

On the other hand, this trend towards concentration – and marketing – has also transformed journalists' perceptions of problems. Their creative freedom has been much restricted, and the fact that their existence depends on the publishing concerns or on the executive organs of parties forces them (despite often considerable incomes and status) to make adjustments that smack not a little of anticipatory censorship. While their "interpretive function" is still real, the interpretation has to take a character that does not depart too far from the pre-set "product" definition. The argument that, nevertheless, there is a plurality of such products does not touch the heart of the matter, if only because access to the media by the population remains restricted and much supposed exposure to media ideas is symbolic only, involving merely a reinforcement and rigidification of previously held opinion. What is important is that the differentiation and openness of views fades away, with complexity not being broken down in the cause of enlightenment, but merely symbolically reduced.

Unfortunately, the area of mass communications still lacks the necessary empirical studies to chart the finer detail of this situation and its trend of development. In particular, there are no micro-analyses studying the processes of opinion formation with a view to exploring the short- and long-term consequences of the interaction between media products and the population. Of great importance for further understanding the nature of party government would be greater knowledge of the effects of the media on electoral behaviour, i. e. the legitimation processes. Governments may be "talked up" or "talked down". One thing is however very clear: the extreme importance of a transformation of the media scene! In the Federal Republic, for instance, the decisions in principle by the Constitutional Court have not, despite their unambiguous normative commitment to avoiding media monopolies or oligopolies, been sufficient to prevent the major private concerns from their product policy in this area so central for democracy. The same goes, incidentally, for the much-vaunted liberal patterns of attitudes in the Anglo-Saxon countries. It is less a question of ownership of the means of production, but is rather a matter of the limitations to which the power of disposing of these means is subject.

VII. International Interpenetration

Among the circumstances that determine the peculiarities of contemporary party government, there is one further central aspect. If one proceeds from the assumption that the struggle for re-allocation of the social product will constantly increase and that this necessitates complementary increases in productivity, then one must ask whether national party governments will be able to continue to carry out the conflict regulation function that is ascribed to them. Firstly, national resources are too constrained for the assumption to hold that the politically necessary decisions can be taken separately in the national centres of power: in Whitehall, the Bonn Chancellery, the Elysée Palace or other seats of government. Secondly, the global political and strategic situation is leading not only to a growth in the military budget, with its setting of planning, production and implementation targets years in advance, but also to an extreme complexity of decision-making. The sheer extent of the totality of demands faced by national governments is quite unprecedented. Thus, the policies called for presuppose an integrative information and decision process, which, for cognitive and institutional reasons, national governments are currently – and, perhaps, in the future – incapable of providing.

Moreover, such national governments must seek support for highly complex policies from a population with a wide range of information and a high capacity for independent evaluation (cf. Wildenmann, 1983). De Tocqueville's dilemma that democracy promotes equality and properity at home, but, given the national goals of his times, namely the preservation and extention of power, cannot pursue a continuous foreign policy (something only an aristocratic government is capable of), does not suffice to describe the situation of party government. Long-term continuous policies aiming for "participation" are called for in all areas of politics, and these policies are by their very nature conflicting in kind. The conflict formulated by the former German President, Gustav Heinemann, as long ago as 1950 (in his resignation speech as Federal Minister of the Interior) between "social" and "military" armament is only one example, far-reaching though it be, of such conflicts of objectives and resources. The theme: "the people's peace and the tyrant's war" (Hermens, 1944) is still on the agenda.

The realisation that there were a variety of political problems which could not be tackled within a restrictive national context was present immediately after the Second World War. The moves towards European unification, up to and including the European Community (EC), drew their inspiration from this realisation together with the overriding need once and for all to put an end to European wars. However, it seems that the supranational institutions are now in a regressive phase; the original driving forces seem to have got bogged down in the day-to-day activities of arranging subsidy agreements and devising bureaucratic regulations.

Characteristically, resistance to a policy of European integration was very considerable from the outset in Britain, the country of party government *par excellence*. There was, in fact, scarcely any willingness for anything that went beyond "cooperation" (Beloff, 1960). The ostensible reasons for this have been sought mostly in the "special" position of Britain, with its Commonwealth ties and national insularity. However, on our hypothesis linking national party governments with a restrictive international stance, much more effort should have been made to find out whether the party governments which have since arisen in other countries, with their clearly national structures and legitimation requirements, have not considerably contributed to this regressive movement. At any rate, within and beside the European Community, the European Political Community (EPC) has brought about a degree of political and administrative cooperation of nationally oriented party governments; but its scope and effectiveness are difficult to predict. At least for those involved – ministers and top officials – there is no requirement of legitimacy and consensus, but at most a strictly national focus. In other words, what has developed supranationally is wholly in line with Max Weber's definition of bureaucracy: the international bureaucracy plans and executes policy itself, and irrespective of its effectiveness it is quite clear that such a development cannot be compatible with democratic norms.

If we adduce Weber's definition of the state analytically and heuristically, then the European Community manifests the following characteristics: The legal system is still wholly national. The harmonisation processes, already well advanced by 1954, collapsed along with the European Defence Community with which that harmonisation process was bound up. The European Community Treaty did, admittedly, create a (partly) common code of international law and a Court of Justice – this latter actively engaged in creating a joint legal framework (cf. Weiler, 1985) – but the normative regulation of society generally continues to be matter for the national governments. A common currency has not come into being, and the attempt to fashion a common monetary policy is a complex and difficult business of cooperative interaction between governments and international banks (cf. Gleske, 1982). The EC has no tax revenue as such, but really only special subventions (serving to transform its organs into interest groups defending their own corner). The Parliament lacks decision-making powers that would make it into a "governing" assembly. Civil order remains a matter for the national governments. A monopoly of force does not exist, any more than does a Community defence or foreign policy. The influence of Community bodies on politics within and outside the Community may be greater than is sometimes publicly thought, but on the whole this is an "organisation" in which the element of "rule" as a legitimised order has developed just as one-sidedly and fragmentarily as its general public legitimation, despite direct elections to the European

Parliament. That nationalistic orientations, in the form of the domination of nationally perceived interests, were increasing was already visible from an early date (Deutsch, Edinger, 1964).

Whether and in what way party government as a nationally responsible institution can regulate the distinctive social and economic problems of the modern state is, therefore, not merely a question of the restrictions to which it is subject in virtue of its internal nature, but is also dependent on the limitations imposed by the international bureaucracy and by the interdependence of political and strategic developments. Whilst the prognosis is at this time anything but hopeful, there is, on the other hand, a great opportunity for modern democratic development waiting to be exploited here.

VIII. Looking to the Future

The discussion above has identified a range of major problems of democratic party government, which may be summarised in terms of internal and external factors. The most important internal factors are:

- the nature of the competition implicit in a given electoral system, which may have very diverse effects on the distribution of power;
- the distribution of party-oriented ideological preferences among the population on the basis of social stratification;
- the nature of communication and mobilisation in the political process, including the structure and functioning of the media;
- the constitutional structure, including the degree of concentration of political decision-making and the degree to which decision-making is devolved to non-governmental institutions;
- the structure of the social positional elites and the networks between them;
- the nature of internalised norms, including legal norms, and the internalised social and political concepts of order.

The most important external factors are:

- the nature of the inter- or supranational institutions with which the party governments are interwoven;
- the global political and strategic situation as a central aspect of international security;
- international social and economic developments.

As a force for purposive action and as focus of popular identification, party government has, as a consequence of these factors, itself become more problematic in recent times. Paradoxically, it seems less able to solve conflicts democratically, the more politics penetrates the whole society. Grewe's question from which we started: "the party state — and is there any alternative?", remains firmly on the agenda. In what way could and should party government be transformed so as to reduce the risk of catastrophic developments?

The ideas which have been put forward in this context are very far from satisfactory or helpful. This is especially true of two opposed conceptions: the one, that the force of the "state" must be strengthened, the other, that more "direct" democracy is necessary. A stronger state can be taken to mean greater internal security and more police, and this idea has, in fact, been used to justify the strengthening of the forces of "law and order". On the other hand, more citizens' initiatives could imply greater anarchy, and have already led to such consequences. What is called for is a new democratic concept of government, and this must necessarily involve a complex transformation of the normative requirements of such a change into revised institutional arrangements.

In light of this discussion, we conclude our analysis of the general framework of the problematic of modern party government by advancing a series of criteria for the further development of party government; they constitute not merely a means of charting the future, but also simultaneously demonstrate the weaknesses of democratic developments at the present time.

A. The Criterion of Competition

The nature of the electoral system is the chief determinant of the relationship between voters and elected leaders, the selection of public officers and the distribution of power among electoral offices. Leaving aside the Federal Republic, where the electoral system – following a few crises of legitimation and despite some specific problems – is generally accepted, there are in Britain, the Netherlands, Italy and France obvious signs of crises of legitimacy concerning fundamental aspects of the electoral process. It is clear that the parliamentary and governmental configurations resulting from these electoral systems no longer command wide general consensus, but, nevertheless, the discussion of these issues is sometimes lacking in consistency. In Britain, for instance, there are criticisms that the percentage distribution of votes does not correspond with that of parliamentary seats (most blatantly illustrated by the election of June 1983), because the electoral system is based on the "winner-takes-all" formula in single-member constituencies. *De facto,* however, it was the split of the opposition into Labour, SDP and Liberals that made the Thatcher victory possible, i. e. the electoral system is based on the legitimisation of governments by each party competing to win an absolute majority of seats, and it can hardly be assumed that the voting population in Britain would wish to refrain from choosing a government. Again, in the Netherlands, it was argued after the 1982 elections that, as the Labour Party emerged from the elections as the largest single party, it should have participated in government. But this involves a confusion, since the very nature of a proportional electoral system, such as that in the Netherlands, forbids public intervention in the choice of a government. That is the task of the politicans after the election, and in the coalitional strategy adopted electoral gains and losses are but one of many considerations.

Since the most important instrument for the legitimisation of rulers is periodic elections, what is required is a basic decision about what is really wanted of the electoral system. Differently designed electoral systems have diverse legitimation consequences and the crucial factor here is the effect of the workings of the electoral system on the capacity for consensus of the decision-making bodies, despite competition. It is ruinous competition amongst parties for governmental office, not competition as such, that needs to be overcome by institutional innovation. Furthermore, there needs to be consideration of the extent to which referendums might be instituted to supplement party competition, since evidently political self-awareness today generally seeks a far closer relationship between voters and leaders than the major parties with their publicity-ridden electoral campaigns can possibly offer.

In most European countries and the United States electoral volatility has become so great — because of the multidimensionality of political orientations — that structural minorities scarcely require any specific protection. Fundamentally, in decisions concerning the structuring of electoral systems as instruments of the voters and of the party leaderships, there has to be a balance achieved between the need to form a government able to act and the need for the voters to have some control over the goals, contents and methods of such governments. The question needs to be decided pragmatically and the solutions adopted are likely to differ from country to country. The issue is a specific one of constitutional policy and not a matter for (one-sided) constitutional theory. The difficulty lies, however, in the fact that a decision once taken sets in motion almost irreversible political processes, creates fundamental voter predispositions and also evokes fixed behaviour patterns on the part of politicians.

B. The Recruitment Criterion

The one-sidedness of personnel selection in virtue of the ability of candidates and office-bearers rather cuts across the requirement for differentiated decision-making. However, selection by expertise, as is customary in central banks, constitutional courts and welfare institutions, is in itself scarcely likely to generate lasting democratic trust between those so (s)elected and the population. There is a steadily declining linkage between the selection of experts on the one hand and party politicians on the other. The problem, as first formulated by Bagehot in *The English*

Constitution (1867) is as virulent as ever: it is not enough either to know nothing about everything, like the generalist, or everything about nothing, like the specialist. Bagehot had, in his day, deduced from this requirement that government and parties ought to find a means of coordination between the various selection criteria. Today, the need is essentially to combine a relatively medium-term circulation of positional elites, chosen according to criteria of expertise required by their offices, with an appropriate degree of candidate selection by the parties. As we have already shown, the real problem of political recruitment under the conditions of contemporary party government is the disproportionate likelihood that politicians will be (s)elected from the professional class of those employed by the state – only they can guarantee the time necessary and ensure themselves against the risks of politics. This problem is a central issue for a democratic, and at the same time rational, future development. Finally, electoral systems themselves have a great impact on the qualities of those recruited, and this is yet another matter that must be considered in pragmatic electoral engineering.

C. Problems of Information Flow

In this connection two very different issues must be distinguished: the information flow within decision-making bodies and the information processes within the population. The former is a matter of ensuring the quality of the information gathered; the latter, a matter of the nature of the media, of political interest and of credibility. In democracies there will always be – in spite of all efforts to increase the quality of information gathering by parliamentary services and the like – a lack of fully adequate and structured information available to parliaments. The cabinet system has the advantage that it may compensate for the lack of structured information in the parliamentary arena through the activity of party governments, but this is only the case where such governments acquire their information systematically. There is, however, a real difficulty in sorting out useful and relevant information – the "gold-digger" problem, sorting the mass of dross from the tiny nuggets of gold. Enormous quantities of information are on offer from both the administration and the interest organisations. Apart from the problems of evaluation, the issue also arises as to which parts of the information are reliable. Who checks what? According to Max Weber, this task should fall to the administration, but this is, indeed, an "ideal" model, and the quantitative expansion of the administration, with the increased size of the administrative apparatus, has intensified rather than alleviated the difficulty.

The real problem is then to provide information which can serve as the basis for government decisions which is secured by legally backed methods, as expert as possible and procured from a range of diverse (and mutually checking) information sources. The idea contemplated in the United States in 1975 (proposition by Senators Javits and Humphrey) of setting up a single "information institution" (particularly in respect of economic policy), although hardly feasible in a presidential system, was an approach to the realisation of these criteria. (Independent of these proposals, see Milbrath & Wildenmann, 1975). It would be easier in cabinet systems which accentuate the importance of office to a higher degree than the individual incumbent. Nor would such institutional innovations be at variance with the general demand for open government. On the other hand, there are areas, such as defence policy, where demonstrably neither the defence ministry nor parliament have qualitatively reliable information (for the Federal Republic, see Schatz, 1969); nor can they procure it for themselves. The predominant models of information procurement are no longer sufficient. The point is not that the state should be strengthened vis-à-vis the interest organisations, but that the decision-making bodies should be informed better and more responsibly and that a consensus should be developed on the decision-making rules to be adopted in the case of dubious or deficient information.

As regards information processes within the population, the situation as revealed by survey research suggests that some 20% have an high degree of political information and a further 20% have a moderate degree. 40% are more or less uninterested, whilst the remainder are highly committed without having any interest in acquiring substantial information (see Barnes & Kaase, 1979 and Muller, 1979). Technically, possibilities today exist for a gradual improvement – that is, an increase in objectivity – of the information flow. This is not, however, a question of the introduction of new mass media techniques, but of the way in which they are handled and given form.

The call for universal and comprehensive information for the population as a whole is utopian and problematic to boot – for instance, nobody would expect us all to become lawyers in order to guarantee the legal system! What should be achieved, however, is a greater credibility in information processes. Quasi-monopolies like those of the television companies, especially when journalistic standards are replaced by a pushy know-all tendency to be "fellow-politicians without a seat", along with the pursuit of ideological inclinations of whatever kind, reduce credibility and detract from the pluralism of the media. S. M. Lipset has recently put forward the thesis in this connection that television news reporting has an impact in weakening the credibility of democratic government systems. Whether this somewhat conservative view is wholly true, information as a precondition for the balancing of interests is hardly likely to be facilitated in a situation where personalisation of the information flow is combined with idiosyncratic newscasting.

If, given the present burden of problems faced by democratic party governments, we are to seek a moderately rational form of decision-making that can be legitimated among the population, then a reshaping of our media system will become inevitable. This is all the more necessary because the nature of personal communication about political situations has been considerably altered by processes of social change. There is, for instance, an increase in the population of those who, while little informed and interested in political information, display a fundamentalism and rigidity that contents itself with symbols. This tendency is furthered by the oversimplification of much media reporting. The increased forcefulness of movements of such individuals is a strong pointer towards the shortcomings and democratic dangers inherent in uninformed interest mediation.

D. Problems in Decision-Making

The core of the party government problematic – looking at it as we have done – is the nature of decision-making in the modern state, and particularly the question of how decisions can be legitimised. The normative assumption inherent in the party government model, that free discussion, especially in parliaments, will lead to the formation of workable majorities, cannot be realised without specific preconditions. Furthermore, that assumption does not touch on the important matter of the reversibility of such decisions once made. Parliamentarism, understood as an institution of decision-making, initially presupposes – and to say it verges almost on the tautological or trivial – that such decisions will genuinely be taken by parliaments and that they do not become mere rubber-stamps for decisions made elsewhere. This precondition is only met partially for, as we have seen, there has been a shift in the locus of decision-making, accompanied by a reduction in the quality of information available to decision-makers and a greater complexity of the decisions themselves.

In the case of a cabinet system, it is further necessary that the coalitions which form the government are able to obtain a working majority. This need not exclude freedom of representation, but does call for high levels of party discipline. Such discipline is, however, somewhat incompatible with demands for greater direct democracy or with the sort of idiosyncratic parliamentary behaviour, which now, as often in the past, has used that conception as its justification. Presidential forms of government are, perhaps, rather more consistent with this kind of individualistic behaviour (and are, therefore, now somewhat in vogue and not merely amongst liberals), but on the other hand have the drawback of inconsistent policies combined with high populistic expectations – the enduring problem of the American constitution.

The proponents of direct democracy sometimes confound this with an allegiance to an "elementary" democracy, which sees organised politics as an evil. However, this claim altogether passes over a further criterion of the decision-process that we have already discussed; namely, that it provides the most comprehensive possible interest mediation in order to provide for the rational organisation of political life. Moreover, a new mode of access by diverse groups of the population can lead to new ways of pursuing interests. "Citizens' movements" are, on the one hand, an index of a lack of openness in the decision-making apparatus and, on the other, an indicator of a lessened understanding of the nature of representative democracy.

Finally, openness in coalition formation is called for. The Federal Republic is fortunate enough not to have the problem that makes Italy, France, Spain and Portugal so hard to govern democratically; namely, the existence of political groupings that cannot be brought into coalitions – and not only so-called Eurocommunism. However, since the 1970s, a form of dangerous competitive party government has also developed in the Federal Republic, and, in particular, the FDP, which is crucial to coalition-formation, but is increasingly finding itself unable to fulfil its own demands for flexibility, has progressively got into difficulties. Moreover, the Federal Republic seems recently to have manifested some tendency towards a centrifugal movement in its ideological spectrum. This is by no means a natural phenomenon, nor can it be attributed to developments in the social structure; the basic three-class configuration of workers, employers and those supported by the state has no inherent tendency to this type of ideological drift. The real cause must be seen in organisational petrification, which, in a period of sharper conflict over distribution, may very well intensify further.

E. The Initiative Criterion

The generation of the necessary initiative to renew political goals and institutions is, as history shows us, a particularly thorny problem. On the one hand, parliamentary democracies are, by their very nature, very slow (sometimes, incapable) to achieve the consensus necessary for basic reform – Italy is a classic example of how difficult the process can be. On the other hand, the long-term continuity of democratic institutions is in itself an important value, because, given the importance of enduring issues, trust and identification with the system can only be built up over long periods of time. Several structuring criteria therefore overlap.

A party government has the great advantage, presupposing a genuine likelihood of periodic changes of government, of new goals and initiatives filtering into the political process. Britain, France, the Federal Republic and the United States (within the American presidential system) have in the last thirty years shown impressive examples. There has, indeed, been no lack of new policy initiatives or of opportunities to realise them. However, whether this is equally true of all areas of politics is an open question. The phraseology of party leaderships, developed in competitive struggle, frequently conceals how small the room for manoeuvre for "new" policies really is an the extent to which there is, in reality, a "body of orthodoxy" that extends above party-political nuances. This is true of economic policy (all the states under discussion have "mixed" economies), of foreign policy (NATO doctrine), in respect of prevailing social welfare standards and with regard to policy toward the Third World.

Essentially, the question of a party government's capacity for innovation is one of the composition, circulation and decisiveness of positional elites. In general, the view may even be defended that the rule of positional elites is crucial for a democratic consensus (see Higley, 1982). To date, the controversies over "pluralism", "consociationalism", "neo-corporatism" or "elite structures" have failed to resolve these problems. Moreover, it remains unclear whether positional elites are only more articulate interpreters of political and social developments, and are thus themselves parts of a more comprehensive macro-process, or whether they autonomously generate new initiatives.

From a normative standpoint, it is comparatively easy to set out how the relationship between the mass population and the positional elites should be shaped. However, providing an institutional and organisational reality is, amongst other things, a question of the parties involved in a particular party government. Thus, it could be argued that the position of the FDP within the German ruling organisation, with its ability to determine the complexion of the ruling coalition, did not merely involve an ideology designed to maximise its own personal patronage, but was a device which permitted the introduction of new initiatives (although the most recent government formation in 1982/3 would allow of a quite different interpretation). It does, at least, give some pause for thought that, in a number of European countries, the German model is seen as an exemplar of party democracy, and that at the same time there are demands for a similar electoral system, provided that it will lead not merely to articulation of the interests of the state-supported class, but also to structured initiatives in respect of constitutional policy.

F. The Integration Criterion

The range of problems which come under this heading are quite fundamental to the further development of party government. In my own terms, the issue is, centrally, one of "power" and "consensus" in a democratic state (cf. Wildenmann, 1964); the question one of how to achieve sufficient harmony between decision-making institutions and the expressed wishes of the citizens in order that conflicts be resolved.

In many ways this has been our theme throughout this essay and, in bringing this discussion of the problematic of party government to a close, we wish only to underline the important way in which the problem of power and consensus is linked to the major areas of conflict in industrial societies (see above, pp. 12—13), in particular, conflicts relating to economic capital, mutual solidarity and conditions for creativity. In other words, we wish to emphasise the interconnection between the problems of integration and questions of class (in the sense of Lepsius's three-class model — Lepsius, 1979), the welfare state and the means by which, despite the constraining implications of rule by party government and of the achievement of social equality, the diversity of individuals can be allowed genuine development. One cannot escape from defining welfare, equality of opportunity and freedom (in terms of principles and not merely as liberties) as the core of government action in the democratic modern state. The class structure that resulted from nineteenth century developments, now overlaid by neo-corporatist phenomena and differentiated by the emergence of a state-supported class, determines the real conditions that are necessarily to be changed. The realisation of human values is just as much at stake here as are welfare guarantees. The welfare state has largely accommodated the social risks of the population, but has simultaneously weakened the motivation for self-determination, since the basic thrust of the development has been to provide collective security where individual security was previously lacking. Whatever the virtues of such a transformation, the way in which it has come about is such as to undermine creativity and individually chosen life-styles, and the "mass" symbolic movements which enshrine such a development in the contemporary state are in many ways contrary to what is intended to be the goal of democratic government.

Bibliography

Bagehot, W. (1964) *The English Constitution.* London: Watts.

Barnes, S. H., M. Kaase et al. (1979) *Political Action: Mass Participation in Five Western Democracies.* Beverly Hills: Sage.

Beloff, M. (1961) *New Dimensions in Foreign Policy.* London: George Allen and Unwin.

Benda, E., W. Maihofer and H.-J. Vogel (1983) *Handbuch des Verfassungsrechts der Bundesrepublik Deutschland.* Berlin: de Gruyter.

Cayrol, R. and P. Perrineau (1982) "Governing Elites in a Changing Industrial Society: the Case of France", in M. M. Czudnowski (ed.), *Does Who Governs Matter? Elite Circulation in Contemporary Societies.* Bloomington: Illinois University Press.

Deutsch, K. W. and L. J. Edinger (1967) *France, Germany and the Western Alliance. A Study of Elite Attitudes on European Integration and World Politics.* New York: Scribner's.

Eden, Sir A. (1960) *The Memoirs of the Rt. Hon. Sir Anthony Eden. Full Circle.* London: Cassell.

Field, L. G. and J. Higley (1982) *The States of National Elites and the Stability of the Political Institutions in Eighty One Nations, 1950—1982.* EUI Working Paper 37. Florence. European University Institute.

Finer, S. E. (1980) *The Changing British Party System 1945—79.*, Washington: American Enterprise Institute for Public Policy Research.

Flora, P., J. Alber and J. Kohl (1977) „Zur Entwicklung der westeuropäischen Wohlfahrtsstaaten", 4 *Politische Vierteljahresschrift,* 705.

GLESKE, L. (1981) *The European Monetary System — Present Situation and Future Prospects.* EUI Working Paper 5. Florence. European University Institute.
GREWE, W. C. (1951) "Parteienstaat — oder was sonst", 36 *Der Monat* 563.
HERMENS, F. A. (1944) *The Tyrants' War and the Peoples' Peace.* Chicago: University of Chicago Press.
KAASE, M. (1981) "Politische Beteiligung und politische Ungleichheit. Betrachtungen zu einem Paradox", in L. Albertin and W. Link (eds.), *Politische Parteien auf dem Weg zur parlamentarischen Demokratie in Deutschland.* Düsseldorf: Droste.
LEHMBRUCH, G. and P. C. SCHMITTER (1982) *Patterns of Corporatist Policy-making.* London: Sage.
LEIBHOLZ, C. (1958) *Strukturprobleme der modernen Demokratie.* Karlsruhe: C. F. Müller.
— (1960) *Das Wesen der Repräsentation und der Gestaltwandel der Demokratie im 20. Jahrhundert.* Berlin: de Gruyter.
LEPSIUS, R. M. (1979) "Soziale Ungleichheit und Klassenstrukturen in der Bundesrepublik Deutschland", in U. Wehler (ed.), *Klassen in der europäischen Sozialgeschichte.* Göttingen: Vandenhoeck und Ruprecht.
LIPSET, S. M. and S. ROKKAN (1967) "Cleavage Structures, Party Systems and Voter Alignments: An Introduction", in S. M. Lipset and S. Rokkan (eds.), *Party Systems and Voter Alignments.* New York: Free Press.
MAIHOFER, W. (1983) "Prinzipien freiheitlicher Demokratie", in E. Benda, W. Maihofer and H.-J. Vogel, *Handbuch des Verfassungsrechts der Bundesrepublik Deutschland.* Berlin: de Gruyter.
— (1983) "Kulturelle Aufgaben des modernen Staates", in E. Benda, W. Maihofer and H.-J. Vogel, *Handbuch des Verfassungsrechts der Bundesrepublik Deutschland.* Berlin: de Gruyter.
MILBRATH, L. W. and R. WILDENMANN (1975) "New Forms of Governance for an Equilibrium Society". Presented at the Conference on 'Limit of Growth'. Houston.
MULLER, E. N. (1982) *Aggressive Political Behavior.* Princeton: Princeton University Press.
NEDELMANN, B. (1970) *Zur Parteienentstehung in Schweden (1866—1907). Historisch-soziologische Aspekte der Institutionalisierung politischer Organisationen.* Diss., University of Mannheim.
REIF, K. (1982) *Parteienregierung in Frankreich. Die Transformation des Parteiensystems durch die Institutionen der V. Republik.* Habilitationsschrift, University of Mannheim.
RIESMAN, D. (1953) *The Lonely Crowd. A Study of the Changing American Character.* New York: Doubleday.
ROSE, R. (1980a) *Challenge to Governance: Studies of Overloaded Politics.* London: Sage.
— (1980b) *Coping with Government.* London: Sage.
SARTORI, G. (1976) *Parties and party systems: A framework for analysis.* Cambridge: Cambridge University Press.
SCHATZ-BERGFELD, M. (1974) *Massenkommunikation und Herrschaft.* Meisenheim/Glan: Anton Hain.
SCHEUCH, E. K. and R. WILDENMANN (1965) *Zur Soziologie der Wahl,* Sonderheft 9, *Kölner Zeitschrift für Soziologie und Sozialpsychologie.* Köln und Opladen: Westdeutscher Verlag.
SCHLETH, U. (1973) *Parteifinanzen — Eine Studie über Kosten und Finanzierung der Parteitätigkeit.* Meisenheim/Glan: Anton Hain.
WEILER, J. H. H. (1985) *Il Sistema Communitario Europeo.* Bologna: Il Molino.
WILDENMANN, R., W. KALTEFLEITER and U. SCHLETH (1965) "Auswirkungen von Wahlsystemen auf das Parteien- und Regierungssystem der Bundesrepublik", Sonderheft 9, *Kölner Zeitschrift für Soziologie und Sozialpsychologie,* 74.

WILDENMANN, R. (1953) "Der Hang zur Bürokratendemokratie: Im neuen Bundestag spielen Beamte und Funktionäre eine allzugroße Rolle", *Deutsche Zeitung und Wirtschaftszeitung*, Nr. 81, 10. 10. 53, 3.
— (²1955) *Partei und Fraktion*. Meisenheim/Glan: Anton Hain.
— (1963) *Macht und Konsens als Problem der Innen- und Außenpolitik*. Frankfurt am Main/Bonn: Athenäum.
— (1968) *Gutachten zur Frage der Subventionierung politischer Parteien aus öffentlichen Mitteln*. Meisenheim/Glan: Anton Hain.
— (1983) "The Problem of Political Information Processes", 18 *Government and Opposition* 131.

Chapter II

Party Government: A Rationalistic Conception

RICHARD S. KATZ

Contents

Political parties have been considered the central institutions of democratic governments at least since the enfranchisement of the working class. Disraeli wrote, "I believe that without party parliamentary government is impossible" (Rose, 1974: 1). Schattschneider (1942: 1) tells us that "modern democracy is unthinkable save in terms of party," whilst to Sartori (1976: ix), "Parties are *the* central intermediate and intermediary structures between society and government." Although as Rose (1969) points out, "operational control of government" by parties is often assumed rather than demonstrated, the literary theory or the dominant ideal-type or myth of democratic government in Western Europe has been the model of party government. Whilst party government has not been accepted quite so readily as a description of government in the United States, it has been widely accepted as an ideal there as well (Kirkpatrick, 1950). With varying degrees of sophistication and with more or fewer caveats, elaborations, and qualifications, this has been true of political scientists, journalists, and the general public. The character, as well as the success or failure of governments both in solving particular problems and in providing effective long term stability and leadership, is most commonly attributed to the state of the parties and party system (Briggs, 1965; Allum, 1973).

Like other idealisations of government — for example that the king and then that the legislature ruled — the party government model is both descriptive and justificatory.[1] At the descriptive level, the party government model assigns to political parties a number of key functions in the governing process, including mobilisation and channeling of support, formulation of alternatives, recruitment and replacement of leadership, and, when in power, implementation of policy and control over its administration. At the normative level, the party government model implies a particular view of democracy, in which the system is made democratic by the electoral role of the parties. Structures or individuals other than parties and their leaders could perform the functions attributed to parties and could contribute to the governing of society, but only parties offer the whole public a choice among comprehensive and comprehensible alternatives. An electorally victorious party or coalition of parties is entitled to control the decision making and implementing functions of government because it has been authorised by the whole people to do so (Ranney, 1962).

The preceding paragraph ignores many thorny problems. Like other idealisations, the party government model is oversimplified, and is not intended to be taken as a complete description of any particular government. Its English origins are quite obvious, and both its descriptive and its normative elements require modification before they can be adapted to other political systems. Nonetheless, until recently it was generally accepted as a desirable ideal and also as a reasonably accurate description of the operation of European, if not necessarily of American, democracy.

In recent years, however, widespread concern has been expressed generally about the governability of industrial or post-industrial societies, and particularly about the ability of parties and party governments to cope with

[1] Throughout this chapter, I intend to limit attention to democratic governments, thus ignoring questions of whether totalitarian parties are properly parties and whether government by such parties is party government. For a discussion of these issues, see Sartori (1976).

contemporary problems (Crozier, 1975). A variety of events, social changes and results of academic research have called the party government model into question, both normatively and empirically. Heightened awareness of the independence of bureaucrats and of their relationship with organised interests has raised the question of whether parties have been, or can be, in effective control of policy. The broadening of government functions and the proliferation of governmental and quasi-governmental agencies indeed has raised the question of whether anyone can exercise comprehensive control. The rise of social groupings and issues not reflected in existing party systems has introduced new strains that threaten the stability of existing institutions and raised doubts regarding the adequacy of representation by parties (Inglehart, 1977), whilst the effective penetration of organised groups into the governmental apparatus has challenged the assumption that parties are necessary for representation. Moreover, the suspicion that partisan bickering is responsible, at least in part, for the apparent incapacity of western governments to deal effectively with contemporary problems has raised doubts about the very desirability of adversarial party government (Finer, 1975).

These doubts have contributed to a feeling that there is a crisis brought about by a lack of *capacity* on the part of the *parties* which is threatening the *persistence* of *party government* and of *democracy*. This suggestion raises questions clustering in three main categories. Firstly, to what extent, and under what circumstances, do governments conform to the party government model? Put somewhat infelicitously, what is the level of "party governmentness" of contemporary regimes, how is it to be explained, and, projecting into the future, what changes in party governmentness should be expected on the basis of other political, social, economic, and cultural developments? Secondly, how and under what circumstances is the level or organisation of party government related to a political system's capacity and persistence? Thirdly, is party government necessary for democracy or, less demandingly, is party government the only alternative to authoritarian, autocratic, or dictatorial government? How much party government is there; can it survive; should one care?

These questions could be approached as historical descriptive problems to be addressed relatively atheoretically. There is much still to be said about the role of parties in the governing of past and present societies at a purely descriptive level. If valid cross-national comparisons are to be made, if events are to be explained, and especially if an assessment of the consequences of potential or future events rather than only those that have already occurred is to be attempted, however, a more developed theoretical framework will be necessary. In this chapter, I want to explore one possible such framework. The remainder of the chapter is divided into three main sections. The first section is concerned with the choice of an overall theoretical approach, or paradigm. The second section then addresses some conceptual problems, in particular the definition of the terms italicised in the last paragraph. Finally, the purpose of the third section is to relate these concepts to one another, drawing theoretical connections among them and suggesting hypotheses and a framework for interpretation. Although examples will be given when possible, more developed empirical assessment of this "prototheory" is left to the second volume in this series.

I. Choice of Paradigm

Before any definitional problems can be resolved or theoretical propositions advanced, one must choose the paradigm within which the work will take place. This involves deciding on the nature of the universe to be explained or studied – the "units" or "things" out of which it is made, the kinds of relationships that are important, and the forces that might produce or modify those relationships. In effect, a paradigm is a framework for the construction of an empirical theory and the choice of a paradigm is the choice of the language in which the theory will be built and the research carried out. Although research based on one paradigm may be useful to work in another, all but the barest facts (and sometimes those as well, depending on operational definitions of concepts) require translation.

Paradigms are not falsifiable. They provide structures within which falsifiable empirical hypotheses may be formulated but have no empirical content themselves. Rather, a paradigm is judged by its usefulness, that is by whether the theories advanced within it are verified and whether it contributes to understanding. Ultimately, the test of a theory, and thus indirectly the measure of its parent paradigm's usefulness, is the "objective" standard of accuracy. To date, however, no social science theory has achieved a level of accuracy such that it can stand on that ground alone. Thus, "generality, plausibility and auxiliary implications" must remain important bases for judging theories and choosing paradigms (Fiorina, 1981: 190).

Unfortunately, one implication of this is that the choice of paradigm is largely a matter of taste based on intuition. Moreover, the paradigm that appears most useful for studying one class of phenomena may be different from that which appears most useful for another (Kaplan, 1964: 258-326). It is not surprising, then, that there has been no consensus reached within political science, or even within its subfields.

This chapter is not the place to debate the relative merits of all the competing paradigms in political science, a task which has been undertaken elsewhere (Barry, 1970; Holt and Richardson, 1970). Instead, in this section I only want to lay out the basic elements of the paradigm I propose to adopt, that is the rationalistic (in Barry's terms, the economic) paradigm.

The basic unit for the rationalistic approach is the goal-oriented rational actor. Goal-oriented actors are individuals who perceive that they have goals and whose actions are motivated by a desire to achieve those goals. People do not just act, they act so as to bring about a situation that they value more rather than one that they value less; if there is behaviour that cannot be regarded as purposive, it is inexplicable within the rationalistic framework. Rationality implies that in attempting to further their goals, actors always try to maximise their attainment with the minimum expenditure of resources. As Locke (1975, section 131) put it, "no rational creature can be supposed to change his condition with an intention to be worse."

Stopping here, one would not have said much, for it seems apparent that all behaviour is rational. Indeed, if a psychotic's withdrawal from reality lessens his pain, even that would be rational (Kelley, 1957). Unless the goals being pursued are known or assumed, the rationalist can be expected to produce little beyond vacuous or *ex post* explanations of the form "He did what he did because he wanted to." Rationalistic work advances beyond this by specifying the ends to be pursued, but at this point one advances from the level of paradigm to that of specific theories. The problem of what goals to consider with specific reference to a theory of party government is discussed below.

It is important to be clear as to what this notion of a goal-oriented rational actor does *not* imply. Firstly, it does not imply that an individual's goals will be mutually compatible in the sense of being achievable simultaneously. There may be trade-offs necessary in any particular choice of action; one can with perfect rationality desire both low taxes and a high level of public expenditure for education. Indeed, the basic assumption of the most rationalistic of the social sciences, economics, is that people simultaneously desire both guns and butter in incompatible quantities. (See, however, Converse, 1964: 209.) Secondly, it does not imply that an individual's goals are sensible as seen by an outside observer. Some goals are simply matters of taste; that I consider something to be objectionable, immoral, or self-destructive does not preclude its pursuit by someone else. Other goals are instrumental and thus based on reality judgements. In this case, an objective observer might decide that they were foolish or mistaken, but this raises the third point. Rational actors are not assumed to be omniscient; indeed the costs of obtaining reliable information may be such that a rational individual would consider a blind guess to be more cost-effective than an informed judgement. Fourthly, rational actors need not make involved cost-benefit analyses before taking every action. Rules of thumb and standard operating procedures are rational if they have been proven satisfactory by experience, either real or vicarious. The search for an optimal strategy may prove suboptimal if excessive search and decision costs are incurred. What is assumed is that individuals behave *as if* they made cost-benefit analyses based on the goals they choose to pursue, with the resources available to them, and in the circumstances in which they find themselves.[2]

The rationalistic paradigm is self-consciously individualistic. Neither groups nor organisations exist as primary units within its framework. Instead, they are viewed fundamentally as collections of individuals whose cooperation or cohesion must be explained (Olson, 1965). In a fully elaborated theory, organisations would be dependent phenomena rather than individual actors; organisation is a strategy that may be pursued by some sets of individuals.

This does not mean that organisations or social groups may not enter rationalistic theories for analytic simplicity. Theory building and testing within the rationalistic paradigm proceeds by successive approximations. Simplifying assumptions regarding the nature of the actors, the goals they pursue, the environment in which they operate, or the strategies open to them are posited, and, on the basis of the consequent model, hypotheses are deduced concerning their behaviour. These are tested and to the extent that predictions fail to fit reality the model is modified. In considering the interactions among organisations, it may be productive initially to regard them as unitary actors. Downs' (1957) treatment of parties is a classic example of this. Although many suggestive conclusions could be derived from this simplification, many anomalies remained. Others (e. g., Robertson, 1976) later relaxed this assumption, obtaining a closer fit with reality.

Organisations and institutions may also play a role in rational theories as exogenous or situational variables. From the point of view of the individual(s) whose behaviour is to be explained, an organisation may appear to be a fixed structure like any other institution. Behaviour is decided on and takes place within an institutional structure. Since this partially determines the results of any particular pattern of behaviour, it influences the likelihood that such behaviour will occur. For example, behaviour on the part of a candidate that would be rewarded in a proportional representation system might be counterproductive, and so less likely, in a plurality system. Cultural expectations similarly condition the expected responses from others and anticipation of those responses will influence the actor's initial choice of behaviour. Social and economic variables may be considered in the same way.

Social structure may also be relevant to a rationalistic theory through its influence on the goals of individuals. Whilst the rationalistic paradigm does not recognise social classes as entities distinct from the individuals

[2] Ronald Rogowski (1974: 32). When the individuals in question are in competition, as in the economy or electoral politics, one ground for believing that they will behave, for whatever reason, as if they were making careful cost-benefit calculations is that those who do not behave "rationally" will not survive.

who comprise them, commonality of socialising experiences and similarity of objective situations may lead members of a social class to have similar interests and goals. Moreover, among the values inculcated by these experiences may be a subjective identification and consequent desire for group solidarity and conformity to perceived group norms. Again, however, class solidarity and class consciousness are seen not as natural but as needing explanation. Similarly, whilst "working class Tories" may be exceptional in some countries, the rationalistic paradigm does not regard them as theoretical anomalies.

The rationalistic paradigm is a way of looking at the world and a style of explanation. In this view, whatever the ultimate influence exercised by social forces or institutional/organisational arrangements, the immediate cause of a political event is always the conscious choice of individual human beings. Whilst social, economic, cultural, or political differences may lead individuals who are otherwise similarly placed and pursuing the same goals to make different choices, it is only through those choices that the influence of impersonal forces can be manifested.

II. Conceptual Problems

A. Party and Partyness

The consequences of adopting a rationalistic approach begin to appear as soon as one thinks about parties. In general terms, there are two different ways in which parties may be viewed. The one most common among adherents of the various "sociological" approaches, and the one often implicit in analyses of the functions of political parties or in assertions that parties do, or ought to do, certain things, as well as in comparisons of the behaviour or "gestalt" of different types of parties, is to see each party as an organic entity. In this view, parties seek to control the government and, in this attempt, may either conflict or cooperate with other organisations or structures in society such as mass media, bureaucracy, interest groups, business firms and the military.

From the rationalistic perspective, however, party must be seen as a "they" rather than as an "it". Moreover, once one tries to develop a rigorous theory or to operationalise the concepts necessary for empirical research, the corporate view of party leads to great difficulties. Two may be mentioned here. The first concerns the coherence of party. If party is to be regarded as a whole, it ought to be possible, for example, to identify its goals. As constant conflict and debate within the British Labour Party make clear, however, it is not always a simple task to identify a party's authoritative voice so as to identify its goals. Similarly, in factionalised parties the decision of constitutionally authorised party organs may not bind the party's constituent parts.[3] Far from rescuing the corporate view, attempts to regard each party as a microcosmic political system simply underline the inadequacy of the original conceptualisation.

This is underscored by the second problem which is in many ways even more difficult. The corporate view must assume parties to have distinct boundaries that set them apart from other structures (Eldersveld, 1964: 1). In fact, there obviously is a deep interpenetration of these supposedly rival and autonomous power sources. What, for example, is one to make of the situation in which a church or trade union controls policy by creating a "captive" political party to do its bidding? Although the British Labour Party has grown more autonomous than it was orignally, the trade unions still dominate its conference. Is it a separate institution or an arm of the trade union movement? If the bishops dictate policy to a christian democratic party, is the church simply a successful pressure group, or is the party an arm of the church? And what of the converse case, when a party creates ancillary organisations that behave like other interest groups? Is the Italian CGIL the Communist party in another form or an autonomous and potentially rival group? In either case, total autonomy and total subservience are both overstatements; there are both connections and differences. This reality is easily lost in viewing party as a distinct organism.

The alternative view is to deny the independent existential basis of party, as well as of other groups. Instead, party is seen as an organisation of, or structured pattern of interactions among, individuals in pursuit of their own goals. Rather than being an independent actor, party is an instrument or conduit or basis of influence used by individuals. In this case, one properly speaks of functions being performed within or through political parties rather than by them. Especially, one is alerted to the possibility that "party functions" might be performed elsewhere or not at all, even whilst organisations calling themselves parties exist.

This highlights a clear problem with functional definitions of parties. If parties are defined by their functions, party nonfeasance becomes a logical impossibility. Likewise, it becomes impossible for the defining functions of parties to be performed by any other institution since it would thereby become a party. One may, of course, still refer to the functions of political parties in the sense of "things done by individuals through the mechanism of party" and be concerned with the importance of those things and with the importance for the political system, of having them done through

[3] An appealing way to conceive and measure party government would be to identify the goals of those parties in power and the goals of rival organisations or structures, and then to compare outcomes with those goals; the closer the fit of results to party goals, the more party government there must have been. This approach is precluded, however, by the indeterminacy of *the* goals of the party.

parties.[4] As Smith (1982) observes, however, "It is one thing to provide a functional 'check-list,' but quite another to imply that a party, a party system or an arrangement of party government exists in order to 'perform' certain functions. The approach readily lends itself to distortion. It implies some kind of over-arching system rationality without ever being called upon to demonstrate its presence ... Without necessarily committing itself, the functional ordering additionally takes on a static emphasis, tending to look for a fixed relationship between structure and function." Whilst the rationalistic approach assumes that individual actors are rational, it makes no assumptions about the "rationality of the system," and indeed research has shown that individual rationality may lead to collective irrationality (Hardin, 1968).

What kind of an organisation is a party and how is it distinguished from other structured patterns of interaction? The answer lies in the functions of political parties, not for the political system as in a functional analysis, but for those who use them. Political parties developed in the nineteenth century with the rise of mass suffrage and regularised political participation. They were created to support and assist their organisers who were already in government (in the case of parties of intraparliamentary origin) or who wished to get into government (parties of extraparliamentary origin).[5] They replaced combinations of members of parliament who supported or opposed the government of the day on the basis of their personal interests or preferences, the interests or preferences of their sponsors, or in return for particularistic rewards. Party represents a strategy by which support in the mass public may be cultivated and converted into political power in an electorally oriented democratic society. The key change was ultimate dependence on popular election, and the central distinctions between parties and other groups are that parties contest elections and that they rely on their success in elections for their claim to legitimate participation in government.

Left at this, personal campaign organisations would qualify as political parties, and to a limited extent and especially in presidential systems they should. Presidential systems require special treatment because personal and party victory in a presidential election are synonymous; whichever person/party wins that one election wins control of the executive branch of government.[6] In parliamentary systems — and in the legislative branch of

[4] The term "system" is used here only to mean the collection of political institutions and activities. It is not meant to imply any of the systematic interconnections implicit in systems theory or the systems approach.

[5] See Ostrogorski (1964). This view contrasts with Eldersveld's (1964: 2) assertion that "Parties came into existence to perform certain functions for the system."

[6] Systems with plural executives, even if directly elected, would be more like parliamentary systems. The same would be true where a president was elected by an independent electoral college (e. g., Finland).

presidential systems — the real prize comes not from a single candidate's victory, but from the formation of a legislative majority. Political parties are further distinguished by their cooperative seeking of majorities, and the concomitant right and obligation collectively to govern and to be held responsible for governing.

Fundamentally, parties represent to the voters alternative teams of rulers and to the members of those teams a device for mobilising support to compete with the members of other teams. The basis of this competition may be programmatic or ideological, but it need not be. In particular, conservative parties may have no concrete programme, only a broad philosophy and a belief in their own ability to rule in the national interest (Beer, 1969: 99; Amery, 1953: 4-31). Other parties may have no articulated goal beyond supporting a particular leader. The party politician is committed, or acts as if he were committed, to a cooperative quest for power, not just a personal quest for office, whilst the party voter is voting for a team in addition to a particular candidate.

This conception of party has obvious roots in the responsible parties doctrine. In that notion, parties are the link between the public as a whole and the government as a whole. For parties to serve this function, voters must be able to treat them as collective entities. Only if parties behave cohesively in the discharge of public office, and only if their candidates are prepared to stand or fall as a team on the basis of the party's collective record in office and proposals for the future can voters, whose electoral vocabulary is necessarily limited, have a chance to speak effectively (Lowell, 1913: 67-69). Party is defined here with at least an eye toward this theory.

In admitting this, it becomes necessary to consider three further questions. The first concerns the nature of party unity and indirectly the question of internal party "democracy" in the case of parties with mass memberships. The "party democrats" have seen parties as "huge associations of partisan voters," and have insisted that they be internally democratic (Kirkpatrick, 1950: 22-23; for a critical view, see Schattschneider, 1942: 54). This has naturally raised some complaints that internal party competition is incompatible with collective action in government. Whilst this point may be valid empirically, it is theoretically possible to argue that internal party democracy requires not only that there be competition within the party but also that all party people, including the losers of this internal competition, behave cohesively vis-à-vis the external world in support of the victorious position. It is only this point that is required by partyness. Whatever the internal organisation or rules of the party, and whatever the level of consensus or dissensus among party people, in their relations with nonparty individuals and groups, those following a party strategy of political action must behave as a team.

The second question concerns the nature of the competition among those teams. The responsible parties theory of democracy generally is associated with the requirement that parties present clear and distinctive platforms, spelling out the policies they will follow in office. Because the party that wins an election (assuming a single party does achieve a majority) can be trusted to put its manifesto into practice, this allows voters to exercise *prospective* control over policy. Parties also compete on the basis of their records in office (Budge and Farlie, 1977: chap. 5). In this case the control exercised by voters is *retrospective,* and might be based either on policies or on outcomes (Fiorina, 1981: chap. 1). Indeed in the last case, the choice of the voters – and correspondingly the competition among the parties – may be based on confidence in a particular team of leaders without conscious regard for the policies they have pursued in the past or would pursue in the future. Whilst these differences are important, they do not bear on a party's claim to that name. All that is required is collective accountability, made possible by the expectation of collective action in office.

The third question concerns party membership. Who is the party? Most broadly, one could argue that a party consists of everyone who votes for or sympathises with it. Demands for internal democracy based on an institution like the American direct primary implicitly assume this view. Except for reaching an electoral decision, it is hard to imagine such an "organisation" taking any sort of collective action; "members" make no promises of loyalty and may not have even to admit their membership publicly; there can be no regular communication among members, only from leaders to followers; no sanctions can be imposed against deviants. A more restricted view would be to look only at formal members in the European card-carrying sense, but this implies a mass membership party. Even this, however, confuses supporters with participants. Although the individualistic orientation renders the whole problem of only marginal concern, the view taken here is that the leadership is the party, and when party is discussed as an actor, it is to the collective leadership that reference is meant. This is the only group small enough and in sufficiently constant communication that consciously concerted action is possible. This is not to deny the importance of mass membership in some parties, and of the decisions of supporters for all parties. Members may take many policy decisions – although always subject to the interpretation of party leaders. They may also choose the leaders. Nonetheless, they are no more "the party" than citizens are "the government" in representative democracies. Finally, as suggested above, mass membership is not necessary for a party at all.

The three requirements or defining characteristics of an ideal party thus are: 1) cohesive team behaviour; 2) orientation toward winning control over the totality of political power exercised by elected officials and those appointed by elected officials; and 3) claiming legitimacy on the basis of electoral success. Organisations with many different structural forms could satisfy these criteria and properly be called parties. On the other hand, organisations that call themselves parties might not. For example, clandestine groups that do not contest elections – even if only because they are legally barred from doing so – would not qualify as political parties as the term is meant here.[7] More generally, organisations can vary in the degree to which they satisfy each of these requirements. This implies that one should be concerned with the level of partyness of a group, that is with the degree to which a group approximates the party ideal type, rather than with the dichotomous choice of whether or not to call the group a party. In these terms, the British Conservative party is higher in partyness than the Italian Christian Democracy, whilst both are higher in partyness than the American Republicans, who are in turn higher in partyness than the American Prohibition party.

B. Party Government, Partyness of Government, and Party Governmentness

In defining party government, one is again confronted with a choice between a dichotomy and a range. There has been some tendency to regard party government as a category into which a system either does or does not fit. For example, Mintzel and Schmitt (1981a; see also 1981b) say "Party government is that form of societal conflict regulation in which a plurality of democratically organised political parties play a relatively dominant role both in the socio-political mediation sphere and in the actual process of political decision-making (government sphere)."

If one is interested in the causes, consequences, and future of party government, however, this approach is of little help. Leaving aside Mintzel and Schmitt's questionable insistence on democratically organised parties, presumably a reference to their internal arrangements rather than to their commitment to democracy in the wider governmental sphere, if party government is a category, it evidently includes all modern Western democracies with the possible exception of the United States. If this is so, then the concept is of no empirical utility, since the corresponding operational variable will have no variance. Moreover, if party is an ideal type that is only approximated by real organisations, then party government also must refer to an ideal type which real governments may approach to greater or lesser degrees. Correspondingly, the operational definition of party government must allow for a range of values as well.

Party government is an abstraction of European parliamentary democracy in the era of mass suffrage. Although most clearly based on academic interpretations of British practice, the party government model is an

[7] This means only that generalisations about the behaviour of parties and party politicians or activists may not apply to these groups, and does not imply any normative judgement about them.

intellectual construct whose logic is far more coherent than is the actual operation of any real government. In historical terms, the party government model represents the adaptation of the institutions of bourgeois parliamentary democracy (which were adaptations of the institutions of royal government) to democracies with electorates numbering in the millions rather than the thousands. For democratic theory, the party government model makes government accountable to the general public by entrusting it to individuals organised into parties that owe their positions to electoral approbation. More concretely, party government involves at least three conditions.

Firstly, all major governmental decisions must be taken by people chosen in elections conducted along party lines, or by individuals appointed by and responsible to such people. It is not necessary that parties compete on the basis of alternative policy proposals, but whatever policies are made must be made by individuals who owe their authority either directly or indirectly to the electoral success of their parties. Recognising that a permanent bureaucracy is an essential feature of all modern governments, this condition is violated to the extent that bureaucrats exercise independent policy making authority. It is similarly violated whenever rule making power is turned over to individuals who cannot be removed by elected officials[8] or to functional boards whose members owe their positions to their roles in interest groups or the like rather than to party appointment or election. The party government model requires that party based leaders be able effectively to control the bureaucracy and other public or semipublic agencies. (For an extended discussion of the relationship of party government and the bureaucracy, see the later chapter by Freddi).

Secondly, policy must be decided within the governing party, when there is a "monocolour" government, or by negotiation among parties when there is a coalition. Not only must policy be made by elected officials, a condition met for example by the American Congress, it must also be made along party lines, so that each party may be held collectively accountable for "its" position. This condition is met only rarely by the Congress. Similarly, frequent cross-party negotiations among factions, as has occurred in Italy, lessen the degree to which this condition is met.

Thirdly, the highest officials (e. g., cabinet ministers and especially the prime minister) must be selected within their parties and be responsible to the people through their parties. Positions in government must flow from support within the party rather than party positions flowing from electoral success. For example, the British practice whereby the leader of the majority

[8] Entrusting courts with rule-making authority thus violates this condition of party government unless the judges are chosen in partisan elections or removable in the normal course of politics. Recognition of this suggests that strict adherence to the norms of party government may not be entirely desirable.

party in the House of Commons becomes prime minister is consistent with the party government model whilst the American usage of declaring the winner of enough primary elections to be nominated for president, or of enough electoral votes to be elected president, therefore to be the leader of his party is not. That British party leaders often remain as leaders even after their parties are defeated but are unlikely to survive a substantial intraparty defection even if they formally win the "vote of confidence," whilst a presidential candidate's "party leadership" can withstand major internal defections but not electoral defeat, is indicative of this distinction. The French case is more complicated, but closer to the party government model than to the American model. Mitterand became the presidential candidate of the Socialist party because he was the party's leader (although clearly his presidential appeal was a condition for his rise to party leadership); he remained party leader even after his defeat in the 1974 election. Giscard was similarly party leader first and president second. His leadership of the larger French right whilst he was president, however, was more in the American mold.

A number of observations must be made regarding this definition of party government. Firstly, it represents an ideal type, rather like but in contrast to Dahl's (1971) ideal type of polyarchy. As such, it represents an extreme that may be approximated but is neither realised nor realisable in the ultimate sense. It is also a multidimensional concept. Thus a particular system may closely approximate the ideal type in one respect but not in another. For example, ignoring for the moment the relative partyness of American and British parties, it is apparent that whilst the importance of party in American congressional-presidential relations is extremely low in comparison to its British parliamentary-cabinet counterpart, the role of party in the American bureaucracy is greater than in the British. Similarly, even within a single political system the degree to which many dimensions of the ideal are approximated may vary from one policy area, time, or set of circumstances to another.

Secondly, party government is not a complete description of government or institutions. Whilst perhaps more clearly derived from consideration of adversarial or majoritarian systems in which elections choose between rival and alternating sets of leaders and policies, the basic logic of the model is equally applicable to consociational or coalitional systems.[9] Although perhaps more difficult to achieve in presidential and/or federal systems (empirical hypotheses, on which see below), party government is logically

[9] Lijphart's (1975) description of consociationalism in the Netherlands as government by elite cartel fits nicely with the party government model to the extent that party elites were the leading figures in each social pillar. The Swiss system described by Steiner (1974) fits far less well.

compatible with these institutional arrangements as well as with parliamentary and unitary systems.

Together, these two observations imply that many different approximations of the party government model are possible. Assuming that a single quantitative measure of party government were devised, it would combine several dimensions with the result that two systems could achieve the same "party government score" whilst standing quite differently on the individual dimensions. Whether the dimensions that comprise the overall concept of party government are sufficiently coherent that this does not occur, or whether the dimensions of the overall concept must be considered separately, is a question for empirical research.

In the same way, similar "party government scores" might be achieved by countries with very different party systems. Two party competitive systems, systems with alternating coalitions, systems dominated by a single party or coalition with a semipermanent opposition (so long as it is permitted to contest elections freely), and systems with grand coalitions all are potential party governments. Whether similar levels of party government are produced by similar conditions and whether they lead to similar consequences in these differing systems also must be resolved empirically.

Finally, this definition of party government is intended to distinguish party government from other forms of government. It speaks to the "partyness of government" as a characteristic of the formal institutions of government and indicates the proportion of formal governmental power exercised in accordance with the party government model. To the extent that a system is high in partyness of government, what formal government there is will be party government. There is no guarantee, however, that there will be any effective formal government at all. Whilst the "authoritative allocation of values" goes on in all societies – even those with no "political" institutions – the government of the party government model may be more or less relevant to this process.

This observation has two consequences for the definition of party government. Firstly, it means that those conditions which define or promote government in general must be appended to those specifically relating to party government. Secondly, adding these considerations to the definition of party government underlines a distinction between *partyness of government,* referring to a narrow institutional sense of party government as party control of the formal government apparatus, and *party governmentness,* referring to a broader sense of party government as a general social characteristic. For example, in a laissez-faire economy, high partyness of government would still leave parties in a relatively marginal position in the authoritative allocation of economic values. Correspondingly, if the power of government grew whilst the party politicians' relative ability to control it shrank, parties might become absolutely more important in the overall allocation of values even whilst the partyness of government declined. The broader concept, party governmentness, refers to a characteristic of the *Herrschaftsorganisation* of the overall society, and indicates the proportion of all social power exercised by parties within the framework of the party government model.

C. System Capacity

Looking at the chronic economic problems of many Western countries, or still more at the collapse of democratic regimes in the interwar era, there is a strong temptation to attribute these difficulties to a lack of capacity on the part of the government or parties. There is an element of truth to this. Assuming that those governing the contemporary West want to "solve" their countries' economic problems, and assuming that the leaders of the prewar democratic regimes of Germany, Italy, and Spain "wanted" those regimes to survive, their failure to do so certainly indicates a lack of capacity. This, however, is a tautology, not an explanation; if failure is the definer of low capacity, low capacity cannot be the explanation of failure.

Moreover, in many cases it is not clear that failure as defined from outside really is an indicator of low capacity. To listen to the rhetoric of some left wing politicians, one might wonder whether bourgeois parties really do want to reduce unemployment; after all, it keeps wages low and workers docile. Similarly, inflation is beneficial to some groups, at least in the short run. Beyond the debatability of what a solution to many problems is, the cost of a solution in terms of personal or organisational goals may be so high that politicians choose not to solve the problem. In Thurow's (1980: 44) view, for example, Richard Nixon could have stemmed American inflation in 1972 had he persisted with recessionary policies; he believed that to do so, however, would cost him the 1972 election and so he chose to change his policy. Objective failure thus may be the result of lack of will or lack of foresight rather than lack of ability. Finally some problems may have no solutions. If poverty is relative rather than absolute, then the poor will always be with us.

This suggests that "problem solution capacity" actually consists of four distinct, or semidistinct, elements. The first element is the capacity to get a specific policy implemented. Taking an example from the field of economic management, if the party leadership decides it wants the central bank's loan rate raised, does it have the ability to get that done? More generally, this element also includes the ability to implement one policy without unintentionally disrupting the implementation of other policies.

The second element of problem solution capacity is the ability to frame policies that will produce the desired (by the policy maker) results. Conceptually, this and the first element are confused by the fact that many political ends are means to more fundamental ends, which in turn are means, and so forth. Continuing with the economic example, an increase in the bank rate may be a means to reduce the money supply, which is a means to reduce inflation, which is a means to stem capital flight, which is a means to stimulate investment, etc. If the party chooses to reduce the money supply and nothing happens, does this mean that they lacked the capacity to implement a policy or that they lacked the capacity to choose a policy that would produce the desired result? Empirically, however, it is often possible to distinguish perceived means from perceived ends, and to find circumstances in which a party's orders are scrupulously followed without the desired result being achieved.

The third element of problem solution capacity is the ability to choose the "right" aims or policies. This is the most difficult element to deal with because of the ambiguity and unmeasurability of "right." On one hand, the term is often used as a synonym for the policies the writer prefers. This is a danger to be avoided in an objective analysis of party government. On the other hand, concern with the "right" policies simply pushes the means-ends chain even further along and takes a longer term view. Can the party identify problems before they become crises? Can it choose policies that avert crises in the future? In the economic example, can the party find a balance among economic growth, inflation, unemployment, and conservation of resources that is viable in the long run?[10]

The final element of problem solution capacity is will. Given that a party could identify correct long term goals, could formulate policies that would achieve those goals, and could get those policies implemented, does it do so? Is the party so positioned and so structured that its leaders are prepared to expend the resources and bear the costs involved in formulating and implementing policies?

The economic examples suggest that capacity involves the power to alter social reality, for example to solve the problem of inflation by reducing the inflation rate. There is another sense of capacity that must be remembered, the ability to resolve or defuse problems by altering perceptions rather than situations, in this case to get people to see a higher inflation rate as acceptable or to lower their level of concern. The same elements are relevant to this sense of capacity as well.

D. Persistence and Failure to Persist

Contemporary concern about party government focusses on the possibility that systems with high partyness of government or high party governmentness will be unable to meet the challenges confronting them and, consequently, will not persist. The complementary possibility that the level

[10] Although clearly a difficult problem, the importance of distinguishing between policies as means and final end states as desiderata is underlined by Robertson (1976).

of party government might increase no longer is seen as a cause for concern. As a result, persistence here is defined *ex adverso;* the real concern is not with persistence, but rather with failure to persist.

There are three ways to conceive of the persistence of a system of party government, and correspondingly three sets of circumstances or conditions that would indicate failure to persist. The first concerns the durability of the current party system and especially the continued dominance of those parties most regularly in office. In Italy, for example, this would mean the Christian Democrats would continue to dominate all cabinets, whilst in Britain it would mean that the Labour and Conservative parties continue to provide alternating single party governments. On the surface, this may be the least interesting. No party system can survive forever in a dynamic society. Even if the party labels remain the same and there is continuity of organisation, the issues raised by the parties, the social groups allied with each party, and the party leaders all will change. Realignments, the rise of new parties and the collapse of old parties all may occur without causing more than cosmetic changes to the society's system of governance. Indeed, the rise of a new party such as the British Social Democrats or the attainment of government status by a party previously consigned to permanent opposition may be indicative of the underlying strength of the polity. On the other hand, the persistence of the current party system is likely to be of great importance to those owing their positions to it.

The second aspect of persistence of party government relates to the continued adherence of political actors to the party government strategy. The alternative would be a voluntary abandonment of this strategy and thus the supersession of a system that highly approximates the party government ideal by one in which parties were far less important.[11] This could come about if the combination of goals and circumstances that led originally to the establishment of party government were to change. For example, exogenous changes such as the rise of television or strengthened interest group systems might encourage even those who have gained power through party to adopt other strategies and certainly would alter the attractiveness of alternative avenues of influence for succeeding generations of political activists. The long run effect would be to change the balance of political forces to the detriment of party government. Moreover, the interplay of short term and long term goals could lead those in power in a government dominated by parties to make choices that ultimately undermine that very system from within. The creation of nonparty independent boards such as the British Electricity Board or the American Federal Reserve Board illustrate this possibility.

[11] The term "supersession" is borrowed from Smith (1982). My use of it, however, whilst strongly influenced by his, is not identical to it. See below.

Supersession, as these examples suggest, would be an evolutionary process resulting from gradual changes and the interplay of many individual decisions over a period of time. Since party government is more a matter of interrelationships among individuals than it is of institutions, it is likely that many of the structures of party government – cabinets, partisan elections, and the parties themselves – would survive a process of supersession, just as the "dignified" parts of the 19th century English constitution had survived their supersession by the "efficient" parts (Bagehot, 1963). Indeed, the persistence of the old institutions might aid in legitimising the new regime. The actual level of party government would decline over time until ultimately one discovered that it had gone. Whilst we have no examples of party governments being fully superseded by some other form, one can look for examples of decline in party government.

The third aspect of persistence is avoidance of precipitate collapse or rupture. In this case, the institutions of the old party government regime disappear. The agents of the collapse may be external, as in a coup or revolution, or they may be internal, with those currently in office deciding to restructure the government themselves. Presumably, rupture could involve the abrupt replacement of one variety of party government by another, as the replacement of the Fourth French Republic by the Fifth ultimately did. It is clear, however, that De Gaulle's intention was to establish a democratic, but nonparty government, regime. The early Fifth Republic in fact would be scored low in partyness of government.

E. Democracy

Much of the concern for the future of party government stems from the close connection of this model with ideas about democracy. Indeed, representative democracy has been defined by some in such a way as to make party government logically necessary for its attainment. This is not the place for a full consideration of the meaning of democracy, but since the question of whether party government is a necessary condition for democratic or nonauthoritarian government in mass societies so colours discussion of its future, this question must be addressed.

The party government model presumes a relatively centralised decision-making process in which a single agency, be it a parliament, a president, or a cabinet exercises supreme control over the full range of government activities. The problem is to democratise that government. In the party government conception, the fundamental democratic principle is majority rule. Because a majority has given their votes to the party or coalition of parties in power and can be said collectively to control them, either prospectively or retrospectively, those politicians are entitled to exercise all the power of the state. Thus, where formal institutions are not centralised in this way, the model assigns to parties the function of making them operate in practice as if they were so organised.

The party government model implicitly assumes the possibility of forming majority coalitions, either within a single party or among a limited number of parties, that are able to agree on a wide range of issues. In its simplest form, the party government model must assume not only that there are two sides to every question (Duverger, 1959), but that there are exactly two significant complexes of positions each represented by one of exactly two parties, one of which is thus guaranteed a majority. Variations based on coalitions relax this assumption, but the notion that political conflict should be contained in the competition of relatively few, cohesive, parties still carries with it the expectation that society will be similarly divided into relatively few cohesive groups, each with its own complex of policy positions or interests. The archetypical example of this is working class solidarity in the socialist tradition of class based politics, but farmers' parties, or parties of religious subcultures could be equally consistent with it.

Laid out like this, it is clear that there are alternative conceptions of democracy imaginable. Two may be mentioned as examples. One is a kind of neocorporatism exemplified by Heisler's (1974) "European polity model." In contrast to the party government model's assumption of centralised decision-making, this model envisions functionally segmented authority. The fundamental value is compromise and the achievement of consensual decisions among those most directly affected by a particular policy, rather than decision by a majority of all citizens. The people are represented in the decision-making bodies of this system, but not primarily in their capacity as citizens. Instead, the emphasis is on representation of affected interests. In Heisler's model, functional boards coexist with a parliamentary system, but as the corporatist bodies gain in influence, the model quite naturally begins to assign primacy to interest groups rather than to parties as avenues of popular participation in the governing process.

The other alternative is pluralist democracy as elaborated by Dahl (1956) among others and approximated by government in the United States. Emphasis is shifted from majority rule to the protection of minorities. This is achieved in part through the *incoherence* of the parties. Instead of each party representing a distinctive social or ideological constituency, the parties overlap so that no party can afford to offend any group. In place of stable majorities, shifting coalitions that often cut across party lines decide succeeding issues. In terms of social structure, this model assumes cross-cutting cleavages rather than coherent groups.

Whether these, or other possible systems, would have the necessary capacity to resolve social problems, whether they could survive, and whether they could remain nonauthoritarian are open questions, but the same is true of party government.

III. Relationships and Hypotheses

As laid out above, party government is less a category than it is a strategy which might be pursued within the category of democratic government. Consequently, the first questions that must be addressed are: 1) under what circumstances would individuals seeking control of government adopt the party government strategy? and 2) what conditions relate to their likelihood of success? A second set of questions then relates the level of party government to the concepts of capacity and persistence: 3) what are the conditions for capacity and persistence? and 4) does the model of party government have any built-in characteristics that relate to capacity or persistence? Naturally, complete answers to these questions are impossible here. The purpose of this section is simply to outline a number of theoretical relationships and to sketch several hypotheses that might be tested in later research.

A. Conditions for Party Government

Political parties were organised to mobilise mass support. They are not the only way in which mass support may be mobilised and channeled. Interest groups, in fact, predate political parties and were used to mobilise support to influence parliamentary and monarchic governments. With increases in education and leisure time and with the growing complexity of societies, the number and range of interest groups have mushroomed. In corporatist or polyarchal models of government, these structures are far more important than are parties. Further, the mass media, especially television, increasingly are able to arouse the public, either on behalf of politicians, who thus no longer need rely on party as their primary channel of communication with the public, or on behalf of other interests, including their own. Moreover, important though it may be, mass support is not the only important political resource. As the complexity of the problems with which the government deals increases, so too does the value of technical expertise. As the need for voluntary compliance and cooperation increases, so too does the value of being able to secure or withhold that compliance. Political parties may be able to mobilise these resources, but they may not. As a consequence, party is a political tool whose relative effectiveness and attractiveness to elites may vary.

To account for the behaviour of politicans (and others) requires understanding of their goals so that the costs and benefits of various actions in terms of those goals may be assessed. The problem of goals may be dealt with in either, or a combination, of two ways. They may be ascertained empirically. This appears most desirable, but actually involves several serious difficulties. To infer goals from behaviour leads immediately to a problem of circularity; if behaviour is the operational indicator of goals, then hypotheses explaining behaviour on the basis of goals are nonfalsifiable. Alhough direct questioning about goals avoids this problem, the practical problems of obtaining frank responses coupled with the impossibility of interviewing those who have passed from the scene render this strategy of questionable value as well. Public pronouncements such as speeches and party manifestos, whilst ostensible statements of goals, are prepared for strategic as well as informative purposes. Moreover, they frequently relate only to one variety of goal, those concerning public policy. Nonetheless, this kind of data, if interpreted with caution, does provide some insight into goals.

The other approach to goals is to stipulate them by assumption. The strategy then is to reason out what a rational actor pursuing the assumed goals would do, compare actual behaviour to the deduced hyotheses, and to the degree that they coincide interpret this as evidence supporting both the general theory and the assumption about goals.

For professional politicians, the most common assumption has been that they "are interested in getting reelected – indeed, in their role here as abstractions, interested in nothing else" (Mayhew, 1974: 13). Whilst an obvious oversimplification, this assumption has been defended on three grounds. The first is the importance of the desire to be reelected as the mechanism on which democratic theory relies to make office holders accountable to the general public. Politicians with no desire to be reelected would have no necessary incentive to worry about the needs or desires of their constituents. Secondly, whatever the other goals of politicians, re-election is an instrument to their realisation. To paraphrase one maxim, if winning isn't everything, losing isn't anything. Finally, the assumption that politicians are single minded seekers of reelection is defended on the ground that it works. A significant range of real world behaviour can be explained in this way.

An alternative approach is to assume the primacy of policy commitments over office. In this formulation, office has purely instrumental value; rational politicians will not compromise their beliefs to win or retain office since doing so destroys the value of victory. There is certainly some truth to this position. Aside from the individual who has given up office for a principle, the continued existence of parties with no likelihood ever of participating in government or even winning a seat[12] and the fervour with which some parties espouse positions they know to be costly electorally imply that there must be some motivation beside office seeking. At the same time, for every "profile in courage," there are corresponding "apologetic

[12] Whether such organisations should be called parties within the framework suggested above is irrelevant here. The point is simply to demonstrate that political activity is often motivated by desires other than office.

statesmen of a compromising kind" prepared to endure anything in order to retain office.[13]

A more realistic view of parties and politicians requires that three types of goals be considered. The first are policy goals. Clearly one reason why people engage in political activity is that they want to achieve or defeat certain social, economic, or political changes. Burke's very definition of party, "a body of men united, for promoting by their joint endeavours the national interest, upon some principle in which they are all agreed" (1839: v. I, 425-26) reflects the importance of this motivation. Whilst politicians and parties differ with regard to the specificity of their policy goals, the degree to which they perceive them to be interconnected (ideological) or isolated, the range of compromise they are prepared to accept, and the overall importance they ascribe to policy, it would be difficult to find anyone engaged in political activity who was completely indifferent to policy. On the other hand, to assume that all members of a particular party must be agreed on anything but the vaguest of principles is to ignore the tremendous differences within such parties as the American Democrats, the Japanese Liberal Democrats, or the Italian Christian Democrats.

A second set of goals is organisational. Examples include maintaining party unity, increasing the size of the party's membership, or securing some subsidy or competitive advantage. To the extent that party is purely instrumental, these goals are instrumental as well. The phenomenon of "party loyalty" and the agonising of politicians before they desert a party of which they have been long time members, however, suggest that party may become an end in itself, a valued association to be defended even at the expense of other goals. Additionally, since the expected long-term instrumental value of party may outweigh short-term costs to other values, this category of goal must be considered.

Finally, there are personal goals. Politicians are people as well as public figures. Whilst it may make little sense to assume that parties as organisations seek office for its own sake, for an individual the social position, power, salary, or other perquisites that are part of public office may be an ultimate, if rarely the ultimate, goal. Enough has been written about the corrupting influence of office to underscore the importance of such personal goals for leading politicians, and those who aspire to become leading politicians.

Although this discussion has been in terms largely of professional politicians, the same types of goals may be ascribed to party members, supporters, and voters. Left wing policy demands that currently threaten the existence of the British Labour Party are based largely in the rank and file and middle level elites. The sacking of leading MPs for the crime of

[13] The first phrase is John F. Kennedy's (1956); the second is from William S. Gilbert, *The Mikado.*

excessive loyalty to the leader indicates a feeling that electoral victory without ideological purity is not worth winning. At other times, constituency parties have behaved as though nothing were so important as party loyalty, even in the face of abrupt about turns in policy (Ranney, 1965: 281). Similarly, personal goals may be important at all levels of party. Some party members may be attracted primarily by a desire to contribute to party victory as a way of influencing policy for the public good or because they value victory by "their" party in the same way that they value victory by "their" football team, but others may be attracted by the hope of special treatment or patronage from the government, because a party job is preferable to unemployment, or intrinsically attractive, or simply for a social outlet (Wilson, 1962). Whilst my concern is primarily with party leaders, they must take account of the motivations of their followers if they are to be effective.

The interrelationships among these goals may be quite complex. Any of them may be instrumental for the achievement of others. Office or party organisation may be valued because they contribute to the opportunity to control policy, but policy may be manipulated so as to retain office or in the interest of party unity. Similarly, a strong organisation may make the personal rewards of leadership more appealing and realisable, but the achievement of high status may be used to bolster the party organisation. Conversely, no single strategy is likely to be best for achieving all three types of goals simultaneously (Sjöblom, 1968: 158-82). Compromises with other parties required to achieve office or to influence public policy may undermine the loyalty of party activists and thus weaken the party, as the Italian Communists found in the early 1980s, but ideological purity may be maintained only by remaining without office or influence. The internal compromises required to maintain party unity or to advance one's personal career may involve sacrificing policy preferences.

Although under some circumstances rational individuals may decide that a party strategy is the best way to achieve their goals, that strategy will certainly involve costs. Party involves compromise, cooperation, and discipline, and those occasionally mean not doing what one otherwise would like to do. Although his limits of tolerance will vary according to the relative value placed on compensatory goals, unless the party is agreed totally on everything, a party politician occasionally will be compelled by party loyalty to support policies that personally he opposes. A party-oriented voter occasionally will have to vote for his party's candidate, even though he finds a candidate of another party to be more attractive personally. In a party government, bureaucrats occasionally will have to be silent and support policies that they think are ill-advised. The problem of explaining party government is to find combinations of circumstances and goals under which people will be willing to bear these costs.

In speculating about these conditions, one runs a great risk of circularity. The strongest conditioning factor for party government at the present is to have had party government in the past. Political arrangements have a natural inertia. The role models for aspiring politicians, and thus the expectations on which they base their judgements, are the behaviour patterns of their predecessors. Even when there are major structural changes, behaviour is likely to adjust slowly. As Bagehot (1963: 268) observed about so momentous a change as the Reform Act of 1832, "A new Constitution does not produce its full effect as long as all its subjects were reared under an old Constitution, as long as its statesmen were trained by that old Constitution." Change will be even slower without major upheavals.

Further, the defining characteristics of party government are conditioning factors for its continuance. If party dominates the policy making process, then those seeking to influence policy must work through parties. If the only route to office is through partisan election, then those seeking office must become party men. Moreover, many other factors that may provide incentives for party government-like behaviour are themselves consequences of party government. Examples include party control over interest articulation and political communication, the existence of structural biases favouring partisan candidates over independents, or widespread party identification in the mass public. Nonetheless, if some element of this apparently homeostatic pattern of mutual causation and reinforcement were to be modified by an exogenous force, one would expect changes throughout, and ultimately a change in the system's propensity toward party government. What factors ought one to expect to determine the level of party government?

1. *Presidential or parliamentary government*

Party government is more likely in parliamentary systems because party is more useful to political leaders in such systems. A parliamentary cabinet needs a continuous majority (of those voting) to remain in office; even if a pattern of shifting alliances might allow a prime minister to remain in office with a different majority on each vote, his ministry would be changing constantly. Party is a device by means of which stable majorities may be achieved, whether office is seen as an instrumental or as an ultimate value. Party is also useful for backbench MPs. For those interested in office, it provides a career ladder; for those interested in policy, party provides a means of influencing the ministry, whose continuous dependence on party support forces them to take account of backbench opinion even if electoral expediency calls for another course.

Presidential government, on the other hand, both makes personalism more likely and entails two rival arenas for decision-making. Whilst the latter problem may be minimised by institutionalising executive dominance, as in Fifth Republic France, the former is thereby heightened. A president, with the resources of the state at his command, the status and visibility of head of state and head of government, and the security of a fixed term is likely to think of himself as separate from and independent of his party. Presidents, in seeing themselves personally to have been entrusted with administration of the state tend to appoint officials with weak or no party ties to a greater extent than do prime ministers. The officials so appointed owe their positions far more clearly to the president than to their parties. All this weakens party government (cf. Lijphart, 1977: 28-29, 210-16).

Two factors may contribute to a partial overcoming of the anti-party bias of presidential systems. The first is frequent partisan reelection campaigns; the seven year term of the French president, for example, might allow the incumbent so to overshadow his party that they are left with little alternative but to be subservient to him. The second is party control over nomination and renomination. Party government can coexist with a presidential system if only committed party men can become president or if party support is required for reelection. A system in which the president is chosen by a partisan electoral college like that of Finland would be more likely to have party government than one in which the president effectively is elected directly, as in the United States.

The French case requires one additional comment. Although it has been discussed as an example of a presidential system, this actually is a debatable point. So long as the president is supported by a majority in the legislature, the system works as if it were presidential, but only in the same sense that "prime ministerial" government also works like presidentialism. Without a reliable majority, however, a French president could not govern and this dependence on legislative support (a characteristic of parliamentary systems) may be one of the strongest factors encouraging party government in France.

2. *Integration and centralisation*

The essence of party government is that what appears to the public as a single entity, the political party, is in coordinated control of the entire government. Whilst this is possible in a decentralised state, with a tightly centralised party organisation coordinating disparate branches of government, it is easier if the institutions of government are themselves centralised. Moreover, decentralised government also makes centralisation of the party more difficult to maintain (Eldersveld, 1964; Duverger, 1959: 55-56).

This is especially so if the basis of decentralisation is geographic. In this case, implementation of policies initiated at one level may depend on cooperation of officials at another level where government has a different partisan complexion. Responsibility is naturally obscured, and the parties have an incentive to obscure it further, those in control at each level attempting to claim credit for successful or popular policies whilst blaming those in control at the other level for the rest. Moreover, if subnational governments are too powerful, the corresponding level of party organisation may supplant the national party as the primary focus of loyalty. If there are important regional differences in culture or interest, this can seriously undermine the coherence of the national parties and party system. The clearest examples of these problems are the distinction between presidential and congressional parties or between northern and southern Democrats in the United States (Burns, 1963) but Swiss parties show evidence of this as well (Katz, 1981; Kerr, 1974).

3. *Electoral system*

Various aspects of the electoral system should have an impact on the level and nature of party government. Probably the most significant for party unity is the presence or absence of some form of intraparty electoral choice. In some systems, voters can choose only parties; the choice of the particular individuals who will be elected if their parties are victorious is an internal party decision. In other systems, however, voters either can influence or entirely determine the choice of person as well as of party (Katz, 1982). Where a candidate must compete with other candidates of his own party, support of and by the party is unlikely to be adequate for election. Instead, the candidate is forced to develop his own base of support. This undermines party cohesion in two ways. Firstly, it gives the successful candidate an independent base; not owing his election only to the party, he has less reason to be loyal to it. Secondly, in building support for the intraparty competition, the candidate will have made compromises, incurred debts, and developed loyalties different from those of his copartisans. Once in office, these candidates find party unity harder to maintain, especially if the intraparty competition involved questions of policy in addition to personalities (Katz, 1980). Electoral systems in which the choice of candidates may cut across party lines (single transferable vote, PR with panachage, or the open primary) should be particularly inhibitive of party government.

Proportional representation presents a mixed situation. On one hand, it is more conducive than single member majority or plurality systems to high partyness of parties. PR systems' list orientation forces candidates to campaign and voters to think in partisan rather than personal terms. It also encourages a uniform national party system by raising the local threshold for representation (Rae, 1971) — thus discouraging purely local parties — whilst also encouraging parties that present candidates anywhere to present them everywhere. That candidates of a party in all areas of the country face the same multiple competitors should encourage them to take the same, ideological, positions, making party unity easier to maintain. On the other hand, PR also encourages party fragmentation by lowering the costs of party schisms. A fragmented party system, then, will make coalition government more likely, and to the extent that this obscures accountability and encourages instability of government it may make partyness of government more difficult to achieve.

Other things being equal, the more different kinds of elected officials there are, the weaker party government is likely to be. In particular, election of more than one official at the national level (e. g., a president and a prime minister) is likely to weaken party government by multiplying the number of individuals with personal claims to speak for the party. On the other hand, increasing the number of partisan appointed officials makes party government more likely. As government has grown larger and more complex, it has required more people to control and coordinate it. Without adequate loyal personnel, a party government nominally in power has no defense against foot dragging bureaucrats and little hope of keeping fully informed of intragovernmental happenings. Similarly, policy making occurs at many points, requiring a large number of partisans in office if the party is to participate in the making of most policies, let alone if it is to make them itself (Rose, 1969).

4. Size of the public sector

Whilst enlargement of the public sector may increase the party governmentness of society, it is likely to decrease the partyness of government. Firstly, a large public sector makes the ruling party more dependent on experts. Often these will be bureaucrats or representatives of affected interests rather than party people. Moreover, even those who are employees of the party are likely to have divided loyalties, on one hand to the party but on the other to their professional peer group. Secondly, the larger the sphere of government activity, the more difficult will be the problem of coordination and the greater the degree of bureaucratic uncontrollability. Thirdly, expansion of government gives more groups a greater stake in politics, encouraging greater activity and involvement, but many of these groups are rivals for party. Fourthly, as more of the economy comes under public control, the need for stability, the party's desire to evade responsibility if things go wrong, and the party's fear of being totally excluded should they lose the next election all grow. This has led to the creation of nonpartisan and multipartisan boards to control, for example, banking, nationalised industries, and mass communication. Once such boards are created, however, significant areas of policy leave direct party control and the problems of coordination of public policy increase.

5. Private government

Individuals naturally try to avoid responsibility for unsuccessful policies. To maintain the collective responsibility that is the hallmark of party government is easier if the public is denied access to intraparty decision-making. Unable to attribute blame to any particular individual or faction, the voters are encouraged to reward or punish the party as a whole. This, in turn, gives each member of the party a stake in the success of its policies, even if he opposed them initially.

Private government also encourages party unity by making compromise among party leaders more possible. All parties are coalitions, and party leaders frequently owe their positions to the particular support of a subgroup within the party, be it based on personal loyalities, policy preferences, or organisational ties. Not faced with the need to forge agreement themselves, those supporters may not be sympathetic to the accommodations necessary to achieve unity, forcing the leader into the untenable position of alienating his supporters if he compromises, but losing his effectiveness if he does not.

6. *Input, representation, and communication*

When party is the primary channel for public participation, demand articulation and aggregation, and communication from leaders to followers, party government will be stronger. Where other structures, e. g., mass media and interest groups, share in performing these functions, party control over politics will be weaker. In particular, if the party is sufficiently in control of communication effectively to control the political agenda, party government will be stronger. If nonparty agencies are able to set public priorities, however, the position of the parties will be weaker.

7. *Bureaucratic anonymity*

Bureaucrats are both potential rivals for party politicians and potential scapegoats for their failures. Both these possibilities undermine party government, but both can be minimised by an expectation of bureaucratic anonymity. Party government is furthered when politicians cannot avoid responsibility by blaming policies on the bureaucracy and bureaucrats are more likely to implement policies they personally oppose if they know they will not suffer for efforts made in good faith to implement bad policies. Moreover, party government is undermined whenever bureaucrats can appeal around their political masters directly to the public or to a powerful interest group clientele.

8. *Social segmentation*

Where each party represents a clearly discernable interest, segment, class, or viewpoint within society, party unity will be easier to maintain, the distinction between parties will be clearer, and party government will be more likely. Cross-cutting cleavages and overlapping party constituencies will make interparty cooperation, and intraparty dissension, more likely, thus decreasing the level of party government.

Where society is divided into relatively few groups, each of which has a relatively coherent *set* of views spanning the range of public issues, a relatively small number of parties should be able adequately to represent those views. Cross-cutting cleavages force the leaders of each party to ignore many issues, consideration of which would threaten their party's unity. One consequence of this is likely to be increased importance for interest groups that represent those concerns.

As the last several conditions mentioned indicate, party government depends not only on party politicians but also on the behaviour of actors for whom the pattern of goals and structure of incentives may be quite different. Whilst a full treatment of this problem is beyond the scope of a single paper, three potentially rival power wielders should be discussed briefly, both for illustrative purposes and because of their importance.

9. Bureaucracy

The first of these is the bureaucracy. Especially in Britain, there was once a tendency to assume the civil service to be apolitical (e.g., Morrison, 1964: 52, 328-31). As an ideal type, the model of bureaucracy assumes not only that bureaucrats are neutral with regard to the policy questions of the day, but also that they do not have personal goals that might conflict with their public responsibilities. Both these assumptions are false. Bureaucrats have a vested interest in established routines and relationships, and in the policies associated with them. There often develops an agreed "civil service" view of how things ought to be done. Whilst these preferences may not be partisan in a strict sense, they represent a tremendous barrier to a party wishing to innovate. Bureaucrats also have an interest in converting their minister from a member of a party team into a spokesman for their department (Crossman, 1972: 63-65). The bureaucrat's private career interest gives him an incentive to defend his programme and budget, often by building support for them outside the government in the form of a clientele. But as in all patron-client relationships, the patron acquires obligations as well as support. Clientelism gives bureaucrats both the opportunity and often the need to obstruct party policies (Dumont, 1972).

10. Interest groups

The second set of potential rivals for party government is interest groups. In the party government model, groups should pursue their interests through parties, either by offering and withholding electoral support or by becoming affiliated with or penetrating a party.[14] The former strategy is likely to be effective if the group's support can make an appreciable difference and if it can be withheld credibly. The latter is likely to be

[14] LaPalombara (1964: chap. 9) uses the Italian term "parentela" (literally, kinsfolk) to describe the latter strategy.

pursued only if one party is dominant; the price of influence through one party is lack of influence when that party is out of office.

If neither of these conditions is met, and especially if the group's interests are relatively narrow, a clientelistic relationship with the bureaucracy is likely to be most productive. The administrative problems of bureaucrats are greatly reduced if they can establish a working relationship with the representatives of the interest affected by their agency. The group, in return, is guaranteed sympathetic access to those in charge of the policies affecting them. Over time, the bureaucrats come to depend on their clients for political support and administrative assistance. The group's leadership tends to be coopted to a quasi-administrative perspective. As the group's leaders and bureaucrats move together, this kind of relationship can lead to party politicians being presented with *faits accomplis* policies agreed by the bureaucracy and the affected interests and not readily subject to change.

A related alternative to a clientelistic strategy is to press for corporatist decision-making. Again, the interest group gains direct access to and participation in the decision process and the bureaucracy gains a smoothly administerable programme. Establishment of corporatist bodies may be attractive for parties as well as a way of defusing opposition and coopting critics. Although this may be an effective short-term strategy for the particular parties in power, in the longer term party government is weakened as expressions of political interest are no longer channeled exclusively through party. Effective administration requires strong and well-articulated interest groups with which party and bureaucracy may deal, but these then become rival sources of power.

11. Television

Finally, the third rival that requires mention is television journalism. This has assumed many of the functions — oversight, criticism, raising of issues — traditionally ascribed to the opposition. But unlike party oppositions, television is both permanently in opposition, and thus never called upon to do better, and apparently disinterested, and thus credible (Crozier, 1975: 92; Smith, 1979).

Although television journalists may have particular policy views they would like to advance, their greatest impact on the problem of party government comes from their pursuit of professional goals (Altheide, 1974). Television has tended to personalise politics, increasing the visibility of a few party leaders whilst diminishing the salience of party. Investigative reporting has decreased the anonymity of bureaucrats and the privacy of government. In the name of objectivity, television has provided a channel for bureaucrats, interest groups, and dissident politicians to mobilise support without the aid of party. In conformance with the professional norm that "good news is no news," television has undermined public confidence in public institutions, including parties (Robinson, 1976). The immediacy of television news has forced party leaders to give more weight to short-term results, to their personal images, and to goals relating to maintenance of their positions at the expense both of governing and of more general organisational goals.

This is not to suggest that television journalists have undermined party government intentionally. Rather, their pursuit of their own goals has an impact on the behavioural incentives of others to the detriment of party government.

B. Conditions for Persistence

For the social theorist interested in the problem of party government, primary interest in persistence concerns the survival of party government as a form of *Herrschaftsorganisation.* This persistence depends, however, on the aggregate decisions and behaviour of individuals for whom the immediate concern is far more likely to be the welfare of their own parties. Regardless of whether office and party strength are instrumental or ultimate goals, they can hardly be ignored by politicians seeking to achieve anything through party government.

Persistence of a party requires the conjunction of two interrelated conditions. Firstly, the supporters and especially the activists and second level leaders of the party must be sufficiently satisfied that they continue to work for it, and in particular that they do not exercise, either singly or collectively, the exit option (Hirschmann, 1970). How easy this will be depends both on the goals of those individuals and on circumstances.

One way for party leaders to minimise the risk of exit is to make use of voice relatively more attractive, that is by being responsive to the demands of their followers. This may involve substantial costs to the leaders, however. It reduces their autonomy, and perhaps also the value of party leadership. They may resist for this reason alone. The demands of party activists may also be counterproductive for leaders seeking to win elections or enter coalition governments. In two-party systems, the supporters of a single party, representing only half of the political spectrum, tend to prefer policies more extreme than those supported by the median voter. Unless the other party is similarly constrained by its supporters, a party that moves away from such a moderate position is severely disadvantaged in a single member plurality system. The response that Robertson (1976) suggests for party leaders is to satisfy their followers when an election is "unwinnable" or "unlosable," and to satisfy the voters when the election's outcome is in doubt, but this is only possible to the extent that followers will allow. If ideological purity is excessively important to a party's supporters, its leaders may have no alternative but to take electorally disadvantageous positions and suffer the consequences at the polls. Similarly, the accommodations with other parties necessary to form either electoral alliances or coalition governments are only possible if leaders are allowed a measure of flexibility by their followers. In general, if the party's followers can be induced to accept symbolic rewards, especially such as the value of party loyalty, the ability of the party to adapt, compete, and maintain its strength is increased.

Similar observations are relevant to professional activists and MPs. Where policy is important but there are deep disagreements within the party, unity is harder to maintain; where office is important and can best be achieved through unity, it is easier to maintain. For example, at least until the 1974-79 Labour government, discipline within British parties increased as the size of the government's majority decreased, whilst policy differences within the out-of-office Labour movement by 1983 had brought the party to the verge of collapse. On the Continent, the Italian Christian Democrats appear willing to go to any lengths to remain united so long as unity guarantees office (Di Palma, 1977). Where the perceived costs of exit are low, unity will be harder to maintain; where leaving the party is tantamount to retiring from politics, compromises will be more likely. This applies to party leadership as well. If defections are likely to cause loss of office, leaders are far more likely to defer to their followers (Axelrod, 1970).

Both leaders and followers are likely to find party unity easier to achieve when they perceive it to be in their own interests. The other condition for the continuance of a party system, continued electoral support, is related to this. It is far easier to find reasons for leaving a party whose electoral support is eroding than one whose electoral stock is rising. This works the other way as well; a united party is more likely to do well at the ballot box. More importantly, however, electoral success is related to perceived performance in office — the state of the economy, prospects for war and peace, and the like. The problem is that these conditions may not be compatible. Thus one consequence of the DC's unwillingness to risk party unity by taking firm action has been continually eroding electoral support. From the other perspective, one problem for those who want to pursue conservative economic policies is to produce the expected long term revival before the short-term electoral consequences of unemployment and retrenched social services cause their parties to desert them or to collapse.

The second sense of persistence relates to the continued adherence of those in power under a party government to its norms, the alternative being a gradual evolution to some other power arrangement. Party government should persist in this sense so long as the structure of incentives that led individuals to adopt that strategy remains in place. To the extent that this simply involves projecting the conditions for party government into the future, little further elaboration is required here. One point, however, does need to be made. Although party government involves costs for some people, once a system of party government is established, those who come to the top have a vested interest in its continuation, as well as in the continuation of their own parties. At the same time, many of the conditions of party government are subject to conscious manipulation. Thus barriers may be erected against those who attempt to pursue a nonparty strategy. The discrimination of most electoral systems and legislative committee assignment processes against independents and adherents of small or new parties are two examples.

This is not to deny the possibility of changes that would lead to the supersession of party government by some alternative form. As suggested above, technological, social, organisational, or political innovations may create new possibilities or alter the relative attractiveness of old ones. Some of these changes, such as the creation of specialist or corporatist boards, may be brought about deliberately by party leaders as short run responses to political problems. Whilst a thought-out choice on the part of party politicians to abandon an established system of party government seems unlikely, the cumulative effect of their adaptation to new circumstances may be to undermine party government.

To the extent that party government is a system from which evolution through gradual abandonment is unlikely, the third aspect of persistence – avoidance of precipitate collapse – becomes the more relevant. For a political system to avoid collapse, it must maintain an adequate level of support. Whilst this is hard to specify, and certainly varies with load and the visibility of alternatives, some level of positive support coupled at least with general acquiescence is necessary for a free government to survive. How is that support maintained, and can party government maintain it?

Support is correlated with performance relative to expectations. Assuming that a system currently has adequate support, its support could become inadequate as a result of any of three processes. Firstly, the difficulty of the problems confronting the government might increase. Some such increases in load may be imposed from outside the political system. For example, in recent times, the formation of the OPEC cartel and resulting dramatic increase in the price of oil has made the problem of economic management objectively more difficult. Similar increases in the objective difficulty of governing have accompanied economic depressions, failed crops, and natural disasters. Other increases in load result from the politicisation of previously nonpolitical problems (Sjöblom, 1984). In part, this is a problem of expectations, which will be discussed below – natural disasters only pose a threat to the government if there is an expectation that government ought to deal with their consequences. This is a clear example of the political importance of being able to control the definition of the political. On the other hand, increases in the range of politicised problems also make governing generally more difficult.

Secondly, the capacity of the system could decline. Whilst ability to manage problems is related to the difficulty of the problems to be managed – it is unlikely that there was anything the Weimar Republic could have done to avoid dissatisfaction during a world-wide depression – equally some governments are better able than others to cope with problems of comparable difficulty. Conditions relating to capacity will be discussed in the next section.

The third situation that may endanger a system of party government is escalating expectations, either that the government will do more things than currently or that it will do those things that it is currently doing better. Expectations arise from three processes. The first is extrapolation from the past. This source of expectations would be of little concern if apparently good performance necessarily indicated real capacity; in this case there would be every reason to expect performance to continue. If, however, apparently good performance were simply the result of fortuitous circumstances, the system could well prove unequal to the challenge when circumstances become less favourable. This may be precisely the situation in which the Western democracies currently find themselves; having taken credit for the economic boom of the 1960s, they must now pay the price of unfulfilled expectations of continued rapid growth in the late 1970s and 1980s. And as the preceding sentence implies, this is a danger that is exacerbated by the electoral incentive for parties in power to claim personal or partisan credit for good times, whether they were responsible or not.

A second source of expectations is promises. In their campaigns, candidates try to convince voters that good things will result from their election. The danger is that expectations will be raised beyond the ability of the victorious party to perform. In several places Sartori (1966; 1976: 137-76) talks about the irresponsible opposition of extreme parties permanently excluded from office in systems of polarised pluralism. Knowing that they will never be called upon to deliver, they engage in reckless outbidding, constantly promising more and more. In fact, this phenomenon is limited neither to extreme parties nor to systems of polarised pluralism. Although unfulfilled promises ultimately may undermine a party's credibility, in the short run, optimistic promises are beneficial; witness the glowing economic forecasts of governments in power.[15] Especially for a party currently out of office, the temptation to promise more than it can deliver so as to win office can be very powerful. But this can only lead to disenchantment with the entire party system, or more generally with the whole idea of parties and party government.

Rising expectations may also be created by nonparty groups as a means of pressuring the government. By convincing a segment of the public that the government can and should do some particular thing, they increase the cost to the party in power of not doing it. Group leaders may well recognise

[15] The problem is made more difficult by the fact that expectations affect behaviour. Thus optimistic economic forecasts may be a means of influencing economic behaviour.

these demands as strategic and be happy to settle for far less; that their followers will be equally realistic is doubtful.

Although one tends to think primarily of support from the public or from groups outside the political branches of government – interest groups and the military for example – support for the system by those who operate it is at least as important. A problem analogous to a revolution of rising expectations in the mass public is the danger that politicians themselves may develop unrealistic expectations, or alternatively that the system will tend to promote politicians whose expectations are already unrealistic. The frustration that they experience when their expectations meet the reality of limited power can also have a destabilising influence.

Inadequate support, whether resulting from absolute incapacity to deal with social problems or simply from unrealisable expectations, makes a political system extremely vulnerable. Whether it actually collapses depends on the availability of an alternative and the presence of a precipitating crisis.

Of course, support is unlikely to decline overnight to such a level that regime persistence is endangered. Politicians who were unable or unwilling to adapt to societal changes or to meet expectations ultimately may recognise the situation and adapt. Some responses, such as taking a new policy line, may restore support while leaving the essentials of the party government regime untouched. Other adaptations may lead to supersession of the party government system. In this case, party government might appear to have renewed support, but in fact would be adapting itself out of existence, much as the British aristocracy adapted itself to the social changes of the 18th and 19th centuries; whilst the institutions might remain, their significance would be thoroughly altered. On the other hand, the governing elite might do nothing, simply surviving on whatever reservoir of support or inertia of indifference there was. In this case, a crisis eventually would topple the system.

The particular relevance of the first meaning of persistence arises when one considers why politicians would fail to adapt. Historically, adaptation of a party system has usually meant the replacement of one set of dominant parties or leaders by another. Thus, although the long-term consequences of nonadaptation may be system collapse, and total ruin for all concerned, the short-term consequence of adaptation may be very high costs for those who actually make the necessary decisions. They may prefer to let tomorrow take care of itself. Again Italy provides an apt example. So long as the DC stays together and Italian democracy survives, any Italian government will be dominated by the DC. For many years, however, the leaders of the DC assumed that the party could stay together only at the price of nonadaptation, that is by sidestepping the need to address fundamental problems. Each time they did this, however, the future of Italian democracy became more precarious (Battaglia, 1979).

C. Capacity of Party Government

A party that was totally capable both at governing and at managing expectations and desires would never lose office. No party is totally capable. As suggested in the last section, there are forces inherent in the party government model militating against the effective management of expectations. There are also forces inherent in party government that limit its problem solution capacity.

As outlined above, problem solution capacity requires talent in a variety of fields and of a variety of types, cooperation especially from the bureaucracy, and will. Looking first at talent, party government involves turning over power to the winners of elections. The skills and talents required for electoral success, however, are very different from those required for policy formulation and implementation (Cronin, 1980: 19-22). In one respect, party government provides a solution to this problem. With party rather than the individual candidate the object of identification, electorally attractive members of the party team can draw support for administratively competent individuals. This is evident both in Britain, where unexciting candidates can be given safe seats (or life peerages), and in list PR systems, where they can be given high list positions. On the other hand, at the highest levels electoral talents remain more important than administrative ability. The problem is magnified if, in order to prevent the establishment of individual "fiefdoms" or for some other reason, ministers are rotated rapidly from one department to another and thus never develop substantial expertise.

Whilst this may lead to "better" policy by making the political "amateurs" more dependent on the bureaucratic "professionals," only if the bureaucracy is particularly loyal to, and understanding of, the party government of the day can this be said to contribute to *party* capacity. Here there may be a trade-off between capable government and party government. Similarly, rotation of ministers may further party unity by encouraging leaders to take a broader view, but does so at the expense of intimate party involvement in the making of specific policies.

The political heads of party governments are transient whilst the bureaucracy is permanent. Capable government requires the cooperation of bureaucrats. Yet the electoral responsibilities of a party give them an incentive to blame the bureaucracy for their failures. An example from the United States illustrates this problem. Said President Kennedy before taking a foreign policy initiative, "I hope this plan works. If it does, it will be another White House success. If it doesn't, it will be another State Department failure" (Cleveland, 1972: 95-96). Under these circumstances, self-defense by the civil service is more likely than loyalty.

Dependence on electoral support is a necessary condition for responsible party government. Nonetheless, if this dependence leads to obsession with day-by-day changes in popularity, it can lead to paralysis. Many policies involve immediate costs that must be borne in order to achieve future benefits. If temporary declines in public approval are likely to disrupt the leadership's hold over the party, such policies, even when needed or rewarding in the long run, are unlikely to be pursued.

The will to govern is also undermined if the goal of maintaining party unity must be given substantially higher priority than policy goals. Party government is government by a team. This creates problems of co-ordination and internal politics. Cabinet ministers, for example, ordinarily owe their official positions at least in part to their independent personal support within the party; if a single party leader could ignore one or two of them, he can hardly ignore them all and expect to remain as leader. Policy must be formed through a continuous process of negotiation and accommodation, a process hardly calculated to achieve consistent or entirely efficient results.

Party government breeds a crisis mentality and a tendency never to deal with a problem before it becomes a crisis. Personal rewards for resolving a crisis, which is obvious, are greater than for avoiding one, which is not. The status, power, and budgets of those who must deal with crises, whether they are successful or not, are greater than those given to merely "competent administrators." The internal compromises necessary to policy making are easier to achieve in a crisis, when the need for an immediate decision is clear, than at other times. Promoting a feeling of crisis can be an effective strategy for mobilising public support and maintaining party unity.

IV. Conclusions

Party government should be explained and its future projected by focussing on the people who make up the parties, and especially on the party leaders who also fill the central governing roles if there is party government, as individuals rather than on the parties as institutions. Although party government may be "functional" for a democratic system, adherence to the party government model as well as the very existence of political parties comes about, if at all, not because of this but because individuals pursuing their personal goals find party and party government to be rewarding. Prediction and explanation must be based on the goals being pursued by those in power and the relative effectiveness of alternative strategies open to them as determined by resources, environmental conditions, and the goals, strategies, and resources of competing actors. The specific hypotheses or suggestions raised above illustrate this approach and need not be repeated here.

If all relevant actors adhered to the norms of party government, the capacity and survivability of the system would be limited only by the wisdom of voters and politicians. Moreover, if the social preconditions tacitly assumed by the party government model were met and its conception of democracy accepted, the result would be democratic as well. The problems are that the social preconditions of the model are satisfied decreasingly by postindustrial societies, that the party government conception of democracy is debatable, and that given conflicting goals between party and nonparty actors, among individuals within each party, and even within a single individual, a structure of incentives encouraging party government-like behaviour often is lacking.

The negative consequences of ineffective government touch everyone in society. Interest groups, media, voters, and politicians all have a long term interest in avoiding system collapse. They do not necessarily have an interest in party government, and certainly may have no interest in the survival of the current party system. Even leaders of the currently dominant parties have other interests as well. The problem of party government, as of all systems of government, is to arrange a structure of incentives that encourages politicians to value long term policy and governing goals over short term power and personal goals; the paradox is that many features of the party government model naturally incline them the other way.

Bibliography

ALLUM, P. (1973) *Italy – Republic Without Government.* New York: W. W. Norton.

ALTHEIDE, D. (1974) *Creating Reality.* Beverly Hills, Ca.: Sage.

AMERY, L.S. (1953) *Thoughts on the Constitution.* London: Oxford University Press.

AXELROD, R. (1970) *Conflict of Interest.* Chicago: Markham.

BAGEHOT, W. (1963) *The English Constitution.* London: Fontana.

BARRY, B. (1970) *Sociologists, Economists, and Democracy.* London: Collier-Macmillan.

BATTAGLIA, A. (1979) *Le politiche dei partiti e la politica di governo.* Rome: Laterza.

BEER, S. (1969) *British Politics in the Collectivist Age.* New York: Vintage Books.

BRIGGS, A. (1965) *The Making of Modern Britain.* New York: Harper and Row.

BUDGE, I. and D. FARLIE (1977) *Voting and Party Competition.* London: John Wiley.

BURKE, E. (1839) "Thoughts on the cause of the present discontents," in *The Works of Edmund Burke.* Boston: Little, Brown.

BURNS, J.M. (1963) *The Deadlock of Democracy.* Englewood Cliffs, N.J.: Prentice-Hall.

CLEVELAND, H. (1972) *The Future Executive.* New York: Harper and Row.

CONVERSE, P.E. (1964) "The nature of belief systems in mass publics," in D. E. Apter (ed.) *Ideology and Discontent.* New York: Free Press of Glencoe.

CRONIN, T.E. (1980) *The State of the Presidency.* Boston: Little, Brown.

CROSSMAN, R. (1972) *Myths of Cabinet Government.* Cambridge, Mass.: Harvard University Press.

CROZIER, M., S. P. HUNTINGTON, and J. WATANUKI (1975) *The Crisis of Democracy.* New York: New York University Press.

DAHL, R. A. (1956) *A Preface to Democratic Theory.* Chicago: University of Chicago Press.

– (1971) *Polyarchy.* New Haven, Conn.: Yale University Press.

DIPALMA, G. (1977) *Surviving Without Governing.* Berkeley, Ca.: University of California Press.

DOWNS, A. (1957) *An Economic Theory of Democracy.* New York: Harper and Row.

DUMONT, M. (1972) "Down the bureaucracy," pp. 114–17 in R. T. Golembiewski et al. (eds.) *Public Administration*. Chicago: Rand McNally.

DUVERGER, M. (1959) *Political Parties*. New York: John Wiley.

ELDERSVELD, S. J. (1964) *Political Parties: A Behavioral Analysis*. Chicago: Rand McNally.

FINER, S. (ed.) (1975) *Adversary Politics and Electoral Reform*. London: Wigram.

FIORINA, M. (1981) *Retrospective Voting in American National Elections*. New Haven, Conn.: Yale University Press.

HARDIN, G. (1968) "The tragedy of the commons," 162 *Science* 1243.

HEISLER, M. O. and R. B. KVAVIK (1974) "Patterns of European politics: the 'European polity' model," in M. O. Heisler (ed.) *Politics in Europe*. New York: David McKay.

HIRSCHMANN, A. O. (1970) *Exit, Voice, and Loyalty*. Cambridge, Mass.: Harvard University Press.

HOLT, R. H. and J. M. RICHARDSON, Jr. (1970) "Competing paradigms in comparative politics," in R. H. Holt and J. E. Turner (eds.) *The Methodology of Comparative Research*. New York: Free Press.

INGLEHART, R. (1977) *The Silent Revolution*. Princeton, N.J.: Princeton University Press.

KAPLAN, A. (1954) *The Conduct of Inquiry: Methodology for Behavioral Science*. San Francisco: Chandler.

KATZ, R. S. (1980) *A Theory of Parties and Electoral Systems*. Baltimore: Johns Hopkins University Press.

– (1981) "Dimensions of partisan conflict in Swiss cantons." Presented at the annual meeting of the American Political Science Association, New York.

– (1982) "Electoral policy," in S. Nagel (ed.) *The Encylopedia of Policy Studies*. New York: Marcel Dekker.

KELLEY, S., Jr. (1957) "Preface," in A. Downs. *An Economic Theory of Democracy*. New York: Harper and Row.

KENNEDY, J. F. (1956) *Profiles in Courage*. New York: Harper and Row.

KERR, H. H., Jr. (1974) *Switzerland: Social Cleavages and Partisan Conflict*. Beverly Hills, Ca.: Sage Professional Papers in Contemporary Political Sociology 1:06-002.

KIRKPATRICK, E. [ed.] (1950) *Toward a More Responsible Two Party System*. New York: Rinehart.

LAPALOMBARA, J. (1964) *Interest Groups in Italian Politics*. Princeton, N.J.: Princeton University Press.

LIJPHART, A. (1975) *The Politics of Accommodation*. Berkeley, Ca.: University of California Press.

– (1977) *Democracy in Plural Societies*. New Haven, Conn.: Yale University Press.

LOCKE, J. (1975) *Second Treatise of Government*. Indianapolis, Ind.: Bobbs-Merrill.

LOWELL, A. L. (1913) *Public Opinion and Popular Government*. New York: Longmans, Green.

MAYHEW, D. (1974) *Congress: The Electoral Connection*. New Haven, Conn.: Yale University Press.

MINTZEL, A. and H. SCHMITT (1981a) "How to investigate the future of party government?" Mannheim. (unpublished).

– (1981b) "Krise der Parteiendemokratie? Zu Funktionen, Leistungen und Defiziten parlamentarischer Demokratie." 17 *Politische Bildung*, 3–16.

MORRISON, H. (1964) *Government and Parliament*. London: Oxford University Press.

OLSON, M., Jr. (1965) *The Logic of Collective Action*. New York: Schocken.

OSTROGORSKI, M. (1964) *Democracy and the Organization of Political Parties*. New York: Anchor Books.

RAE, D. W. (1971) *The Political Consequences of Electoral Laws*. New Haven, Conn.: Yale University Press.

Ranney, A. (1962) *The Doctrine of Responsible Party Government.* Urbana, Ill.: University of Illinois Press.

— (1965) *Pathways to Parliament.* Madison, Wisc.: University of Wisconsin Press.

Robertson, D. (1976) *A Theory of Party Competition.* London: John Wiley.

Robinson, M. (1976) "Public affairs television and the growth of political malaise," 70 *Amer. Pol. Sci. Rev.* 409 (June).

Rogowski, R. (1974) *Rational Legitimacy.* Princeton, N.J.: Princeton University Press.

Rose, R. (1969) "The variability of party government: a theoretical and empirical critique," 17 *Political Studies* 413 (December).

— (1974) *The Problem of Party Government.* London: Macmillan.

Sartori, E. (1966) "European political parties: the case of polarized pluralism," in J. LaPalombara and M. Weiner (eds.) *Political Parties and Political Development.* Princeton, N.J.: Princeton University Press.

— (1976) *Parties and party systems.* Cambridge: Cambridge University Press.

Schattschneider, E. E. (1942) *Party Government.* New York: Rinehart and Winston.

Sjöblom, G. (1968) *Party Strategies in a Multiparty System.* Lund: Studentlitteratur.

— (1972) "Problemi e soluzioni in politica." 14 *Rivista Italiana di Scienza Politica,* 41–85.

Smith, A. [ed.] (1979) *Television and Political Life.* New York: St. Martin's Press.

Smith, G. (1982) "Party government — adaptation and survival: a typological presentation." Presented at the European Consortium for Political Research Joint Session of Workshops, Aarhus (April 1982).

Steiner, J. (1974) *Amicable Agreement versus Majority Rule.* Chapel Hill, N. C.: University of North Carolina Press.

Thurow, L. C. (1980) *The Zero-Sum Society.* New York: Penguin Books.

Wilson, J. Q. (1962) *The Amateur Democrat.* Chicago: University of Chicago Press.

Chapter III

Problems and Problem Solutions in Politics Some Conceptualisations and Conjectures*

GUNNAR SJÖBLOM

Contents

I. The Rationale of the Exercise

In this essay I will argue:

(a) that notions like (actor-) "problems" and (actors') "problem-solving" are implicitly central in political science, and

* The author wants to thank Francis Castles, Karl W. Deutsch, Giorgio Freddi, Richard S. Katz, Gordon Smith and Rudolf Wildenmann for useful comments.

(b) that they deserve to be made explicit, as their fruitfulness seems to be high (e.g. for the study of political competition, of power structures, of agenda-setting and agenda-shifts, and of the viability of regimes), but
(c) that a number of clarifications and distinctions are necessary to make such notions useful and to develop them into concepts.

Let us look at some examples supporting point (a) above:

- It is often said that a necessary condition for understanding a person's actions and reactions is an understanding of his problem situation – the same may be said of collectivities.
- Politics is often characterised as a problem-solving activity, aiming at the solution of societal problems by the use of collective decisions and actions (cf. Deutsch, 1963). Sometimes it may even be argued that the whole institutional set-up of a society may be seen as an effort to solve some "over-riding problem" (cf. Bell, 1969; Schumpeter, 1950).
- While it seems notoriously difficult to agree on a number of standardised items for a description of "political culture", items of the following type seem intuitively relevant: opinions on what constitutes "normalcy" in politics; what issues are put (or not put) on the political agenda (over time); the ways problems are defined, formulated and located; opinions on what constitute legitimate procedures for public problem-solving.
- Electoral shifts and realignments in a party system may be caused by the voters' perceptions of how the programmes and policies of different parties fit the types of societal problems, which at a given time are regarded as the most salient.
- Shifts in the perception of dominant patterns of societal problems may change the relations between parties at the parliamentary and governmental level, e. g. by leading to break-ups of coalitions and the formation new ones.

This essay represents a preliminary and exploratory effort to see what the conceivable prerequisites are for using "problem" "problem-solving" and, to some extent, the "handling of problems" as some central concepts in political analysis, and to see what are the likely consequences. It is written within the framework of the project *The Future of Party Government*, in which one of the central themes concerns the ability of party governments to handle societal problems.

The title of the project raises (at least) four questions, one at the conceptual level and three at the empirical (but partly conjectural) level. They are here given as a background.

(a) What can be meant by "party government" and which variations of the concept are conceivable?

(b) Which varieties of party government exist, have existed or are likely to emerge?
(c) Under which conditions, if any, are party governments likely to persist (and which types of party governments are likely to be most viable?)
(d) If party governments (or some types of them) are not likely to persist, which are the alternatives and which are the most probable alternatives?

It is obvious that answers to these questions are fundamental for the whole project, but I will here only treat them sketchily, referring to the division of labour in the project (cf., in particular the essays by Katz and Smith in this volume). Just a few comments are appropriate.

The study object of the party is confined to representative democracies. Now, it seems to be a common assumption among political scientists that it is almost impossible to conceive of such democracies if competitive parties do not exist (cf. Schumpeter's well known definition).[1] But the reverse is not the case: we can well have a system of competitive parties without having a democratic system. Hence, a competitive party system is a necessary (but not sufficient) condition for democratic government but not vice versa. A stricter formulation of the theme of the project would have been "The Future of Democratic Party Government".

But if all democratic and representative regimes are supposed to have "party governments", then the notion evidently covers a wide range of political phenomena. Now, two of the most fundamental properties of any regime are: a) the ways in which leaders are selected, appointed and dismissed, and b) the ways in which policies are selected and decided. The role of parties in these two processes may vary widely, from a very weak to a very strong influence. As this variation is central to the research problem of the project, 'party government' has to be treated as a variable concept. This is not the place, however, to try to find out how this should be done (cf. Katz, this volume). But this is a digression. In order to approach the main themes of this essay let us recall question c) in connection with the project title:

– Under which conditions, if any, are party governments likely to persist (and which types of party governments are likely to be most viable)?

For the project, one fundamental working hypothesis, answering (but very vaguely) this question is:

– Party government (in some form) is likely to persist if, and only if, it can solve the important societal problems in an acceptable way.

A roughly equivalent formulation of the same hypothesis is:

– Party government (in some form) is likely to persist if and only if it has a high degree of problem-solving capacity.

[1] Schumpeter, 1950; cf. Downs, 1957. No assumption is made here about the degree of competition.

The rest of this essay will mainly be devoted to some to the conceptual and empirical difficulties raised by these two working hypotheses.[2] The stress is on formal and methodological issues and most of the time I will have rather little to say about the question of whether these working hypotheses seem empirically probable or not. Only in Section VII, below, are they substantially modified as to their explanatory scope by the introduction of some other probable plus-factors for the persistence of party government, viz. the intrinsic value (or "*Eigenwert*") of the party-government regime and the citizens evaluations of alternative regimes.

II. The Problem of "Problem"

Let me illustrate some of the difficulties involved in writing an essay of this sort with a silly-sounding statement: "It is problematical to write about 'problems'". "Problem" in an undefined form seems to be a very common term in political science writings (as it is in everyday language also). It sometimes refers to "difficulties", "obstacles", "complications" (etc.), sometimes to the very stuff or material of politics (cf. "Politics is a problem-solving process"), (cf. Simon, 1969; 1977; Taylor, 1965) and sometimes to the very stuff or material of political analysis (i. e. "research problems", cf. "the domain of a discipline is defined by its problems")[3]. We need, of course, a number of undefined terms to be able to communicate; to ask for strict definitions and distinctions all the time is an effective way of blocking all communication. But if we want to use the term "problem" as a name for a rather central concept in political science, the situation is different: we will then have to make clear distinctions between different types of problems, e. g. actor-problems vs. analyst-problems, "problems as the stuff of politics" vs. "problem as a name for a general feeling of uncertainty and stress" (and many other distinctions).

What follows is a tentative outline of a number of such distinctions and specifications, which, I believe, are fruitful. "Fruitful" here means that it may be possible to formulate a number of research problems and general propositions of informative value if and only if such distinctions are made – or that some types of political behaviour may be understood only by the use of such distinctions. This is, of course, only guesswork until the

[2] A "working hypothesis", as the term is used here, is a preliminary assumption, stated for exploratory and heuristic purposes, in order to structure a more or less unstructured research problem or set of research problems. It is expected that a working hypothesis will have to be a reformulated and qualified by *ex post* analysis (for an example, see Section VII, this essay).

[3] Popper, 1976. On research problems, cf. also Merton, 1959; Eckstein, 1964; Lindblom, 1982. On actor-problems, e. g. Starbuck, 1983.

conceptualisations are applied, but this is a fate which the present exercise shares with many conceptual analyses.

In very general terms, a "problem" exists when there is a *discrepancy* between what is and what is desired? If it is an intellectual problem, there is a discrepancy between what one knows and what one wants to know; if it is a "practical problem", there is a discrepancy between the existing state of affairs and a desired state of affairs[4]. In the first case an answer is needed, in the second case some type of action and its impact. Questions such as "why?" and "how?" have to be answered.

This "discrepancy" is the constitutive component in the definition of 'problem'. The problem may then have all sorts of predicates: small or large, structured or unstructured, simple or complicated, individual or collective, short-term or long-term, tractable or intractable, "benign" or "wicked" (Rittel–Webber, 1973), decomposable or non-decomposable (Simon, 1969), isolated or interdependent, proximate or distant (Hewitt–Hall, 1973), etc., etc. – the identification of such properties is, to be sure, of fundamental importance for the problem-solver, but they are *not* constitutive components of the definition of problem, as used here.

What is a "solution" to a problem? In a preliminary way, we can say that a solution to an intellectual problem consists in a "satisfactory" answer to the question "why?"; a solution to a practical problem consists in a "satisfactory" answer to the question "how?". Different people may have different opinions as to what is "satisfactory" in a given context, and there may also be many solutions to a problem, which are more or less "satisfactory". In what follows, I will concentrate on practical problems in social and political contexts.

Does the notion of "problem" always imply that there exists some "solution" to the problem, or can we reasonably talk about "unsolvable problems" without a *contradictio in adiecto*? This raises a lot of further questions: unsolvable for whom? Unsolvable for a certain person but not for another, unsolvable for any individual but perhaps not for organised groups of people, unsolvable because of present lack of data, causal knowledge, technological resources (etc.) or "unsolvable in principle"? Are problems, which are unsolvable "in principle" to be regarded not as proper problems but as "spurious problems", which are not to be solved but "dissolved"?

Questions of this sort point to a very serious complication, namely that the use of the very term "problem" in "practical problem" is based only on a rather incomplete analogy with "intellectual problem" or "cognitive problem"; the same applies to the term "solutions".

[4] Cf. Billings et al., 1980. The argument could be further developed concerning political contexts by using the distinction "goal"/"goal image" – cf. Deutsch, 1963.

There may also exist another important difference between intellectual problems and practical problems, at least to the extent that the latter refer to politics. When an intellectual problem is solved, it is no longer a problem; if the solution is not lost, you can just return to it (you may later on find the solution less satisfactory, but that is another matter). Most practical problems in politics are not of this character: they have a tendency to pop up again and again. We may distinguish between reversible and irreversible solutions; one way well argue that one fundamental norm in political democracies is that solutions should be reversible as far as possible (at least in principle – actually, they may be irreversible because of great costs of change). – Hence it is common to talk about "resolution" in political contexts (cf., e. g. Banks, 1981).

Now, "problems" are not just there to be detected and then solved – they have to be formulated and defined (problem definition is a vital part of "reality construction"). A problem definition will here mean the description of a) a desirable state of affairs, b) an existing state of affairs, and c) the discrepancy or "distance" between a) and b). Does a problem definition also include the type of solution to be looked for? This will here be left as an open question (cf. Rittel–Weber, 1973). A problem definition according to a) – c), above, will, of course, restrict the repertoire of conceivable solutions but the definition may be more of less open in this respect – sometimes the area of search for solutions may be narrow, sometimes wide. But, evidently, the more you want to define a problem in detail, the more you want to "understand" it, the more you have to consider the extent of the repertoire of conceivable "solutions". (Another point to be left open here is if a definition of a problem also includes an assessment of its relative weight or salience, in other words a ranking of it in the actor's list of priorities).

Is there a "problem" only if somebody perceives something as a problem and tries to define it or could we perhaps talk about "objective problems", which are not necessarily perceived/defined by anybody at a certain moment of time? This is, of course, a matter of debate (the introduction of the attribute "objective" is often an indicator of a high degree of subjective arbitrariness), but presumably nobody would deny the usefulness of notions like "latent problems", "potential problems" or "anticipation of problems".

Are problems always "unique" in each situation or can they in general be reduced to a set of basic existential problems? (cf., e. g. Lindbeck, 1973; Popper, 1976; Tarschys, 1977). – This is primarily a question of analytical intentions, above all concerning the choice of the level of abstraction. Something which is absolutely and genuinely unique can hardly be grasped and analysed by the human intellect – every problem will have to be assessed against the stock of existing knowledge, classified by analogy, etc. An "incorrect" problem definition in this sense may be fatal for the ability to "solve" the problem. Here, it may make a great difference if the problem definition is "fixed", as it were, over time, or if it is fluid, sequential, emergent, or "experimental" (cf. Lane, 1983). This also raises the awkward question of to what extent it is possible to delimit a problem and handle it separately, or if it must be treated as part of a greater cluster (also cf. section V. A, *infra*).

Concerning the discrepancy between what is and what is desired, one may ask: desired by whom? Not necessarily by the actor himself. A schoolboy may be perfectly content with what he knows but his teacher may not be; a politician may be personally satisfied with some existing state of affairs but cannot afford to disregard the dissatisfaction of some voters. Hence, stating a problem may not reflect personal dissatisfaction with some discrepancy but some sort of dependent position.

This can be seen in a more general context: in any polity there may exist a degree of conflict. In principle, it may be possible to characterise a certain polity by its distributional profile on a scale of consensus/conflict regarding problem definitions. Presumably we could say that a high degree of consensus on problem definitions is a sign of a homogenous political culture while a high degree of conflict in this respect is a sign of a heterogenous political culture.

To this may be added a distinction between *proximate* and *distant* problematic situations: "A problematic situation is *proximate* if a person's knowledge of it is direct and unmediated by mass media or by third parties: and the situation is *distant* if knowledge is mediated." (Hewitt—Hall, 1973:373). "The significance of the distinction is that members of contemporary society are increasingly affected by situations far removed from direct view for which they receive information in sketchy form through the media" (*ibid.*) This distinction may be important from a power perspective in the following sense: ability to engage other people in what is to them "distant problematic situations" may be a sign of an actor's social influence.

Another important notion in this connection is that the perception of a problem may be seen with regard to some expected standard, presumably reflecting what is seen as "normalcy" (cf. Lyles—Mitroff, 1980; also Kiesler—Sproull, 1982). If things deviate from this "normal standard", a problem exists. As is well known, there is often a connection between high frequency and what is regarded as normal (in a perverse case the two notions tend to coincide). Put in another way: one may get so used to certain problems that they are no longer regarded as problems. From the point of view of comparative politics this is highly pertinent — perceptions of "normalcy" are culturally and habitually determined; an unemployment rate of, say, 10 percent, may be seen as normal in one country and as catastrophic in another. But, of course, notions of "normalcy" may be highly controversial; in a situation of conflict on problem definitions, there may, for instance, exist a permanent opposition against some states of affairs, which some people regard as "normal".

Even if there exists an agreement as to what constitutes normalcy, "problems" do not only arise as a result of discrepancies between "normalcy" and "existing states". They may also arise as a result of increasing *expectations* among the public (or parts of it), and/or increasing *aspirations* among the decision-makers (or some of them) concerning expected standards (cf., e. g., Brittan, 1975; Scharpf, 1977). (I will return to these phenomena, changes in levels of aspirations and expectations, in Section VI of this essay, dealing with "Problem-Solving Capacity").

As mentioned in the beginning of this essay, the project is mainly concerned with party activities in government. Does the discussion so far give a too "rationalistic" (as it were) picture of parties' decision-making? It may, but the following should be kept in mind: to say that "politics is a problem-solving activity" does not necessarily mean that it is *only* a problem-solving activity; we know, for instance, that "low politics" to a high degree is programmed and routinised, and that there are lots of ritualistic and symbolic activities both in "low" and in "high" politics. This indicates the need to separate "problem-solving" from other activities – if all political activities are named by that term, we have just introduced a redundant notion.

Let me in this context give a quotation, which presumably represents a dominant view among students of organisations today: "Organizations' activities categorize in at least two modes: a problem-solving mode in which perceived problems motivate searches for solutions, and an action-generating mode in which action taking motivates the invention of problems to justify the actions. The problem-solving mode seems to describe a very small percentage of the activity sequences that occur, and the action-generating mode a large percentage". (Starbuck, 1983:91).

The reasoning so far seems to justify the introduction of still another notion, viz. *problem-handling*. (cf. G. Smith, *infra*). This is a more inclusive notion than problem-solving; to solve a problem is one way of handling it, but there are other alternatives. One example is the one mentioned in the quotation, above: to invent problems in order to justify (legitimate) actions. Another is to redefine an untractable problem, which then may or may not be "solved". Still another option is to remove intractable problems from the political agenda (even if this may be difficult to do because of the political competition). A party may, on the other hand, try to keep a problem alive and try to avoid solutions, for strategic reasons – because the problem may lead to the creation of support for the party (a condition for this is evidently that the party leaders believe that they can keep the problem "under control", so they do not get into the situation of the sorcerer's apprentice). Still another way to handle a problem is through so-called non-decision-making: to prevent problems being put on the political agenda and maybe even trying to stop any articulation of the problem. (cf. also Section V, *infra*).

In this section, I have tried to define, or to suggest definitional outlines for notions like "problem", "problem solutions" and "the handling of problems". In Section V of the essay, the discussion of some properties of problems in politics will be continued. Before that, a framework is suggested for the analysis of the types of assessments a political actor must make, choosing between action alternatives (Section III). I then proceed to a rough classification of such problems, which seem relevant for the project of *The Future of Party Government*, (Section IV).

III. Actor Assessment of Action Alternatives

A. Three Types of Assessments

We have characterised a "practical problem" as a perceived discrepancy between an existing state of affairs and a desired state of affairs; the "solution" to this problem is some sort of action resulting in the removal of the discrepancy. (Of course, the existing state of affairs may be seen as desirable but as threatened: the solution is then an action which removes the threat). Alternatively, the solution may be partial – leading to a decreased discrepancy, or even to a minimisation of the increase of the discrepancy in the case of a "defensive situation".

Let us try to reconstruct the decisional situation of an actor, faced with a problem. (The reasoning mainly refers to political parties in democracies but may be more or less applicable to all collective actors). It will be assumed here that an actor such as a political party (in operational terms: the elite of the party) has to make three types of assessment in the selection of different lines of action to take:

– what are the likely results of the action?
– how are the likely results of the action related to the desirable state of affairs?
– how do the results of the action affect the strategic position of one's own party and of competing parties?

I will refer to these three types of assessments made by the actor as:

– the *matter-of-fact assessment* (the instrumental assessment of the probable results of different policy alternatives)
– the *value assessment*
– the *strategic assessment*[5].

In principle, each of these three types of assessment could be made separately from the others:

[5] For some roughly analogous distinctions, see Tichy, 1980.

- You can make a matter-of-fact assessment as to the likely consequences of an action, irrespective of the relation of these consequences to what is regarded as desirable or to what are the strategic consequences for one's own party or other parties (but you cannot define a problem in that way).
- You can make an assessment of what states of affairs are desirable, even if no known techniques exist to bring about these states of affairs, and irrespective of strategic concerns.
- You can make an assessment of the probable strategic consequences of an action, irrespective of other consequences of this action and irrespective of what you otherwise regard as desirable.

In practice, these three types of assessment are of course closely intertwined. Opinions of what constitutes the desirable are normally colored by what is seen as possible and vice versa (as in wishful thinking). (Sjøblom, 1968). To choose a strategically favorable action alternative with very negative results from a value point of view is usually avoided (that would indicate an enormous appetite for power itself) as is the reverse (*"fiat justitia, pereat mundus"*). Actions with a high efficiency but very negative strategic consequences are normally avoided, as are strategically favorable actions with very negative consequences otherwise.

As these examples indicate, goal conflicts are quite common. (For a parallel, cf. Freddi, *infra*, concerning different types of administrative rationality). The ideal action alternative is one which, with the highest probability leads to the most desired state of affairs and which simultaneously is strategically optimal. Such action alternatives are only rarely to be found[6].

A number of empirical complications are ignored in the reasoning above, e. g. if an action alternative, which is negative in respect of what is generally regarded as a party's values, is also likely to be strategically negative, (e. g. by causing lack of party cohesion) or if the use of non-efficient policies is also likely to lead to strategically negative results ("you cannot fool all of the people for all of the time"). (The time factor is also evidently essential in considerations of this type). Some further complications of this sort should also be briefly mentioned here:

- What are the consequences for the three types of assessment of the ways different problems (and hence actions) are connected? (cf. Section V. A. below, on aggregation/disaggregation of problems).
- What happens if the means, used in the action, are valued *per se* (positively or negatively) and not only the projection of the probable outcomes of the actions? It is a prerequisite for rational action that only

[6] Cf. the notion of 'satisfaction' (Simon). Cf. Keeny—Raiffa, 1976; Sjöblom, 1968: ch. 5.

> the desired state of affairs (the "goals") are objects of value, while the means used – provided that they do not contradict fundamental regime norms – as far as possible should be regarded as valuationally neutral?

(In Section VII, I will return to a parallel phenomenon, viz. that institutions usually are seen as having a intrinsic value or "*Eigenwert*" and not only evaluated from an instrumental point of view).

Obviously each of the three assessments involves some cognitive problems, including predictions and/or projections under different degrees of uncertainty and/or ambiguity, (see below, Section V. A.). Making the matter-of-fact assessment requires data knowledge (on existing states of affairs; usually also on earlier states of affairs) and causal knowledge for predictions/projections.[7] Making the strategic assessment is not different in this respect (the data problem may be more complicated because of the competitive situation): also here you need data knowledge and causal knowledge to predict/project the impacts of the action on other actors, whose moves and reactions create the strategic situation (competing parties, one's own party members, voters, other intermediate actors in the political system).

In the case of "policy failures" cognitive and strategic explanations are typically mixed as when political authorities are accused of ignoring "the facts" (or the causal mechanisms) because of an obsession with power and/or because of "ideological blinkers" ("you are not the doctors, you are the disease").

B. The Value Assessment

To what extent does the value assessment involve cognitive elements? – To decide on what is desirable is, of course, in itself an act of valuation, but besides that the assessment requires cognitive knowledge of the present state of affairs. It also requires some sort of operationalisation of what constitutes the desirable state of affairs; in the absence of such "operationalisations", the value component will hardly give any directions for action; the actor will then be more or less "drifting" (cf. the title of an article "If you don't care where you get to, then it doesn't matter which way you go". Wholey *et al.*, 1975 – quoting *Alice in Wonderland*).

Lack of a value system (or even of a reasonably explicit value system) may also lead to difficulties in motivating and legitimating decisions and hence also to trouble with a party's public image of credibility. It will then also be difficult to assess whether different persons among the party elite and the members actually agree on what is desirable.

[7] See, e. g. Abernethy, 1978; Grumm, 1975; Hanf–Scharpf eds., 1978; J. P. Olsen, 1972; Quade, 1979; Reynolds, 1975; Sowell, 1980.

Different desirable end-states must also be assessed and compared for their degree of consistency. They may also require ranking operations which at least contain some cognitive elements.

Many political debates also concern the further consequences if some desired end-states are reached or desired trends continue (e. g. "further economic growth will lead to an ecocatastrophe", "further public regulation of economic life will lead to an authoritarian regime"). While highly conjectural, such statements are in principle cognitive and empirical, despite their valuational overtones.

C. The Strategic Assessment

The main question in the strategic assessment is:

– How are different measures and their probable impacts, intended as solutions of a problem, related to one's own party's and other parties' strategic positions (are they positive, negative, or neutral)?

Measures are strategically neutral when, for instance, the problems they are intended to solve are not politicised in any arena (but their unintended consequences may be strategically relevant).

In the strategic assessment the competition must always be taken into account, not least because the situations are often zero-sum in character: if one party wins parliamentary mandates, one or more of the other parties must lose, if one or more parties form the government, one or more of the other parties must stay in opposition, etc.

The conditions to be assessed in the strategic assessment are usually more fluid than those assessed in the matter-of-fact assessment and much more fluid than those in the value assessment. The importance of strategic considerations may, for instance, vary depending on where one stands in the electoral cycle: voter opinions are highly important close to an election, less so immediately after the election; opinions of the party members may be highly important before and during a party congress, but less so after the congress; opinions of other parties may be decisive in the process of forming coalition governments or in the formation of parliamentary majorities, but less so when these things are not to the fore.

A very large number of strategic questions could be asked in connection with the consideration of different policy options and their likely results; I will confine myself to a few examples:

– are the likely results of a zero-sum character – must benefits to one group be at the expense of other groups?
– from which groups among the voters do the demands emerge – is it, for instance, from groups which actually or potentially belong to one's own party?
– what is the political salience of the problems and different solutions for different voters?

- does a particular stand on a policy question favour or disfavour the party's credibility among the voters?
- does a particular stand on a policy question enhance or damage the party's coalitional options in parliament?
- taking a particular stand on a policy question, is it likely or not that the party will be outbid by other parties?
- taking a particular stand on a policy question, is it likely or not that the party may retain (or create) a reasonable degree of party cohesion?
- what are the long-term strategic consequences (if any) of different policy measures?

The last question deserves some comments. Certain decisions may change the long-term socio-economic composition of the electorate (e. g. lowering of voting age, change in relative size of different occupational groups, changes in educational levels, changes in geographical locations, etc.) *or* they may for a long time determine (positively or negatively) the party's image among certain groups of voters, *or* they may change the conditions for competition between the parties (e. g. changes of electoral laws, rules for party finance, rules for the use of public media by parties, etc.) *or* they may change the decisional machinery itself (large increases in size of public bureaucracies, measures leading to a corporatist decision-making system, constitutional changes, changing the degree of centralisation or decentralisation or the delegation of authority to supra-national organisations). Etc. Changes of the type mentioned are of particular importance for the project on *The Future of Party Government*, as they directly and indirectly lead to changes in the very nature of the *Herrschaftsorganisation*.

IV. Societal Problems — Policy Problems — Governance Problems

Here, I shall try to make a distinction between three types of practical problems:

- Societal problems
- Policy problems
- Governance problems.

A societal problem is a discrepancy between the actual living conditions of people in a society and some expected standard of living conditions.

"Societal" means that at least a substantial part of the population is involved, and presumably also, that the actual conditions are not isolated in their consequences but, have repercussions on other sectors of societal life. Typical examples are poverty, ill health, illiteracy, bad housing, crime, unemployment, inflation, etc. As mentioned before, it may depend on habits, expectations and aspirations, whether, or to what degree, such conditions are perceived as problems; (e. g. "illiteracy" may not be seen as a societal problem in a rather static tribal society, but certainly will be in a society undergoing rapid industrialisation). "Expected standards" are often shifting, sometimes rapidly; expectations may also vary greatly between different groups in society. Most important, different societies and different epochs may vary widely as to whether such problems are the responsibility (and, hence to be handled by) the political machinery of the society (and, if so, to what extent).

A policy problem is a discrepancy between a desired state of affairs and the "social technology" available for bringing about the desired state of affairs (cf. Kerr, 1976).

"Social technology" here refers to knowledge (data knowledge, causal knowledge and "know-how" knowledge), financial and manpower resources, technical equipment etc.

For convenience, "policy problems" will here be confined to "public policy problems", i. e. to policy problems as perceived by decision-makers within the political machinery of a society. Frequently the very definition of the problem is complicated and even more so the location of the problem, i. e. knowing what causal mechanisms should be triggered and knowing in what context the problem should be seen. (Unemployment may be seen as a result of low education, and/or bad health, and/or geographical rigidity, and/or racial discrimination, and/or foreign competition, and/or too high interest rates, and/or some other factors and/or some combination of factors).

Policy problems may be classified in different ways: by substantive contents (cf. a number of classification systems in policy-analysis), by functional criteria (e. g. regulative, distributive, etc.), (Lowi, 1972), or by institutional criteria (e. g. according to what parliamentary committee, ministry or public bureaucracy takes care of them). (Damgaard, 1977).

A governance problem is a discrepancy between what is normatively and functionally expected of public governance and the actual performance in this respect. (Observe that this definition is in systemic and regime-normative terms, not in actor terms.)

As stated previously there are at least two functions common to all types of political systems: political roles must be filled (recruitment) and authoritative decisions must be made and implemented and accepted as binding by the citizens (for whatever reasons).

I will further assume that common to all political regimes is a general standard or norm of efficiency: in whatever way the problems (and, hence, the goals) are defined by the public authorities, those authorities are presumed to select "solutions" according to what they (for whatever reason) think will be effective (lead to, or towards, the desired outcomes) and with considerations of the costs. This may also be called the norm of "subjective instrumental rationality".

Expectations of political governance are further connected to the specific norms of the prevailing regime. (cf. Dahl, 1982). A (democratic) party-government regime is — *inter alia* — a representative, competitive system. An high degree of popular participation is regarded as a desirable (but not necessarily defining) characteristic of a democracy. (Barnes—Kaase et al., 1979; Braybrooke, 1975; White, 1976). The representative[8] authorities are supposed to provide leadership but at the same time not to deviate too much from the electorate concerning opinion distribution. This requires an interactive process: representatives informing the electorate about policy problems (etc.) *and* representatives being "responsive" to demands from the electorate. (Anckar, 1980; Page, 1977). The representatives are also supposed to be accountable to the electorate via the institution of general elections, providing the voters with sanctions (positive and negative) (Sjøblom, 1983; B.C. Smith, 1980). A competitive party system requires the existence of at least two parties, presenting alternative candidates and some (more or less alternative) policies (packages of policies) to the electorate.

In a democracy it is further assumed, that opinion formation is "free", i.e. not based on violence, threats, corruption and the like, and that there is "freedom of expression" (divergent political opinions are not to be suppressed). It is also assumed that the authoritative decisions normally are regarded as legitimate, i.e. as binding, e.g. because they are made according to generally accepted "rules of the game". Only to a limited degree can they be enforced.

What has been said so far constitutes, to be sure, just a minimal list of fundamental functions and norms in a democratic party government regime, but it is sufficient to exemplify a number of *basic governance problems* (some of them general, some of them mainly referring to democratic party government systems):

- if one cannot recruit public decision-makers or if persons are recruited, who are patently incompetent in relation to the problems that are prevalent;
- if the authorities cannot reach decisions (e.g. if majority formation is hampered by fragmentation of the party system and/or divergent opinions among decision-makers, if stalemates are reached, if coalitions cannot be formed, if "decisional costs" are excessive etc.);
- if the implementation of the authoritative decisions deviate substantially from the intentions behind them (if the central public authorities lack supervision and control);
- if the authoritative decisions, when implemented, turn out to be contrary or even contradictory (lack of coordination);

[8] On representation, see Pitkin, 1967; Eulau—Wahlke, 1978. On competition, see Khandwalla, 1981; Downs, 1957; Schumpeter, 1950.

- if the messages from the representatives to the electorate (or vice versa) are systematically misleading;
- if the representatives are unresponsive to demands from substantial (or "strategically located") groups in the electorate (n. b.: to be "responsive" means to be attentive to demands, not necessarily to yield to them; the response may well be "no", followed by arguments);
- if the public authorities lack channels through which they can get correct and sufficient information or if they lack means to make information 'operational' (e. g.: "information overload");
- if parties lack resources to formulate policy proposals in respect of the more important problems and or channels to present these proposals to the electorate;
- if the process of governance is seen by the electorate, or substantial parts of it, as violating fundamental regime norms and/or fundamental "human rights";
- if the public authorities and their decisions are regarded as illegitimate by substantial parts of the electorate (for whatever reasons).
- Etc.
- (Cf. also juxtapositions like "political solutions" – or even "diplomatic solutions" – versus "military solutions").

In terms of these – admittedly rather vague – definitions of some different types of practical collective problems, it is clear that societal problems and policy problems are mainly connected to the *substance or content* of human living conditions, while governance problems are mainly connected to institutions and procedures, to ways and means of coming to collective decisions and getting them accepted as binding. It is important to stress that governance problems arise under conditions of conflict and competition. If it were possible all the time, voluntarily and unanimously, to agree on all measures, 'politics' would not exist. By analogy, if we know that one and only one best solution to a policy problem exists and we have the resources to solve it, no policy problem would exist.

So much for definitions (or definitional outlines). The relations between the three types of problems should, however, be regarded as an empirical problem. Some examples are appropriate. The general growth of the public sector means that more and more societal problems are made into policy problems and handled by the public decisional machinery. This does not make the societal problems into governance problems. Unemployment is (in this terminology) still a societal problem and not a governance problem; if it is handled by the public authorities, e. g. on the governmental and parliamentary level, it is transformed into a policy problem. It may well give rise to governance problems or to conflicts among decision-makers, but this is an empirical relation.

As illustrations of conceivable empirical relations between the three types of problems the following is suggested:

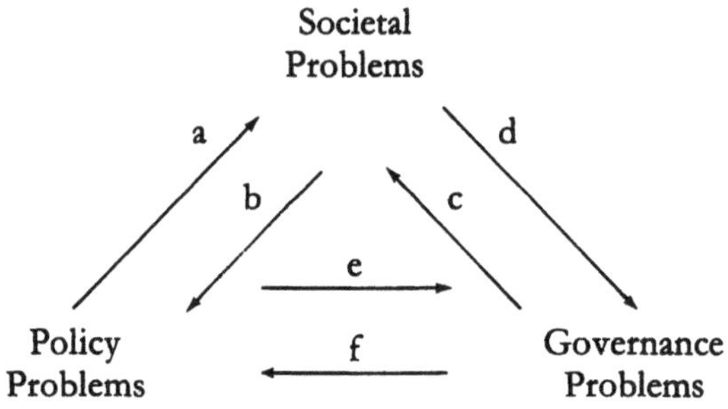

Examples:

(a) No 'solutions' seem to exist
(b) Societal changes make existing policies outdated
(c) Adverse consequences of political stalemate, e. g. excessive inflation
(d) Within party splits because of societal tensions
(e) Coalition breakdown because of divergent policies
(f) Search for new policy options because of coalition formation.

But the three types of problems *may* also be empirically unconnected. A societal problem (as perceived by a substantial group of citizens) may not be taken up by the political system and hence no policy options considered.[9] (Lack of relation b). There is also the important possibility that the relations between societal problems, as experienced by citizens, and the formulation of these problems as policy problems, are indeterminate, e. g. in the sense that the citizens do not "recognise" their problems when these are processed at the policy-making level. Such a lack of congruence may depend on several factors — e. g. direct misperception, structural constraints in the policy-making bodies (cf. Freddi, *infra*), strategic competition among the political parties, etc. The deliberation of policy options may take place among experts, without repercussions on political relations. (Lack of relation e). The same deliberations may have only a very scant relation to societal problems (artificial problems, created by policy specialists). Governance problems may be self-generating, without relation to either policy problems or societal problems (Lack of relations e and d).

V. Some Properties of Policy Problems

A problem may have a great number of properties, (as exemplified by the enumeration in Section II, above). A few of the presumably more important properties (in view of the research problems of the project) will be briefly treated here:

[9] Cf. notions like 'gate-keeping', 'non-decision-making', etc.

- Is a problem structured or unstructured? How is it defined and located? Can it be disaggregated and/or aggregated with other problems? (A.)
- Is a problem avoidable or unavoidable? In the latter case, can it be controlled in some way or must the reaction be just "reactive" (and adaptive)? (B.)
- By what criteria can one assess the "size" of a problem? (C.)
- What is the "time horizon" of a problems? (D.)
- To what arena(s) is a problem assigned? What does this mean in political terms and for the way the problem is conceived and handled? How are shifts of arenas related to strategic deliberations? (E.)

In this section the discussion is concentrated on policy problems, but it may well be that some of the reasoning is also applicable to societal problems and/or governance problems.

A. Structured and Unstructured Problems

A problem is (well-) structured if you know the discrepancy between the actual and the desirable and you know the action(s) that with high probability will remove this discrepancy. The decision is then made under (relative) certainty. A number of routine problems are of this character. Obviously, such problems are rather uninteresting from our point of view.

Problems which involve decision-making under risk and uncertainty are normally also structured. In both cases the discrepancy is defined and a number of action alternatives are available. The outcomes may be calculated with different degrees of probability/uncertainty.

Most policy problems referring to ·societal problems are not of this character however. They do not involve decision-making under uncertainty but under ambiguity. (cf. Mintzberg et al., 1976); March/Olsen et al., 1976 Page, 1976). The description of the actual state of affairs is uncertain, the view of the desirable may be dim; hence, it is unclear what constitutes the discrepancy; hence, the problem is not defined; hence, the action alternatives cannot be defined. Even if the discrepancy is made a bit more precise, no alternatives to handle such problems may be known or one is uncertain if existing "technologies" are applicable. In such cases, the whole problem situation is 'undefined' and the "diagnosis" difficult to make.

Two strategies to try to define the problem in such situations are either to make a horizontal or a vertical connection. In the first case the problem is compared to another one with which it appears to be similar and which may be known and defined; the 'solution' is then based on analogy.

The vertical connection means that you either try to disaggregate the unstructured problem ("decompose" or "factor" it) into familiar, structurable elements; or that you try to aggregate the problems with others to find out to which wider context it belongs. A problem may be very differently defined if it is seen in one context or another (cf. the example of unemployment as given in Section IV).

The question of aggregation/disaggregation belongs, of course, to a class of difficulties which is a plague for both analysts and for political actors: how to draw boundaries "in a reasonable way" (how is a system delimited? How is a decision delimited? How is a role delimited? etc., (cf. Coleman, 1966; Ramos, 1976)). A certain amount of arbitrariness can hardly be avoided, whether the criteria be "effectiveness" or "efficiency" or even "feasibility", (cf. Majone, 1975), but the cognitive difficulties are further increased by the probability that different delimitations have different consequences for the power structure and hence are likely to be selected also from a strategic point of view. The analyst may use criteria such as "informative value" or "fruitfulness", but such criteria are notoriously vague, at least *ex ante* (cf. McGrath, 1981; Sjøblom, 1977); the analyst may also for "operational reasons" (which sometimes is another expression for intellectual laziness) use the actors' own categories ("the language of the sources"), which, however, often leads to a lack of comparability (in time and space) and to a low level of generalisability and hence is likely to score low on more "scholarly criteria".

Skill in aggregating/disaggregating problems is often highly important in strategic contexts. Much is gained if you can get your "influence objects" to accept your problem definition and if the problem is then put on the political agenda. Also, in bargaining and negotiation processes it is very common that one oscillates between aggregation and disaggregation of the issues and that the disagreement concerns how to define the problem(s) (cf. Lyles/Mitroff, 1980).

If a problem is structured there exists a repertoire of actions which are regarded as 'solutions'; the decision of what action to choose then involves some processes of *search* (search strategies). If a problem is unstructured, and cannot be structured by means of horizontal comparison (analogy) or vertical connection (aggregation or disaggregation), a new type of solution has to be created; this is a process of *design*. It is not made easier by the circumstance that unstructured policy problems are more likely to evoke governance problems than are structured policy problems. Between these two situations there is, of course, the one where a solution is found by search but has to be modified or redesigned to fit the present problem. (cf. Mintzberg et al., 1976).[10]

If completely new solutions have to be designed for a large policy problem, the very design process may be very costly and lengthy. For every step the number of options decreases — to "recycle" to earlier phases, in order to open up new options, may be costly, and the decisions taken may therefore increasingly be seen as irreversible, even if doubts begin to emerge as to the efficiency and general feasibility of the solution (cf. the "Concorde-syndrome"). (cf. Edmead, 1982). In relation to some fun-

[10] See Mohr, 1973; Nagel, 1980; Perrow, 1964; Simon, 1964.

damental democratic norms such "solutions" may be very problematical (cf. what was earlier said about reversibility, Section II.)

Taking the political aspect into account – from the points of view of both value assessment and strategic assessment – the problem-solving process described so far may look much too "rationalistic". This has to do – *inter alia* – with the fact (mentioned earlier, in passing) that not only are certain societal outcomes regarded as desirable but often also certain means *per se*, i. e. certain "solutions" (the phenomenon of "instrumental *Eigenwert*", (cf. Section VII. *infra*)). We then get a situation where not only are "problems in search of solutions" but also "solutions in search of problems" (cf. Olsen, 1972; March–Olsen et al., 1976). A socialist has often an inclination to regard "socialist technologies" as solutions to most problems; a liberal has often an inclination to regard "market technologies" as solutions to most problems. Such conditioned reflexes may look ridiculous but they may, on the other hand, mirror a deep insight: measures taken to solve policy problems of larger size also have "side-effects", in particular concerning the institutions that are created, changed or abolished in relation to what policy option is chosen (cf. Anderson, 1977). Political success does not only consist of getting your preferred policies decided and implemented, but also comes from influencing the institutional set-up of the society. (The latter type of success may, by the way, be much more durable and strategically "fruitful" and may be a guarantee for the continuation of the "winning" policies).

B. 'Imposed' versus 'Created' Problems

Some of the societal problems with which politicians are struggling seem to be "imposed" on them: they emerge in the environment (domestic or abroad); only to a limited extent, if at all, are they amenable to manipulation by the politicians with regard to the problem definition or problem perception of the citizens; they cannot be stopped by the gatekeepers of the political system. In the extreme form they appear as "crisis problems".[11]

Another type of problem are those "created" by the politicians themselves, problems which emerge as a by-product of the very game of politics. (They may also be called "opportunity problems"). (cf. Lyles/Mitroff, 1980; March/Olsen et al., 1976). They are not responses to demands, articulated by citizens' groups, but based on what politicians perceive as "wants" or "needs". They would not have been articulated had not some politicians intended them to be.

Between these two extreme types of problems we can conceive all sorts of intermediate forms. In general, the question concerns, first, the origins of problems, second, their degree of inevitability. The notion of gatekeeping

[11] Cf. e. g. Deutsch, 1981; Herman ed., 1972; Lyles–Mitroff, 1980; Zimmermann, 1979.

may give an impression that it is within the discretion of politicians whether a problem should be "let in" or not; but in the case of "imposed problems" no discretion exists, by definition. Moreover, it should not be forgotten that the gatekeeping process in itself is also a matter of party competition, and of competition between the parties and other actors (e. g. in the case of "muckraking journalism" or in the case of pressures from "one-issue movements" or in the case of policy-making administrators).

In the effort to characterise a political system, the degree of "imposedness" of its problem seems to be an important property, telling us what degree of freedom or room for manoeuvre its decision-makers have.

These notions are close to a family of concepts, quite common in contemporary political science, such as "articulation", "gatekeeping", "non-decision-making", "agenda-setting"[12] (activities or procedures in politics) and "issues" and "cleavages" (Rae—Taylor, 1970); Zuckerman, 1975) (the 'material' of politics). Closely related are also notions likc "active" vs. "adaptation". A problem which at one point of time appears to be under control may, if ignored, develop into an "imposed problem" (in the worst case into a "crisis problem"), to which an actor has to adapt and/or respond with 'reactive means', i. e. with a decreased degree of freedom.

C. The "Size" of a Problem

How is the "size" of a problem to be defined? Some criteria (which may overlap) are:

- in terms of the time used for its solving
- in terms of the number of people affected
- in terms of the intensity of feelings of those affected
- in terms of the "centrality" of the problem (its causal relations to other problems)
- in terms of the cognitive "difficulty" of solving the problem (do technologies exist to "solve" it?)
- in terms of the financial costs connected with feasible options for "solutions"
- in terms of the degree of change involved in the solution (routine solutions require only small changes, but some solutions may mean basic structural rearrangements in society)
- in terms of its importance in relation to some fundamental regime norms or norms in the political culture (e. g. does the problem constitute a threat to fundamental 'rights' of individual citizens or groups of citizens?)
- in terms of the degree to which feasible solutions restrict the future room for manoeuvre of the decision-makers (cf. "reversible"/"irreversible" solutions)

[12] E. g. Cobb et al., 1976; McCombs, 1981; Walker, 1977.

– etc. (for a very illuminating overview, see Wiseman, 1978).

Maybe the "size of a problem" can also be described in terms of the uncertainty of the effectiveness of available measures (the higher the uncertainty, the bigger the problem):

– Is a certain measure necessary or sufficient, or both for a "solution" of a problem?

(It may be necessary but not sufficient – hence it has to be supplemented; or sufficient but not necessary – hence alternatives exist; or both necessary and sufficient – hence no alternatives exist).

– How well can existing (and earlier existing) states of affairs be described?
– Are indicators reliable and valid, are they up-to-date, are they "sensitive" to changes but "robust" towards "noise", etc.? (cf. Sylvan–Thorson, 1980).

This last question raises the interesting issue of the aspiration levels of the decision-makers – it is relatively easier to describe, say, unemployment than, say, deteriorating "quality of life" – and decision-makers may have an "operationalist bias" (as many scholars have). It is also probable that rising levels of expectations will require other types of indicators for decision-makers, if they try to respond to such expectations. (cf. Allardt, 1973).

Evidently, the assessment of the "size" of a problem and the ranking of problems in this respect is important for decision-makers as the number of problems is large and can easily be multiplied; hence, some problems have to be ignored and resources of planning and problem-solving concentrated on "big problems". We know, on the other hand, that decision-makers often ignore this general rule; finding some big problems intractable and unpleasant they try to ignore or avoid them and instead engage in petty problems, style issues and symbolic politics ("problem displacement") (Lyles–Mitroff, 1980; March–Olsen et al., 1976). An important question is whether there is anything in the political institution or in the competitive situation *per se* which induces them to do so.

D. The "Time Horizon" of Problems

A different but related aspect has to do with the "time horizon" of problems (cf. Deutsch, 1963; Downs, 1972; T. W. Smith, 1980; Steiner–Dorff, 1980):

– How urgent is the problem (is a quick solution necessary, or is it possible, or even better, to wait and see)?
– What is the 'tempo' of the problem – does it grow slowly or quickly?

These two questions should be separated; while a quick-growing problem presumably calls for quick "solutions", the same may be valid for slow-growing problems, e. g. if they may be "killed" at an early but not at a late stage. The intelligent actor is the one who avoids problems if they are avoidable; who handles them when they are least difficult to handle (never let a problem grow if it can be stopped!) Hence, an important precondition for intelligent acting in the world is "anticipation" (or "lead"); the ability to foresee what may happen — hence only rarely having to act under surprise, time pressure or stress.

- Are the measures taken intended as short-term or long-term solutions?
- Do the measures taken have rapid effects or are the effects to be discovered, if at all, only in the long-term ("lag" of effect)?
- Do the benefit-aspects and the cost-aspects of the solution have the same time perspectives or do they differ? (This last question may be of the utmost political importance — both concerning general effects and concerning the temporal distribution of benefits and costs to different groups of citizens).
- Can the long-term effects of a measure be calculated? Can the side-effects of a measure be calculated?
- Does the problem occur regularly or irregularly? Is it a recurrent problem or an "unique" problem?
- If the problem, according to experience, is likely to be concomitant to other problems, do these problems emerge as a sequence or do they emerge in a cluster?

On this last question: it is well known that it makes a difference for an actor's ability to handle problems if they occur one by one, as it were, or if they emerge all at the same time: in the last case, the total "load" on the decisional machinery may become too heavy (cf. the so-called "crisis theory" in comparative politics (cf. Rokkan, 1970), and also the literature on "governmental overload")[13]. This may or may not be possible to regulate by gatekeeping (this is not possible if problems are "imposed").

- If a perceived trend is defined as a problem, does there eventually exist any countervailing trend, which in due time may extinguish the problem or, at least, reduce it? (cf. Sjøblom, 1983).

E. Problems and Arenas

If a societal problem passes into the public decisional machinery it is transformed into a policy problem; if it becomes the object of conflict among public desision-makers it is "politicised"; the policy problem is then made into an "issue"; a "policy issue".

For an assessment of a political system it is of great importance to specify in which connection (i.e. in which arena) a problem is politicised: in the parliamentary arena, in the electoral arena, in the bureaucratic arena, in the

[13] See Crozier et al., 1975; Douglas, 1976; King, 1975; Huntington, 1974; Lehner, 1979; Offe, 1979; Rose, 1978; 1979; Rose ed., 1980; Schmitter, 1980.

corporative arena? (or whatever distinctions that may be used). Further, what overlap is there in this respect between the different arenas? (cf. McCann—Galbraith, 1981).

The answer to this latter question is of great interest for an assessment of a political system. Assume, for the sake of argument, the (empirically highly unlikely) condition that there is no overlap whatsoever between the policy issues presented in the parliamentary arena and those salient in the electoral arena. This indicates a system which in reality is not 'representative': the contest in the electoral arena is then just a play for the gallery. If there is only a very limited overlap in this respect between different arenas, we may speak of a highly "segmented" or "sectorised" system. (Such segmentation may be an institutional device to structure otherwise unstructured problems) (cf. Olsen, 1981).

Some discrepancies of this sort always exist in "representative" or "delegated" systems, among other things because of the different capacity of different arenas to "process issues"; there is, for instance, some limit to the number of issues that can be put on the electoral agenda. What issues to put there, and what priorities to set between issues, is a matter of competition between parties in electoral agenda-setting. (Many issues, however, are not "policy-issues" but "non-topical issues" concerning personalities, style questions, credibility, and the like) (cf. Sjøblom, 1968). The degree of overlap between different parties in this respect is another question of great interest for political actors and political analysts. If no overlap exists, the parties are competing on different agendas, not on their different positions as to the same issues. The type of competition is different in the two cases. What further consequences for the political system follow if one or the other type of competition prevails?

So far the reasoning has been based on the simplified assumption that a policy issue "is what it is", wherever it appears and whatever the degree of overlap or non-overlap. But this may not be so. In particular two circumstances deserve to be mentioned: the way each issue is presented and perceived in different arenas and the way different issues are aggregated or disaggregated in different arenas. An issue is normally differently presented to, and perceived by, an expert and a layman. An issue may further be perceived and assessed differently, if it is perceived in one context or in another.

In the analysis of party competition, the competence of different arenas to handle problems may be of great interest (seen from a prescriptive point of view, this is the question of how to design institutions and the relations between them) (cf. Anderson, 1977; Metcalfe, 1981). From the perspective of political parties, power relations may be very different in different arenas. Parties in government are normally interested in having issues decided in the governmental arenas. Parties in opposition may call for a dissolution of parliament and new elections if they think that the majority in the electorate has shifted since the last election. Minority parties may call for a referendum on a specific issue if they think they represent a majority position on that issue. Some parties may be inclined to refer some issues to corporative arenas, if they think this will enhance their views. Some parties may speak of decentralisation, if they think that their views are better grounded in regional and/or local representative bodies than in the national parliament. Other parties may try to refer issues to expert committees, or to judicial adjudication for the same reason. Some parties try to take some issues out of the political system, referring them to market decisions. All these are examples of efforts to shift arena for strategic reasons.

It may also be the case that the move of a policy issue from one arena to another is a sign of an increased or decreased degree of politicisation and/or is a sign that a conflict has been transformed; it may also indicate a change of the political agenda, signalling a new ranking of problem priority. Sometimes an issue is moved to an arena, where the decisions are regarded as highly legitimate and, perhaps, irreversible, at least for the foreseeable future: this may be the case when a policy issue is put to a referendum or to the courts.

I am not saying that all views on decisional competence, on the "proper site of decisions", can be explained in such a power perpective. A party often holds principles in such respects which are not obviously to its advantage; it may, for instance, be quite difficult to take positions which are perceived to be contrary to or not consistent with widely accepted norms of a democratic regime. But the perspective needs to be analysed, all the more so as it may reveal that institutions as such are not just neutral frameworks for political competition: they are created and designed (or abolished) with a view to the consequences of competition, and in that respect an often "biased" (such a bias may, of course, also be unintended)[14].

The reasoning so far may seem digressive, but it has served to underline some points of interest for the analysis of policy problems. To summarise a few of the questions:

- To what arena (site, level) in the political system is a policy problem referred for handling? To what extent is such referring controversial? Could such controversies be explained by parties' self-interest, if the power structure of a certain arena is more to their advantage than those of others?
- What degree of overlap exists between different arenas concerning issues? Can differences in degree help us to construct useful typologies of political systems (e.g. based on criteria such as politicisation, representativeness, responsiveness, fragmentation)?

[14] Anderson, 1977; Hirschman, 1970; Nystrom—Starbuck eds., 1981.

- To what degree is it possible to disaggregate a problem into subproblems or to aggregate different problems, and what are the differences in this respect between different arenas? Can the principles for aggregation/disaggregation, as related to different arenas, be analysed in terms of party strategies? What are the relations between different aggregations/disaggregations and democratic norms concerning the information of electorates (with further consequences for the possibilities of the voters to act "in a rational way")?

The relevance for the project *The Future of Party Government* of the distribution of policy problems to different arenas and of shifts between arenas should be obvious: if more and more of the important policy problems are acted upon and decided in arenas where the parties have low influence or no influence at all, then the relative roles of parties in governance will obviously vanish; a new power structure may emerge and we may then end up with another type of regime (cf. G. Smith, *infra*).

VI. "Problem-Solving Capacity"

A number of difficult operational research problems are evidently involved in the research problems formulated so far. One of the greatest difficulties presumably concerns the meaning that should be given to the term "problem-solving capacity"; I now turn to some notes on this notion.

"Capacity" is a term which belongs to the functional family of terms, and it is marred by the ambiguity (and also vagueness) which usually characterises such terms: it may refer to *potentials*, to *activities*, or to *outcomes* (and in the background there is some vague notion of "need") (cf. Sjøblom, 1981). These complications are well-known, but let me briefly illustrate them in our specific context:

- Your potential to solve problems may be high but you may not use it.
- You may be active in trying to solve problems but lack potential to solve them or at least only use part of your potential.
- The outcome may be that the societal problems are solved (in some sense) but this may not be the result of your activities (the problems may be solved irrespective of your activities or even despite your activities).

Whichever meaning is given to the term "capacity" — potential, activities, outcomes — there will be difficulties:

a) If "potential" is chosen we run into operational difficulties and data difficulties — it may be very difficult to find out what the limits of the potentials are. From the point of view of validity, however, "potential" seems to be the reasonable choice: what we want to know is exactly the potentials of different governmental systems for the solution of policy-problems.

b) If "activities" is chosen, the operational difficulties are small (in principle – there may, of course, be difficulties in data access, in sampling, etc.) but "activities" may be an indicator of dubious validity for "capacity"; from the point of view of the matter-of-fact assessment, activities may, for instance, be mainly symbolic; in the worst case they have no discernable consequences whatsoever (they may or may not have strategic effects).

c) If "outcomes" is chosen, there is a high risk of circularity and a number of causal problems may be sidestepped – if problems are solved "by themselves", as it were, or by actors and/or forces outside the political system, or even by actors and/or forces outside the national system, then "outcomes" do not tell us anything about the "problem-solving capacity" connected to constitutive properties of the type of governmental system under study.

So we seem to be caught in a dilemma because of our wish to use a notion like "capacity".

However, I shall leave it here and declare that I will stick to capacity as "potential" in what follows – well aware of the operational difficulties. The capacity of a large collectivity can hardly be directly measured in any reasonable sense – in contrast to, say, the intellectual capacity of an individual or the performing capacity of a sportsman. This does not mean that the notion of collective capacity is empty, just that is very elusive. The research problem has to be decomposed into a number of researchable smaller questions and the answers to them have to be synthesised into an assessment of the "problem-solving capacity" of (in this case) a certain type of party government. (Some indicators are relatively uncomplicated, e. g. institutions for the processing of routine problems; proportions of resources in a budget which are not committed in advance ("slack resources" "redundancy") (cf. Landau, 1969).

Such research will require that at least three further aspects are taken into account:

a) the "location" of the capacity in the overall system,
b) the relation between capacity and the degree of 'difficulty' of the policy problems/societal problems,
c) the impact of different levels of popular expectations on the problem-solving capacity.

a) Like "function", "capacity" may refer to different *levels* of the political system. One specific party may have a certain capacity which other parties lack; so may one party system in relation to another, one regime in relation to another, one political system in relation to another. It is evidently an important but very difficult research problem to assess to which level of the system a certain capacity is connected: does a certain political system manage to "solve" a number of policy problems because of the capacity of a certain party, or does this party solve problems because of capacities inherent in the overall system? What possible connections in this respect exist between different levels? (cf. McIntosh et al., 1977).

The complication here refers to different actors or actors at different levels in the political system. But there may exist another difference in problem-solving capacity among different actors or actors at different levels. A certain regime or a certain party may, for instance, have a high capacity to solve certain types of problems, say problems of a distributive kind, while its capacity is low concerning other problem types, say of a regulative kind or concerning growth and balance of the economy. Different actors, different regimes, etc., may be compared in this respect, which presumably will tell us something important about the various political systems.

b) But the most relativistic complication of all to be treated here is this: capacity must always be related to how *difficult* the problems to be solved are. The likely success of an effort to solve a problem depends on how difficult a problem is: in one type of regime easy problems are solved with complete success – in another regime difficult problems are solved with limited success. If this is all the information there is, very little can be said on the 'problem solution potential' of each regime.

c) As a specification of the last argument: the difficulty of a problem is obviously highly dependent on the level of *expectation* of the citizens – this may for instance, rise to such a high level that virtually all problems are insoluable in the sense that any solution and its effects may cause frustration. To put it *ex adverso:* a "solution" to a problem may then mean that the level of expectation is lowered. This, I assume, is a possibility that deserves close attention, because it indicates that 'problem solution capacity' may not only refer to the ability to solve problems "as they are" but also to the "ability to influence the perception and definition of these problems" and to 'the expected suitability and feasibility of solutions' and to 'the expected impacts of these solutions' – in short, influencing perceptions and expectations. When parties calculate the "costs of solutions", these different options must also be taken into account.

This can be summarised in the following research problems:

- What factors determine the citizens' perceptions and definitions of problems?
- What factors determine the citizens' levels of expectations?

It is likely that efforts by a specific party to influence the citizens' perception and definition of problems and their levels of expectation are highly uncertain, first, because this will be a matter of competition between the different parties, with uncertain outcomes and, second, because these perceptions, definitions and expectations are likely to be influenced by a variety of other factors — e.g. by socialisation, culture, the activities of non-party societal actors like the mass media, etc.

The strategic question to be asked by the elite of a specific party is:

— To what degree, if any, can one's own party influence the citizens' perceptions and definitions of problems, and their levels of expectations?

Evidently the strategic assessment is connected to governance problems: how to select action alternatives in such a way that one can maximise the chances of influencing the collective decisions, directly or indirectly, in the short or in the long term.

Evidently the matter-of-fact assessment is connected to policy problems: how to select efficient alternatives so that the discrepancy between actual and desired states of affairs is removed (or, at least, the gap narrowed, or — in cases where deterioration cannot be avoided — the increase in the gap minimised).

The value assessment has no such one-to-one relation but is relevant in connection with all three: societal problems, policy problems, and governance problems. By definition, a value assessment — to specify what is a desirable state of affairs — is one of the prerequisites for defining a policy problem; the conceivable outcomes of different policy options will also have to be ranked in relation to a value standard. And as the strategic assessment means manœuvering in such a way that the chance of influencing the collective decisions is maximised, you must have some idea of what collective decisions (*cum* outcomes) are desirable — hence, make a value assessment. (However, in the last case there may be pathological situations where the strategic game has its own "*Eigenwert*", a malignant case of "suboptimisation": when you are prepared to take *any* position, provided it is optimal from a strategic point of view (cf. Downs, 1957)).

At the beginning of the paper a basic (but vague) working hypothesis for the project was stated like this:

— Party government (in some form) is likely to persist if and only if it can solve the important societal problems in an acceptable way.

An (almost) equivalent formulation of the working hypothesis was:

— Party government (in some form) is likely to persist if and only if it has a high degree or problem-solving capacity.

Using the distinctions made so far the working hypothesis (and its near-equivalent) can now be reformulated.

— Democratic party government is likely to persist if, and only if:

(a) the more important societal problems are put on the agenda, i.e. turned into policy problems, and
(b) the more important policy problems are solved in an acceptable way, and
(c) the more important governance problems are solved in an acceptable way.

As soon as you ask for arguments in support of the working hypothesis stated here ("Party government ... to persist ... problem-solving capacity"), it is clear that it is based on some implicit assumptions. What these assumptions are is, of course, a matter of interpretation. The following could, for instance, be suggested;

- Any system of government is likely to persist if and only if it has an high degree of legitimacy.
- Any system of government is likely to have an high degree of legitimacy if and only if it has an high problem-solving capacity (and this is actually used).
- Party government, as a system of government, is likely ... etc.

The first proposition may seem patently false as some systems of government which are regarded as legitimate by a majority of its citizens do persist mainly by the use of force, terror and communication control. This taken into account, the reasoning could be changed into a much weaker version:

- Any system of government, normatively based on the voluntary consent of its citizens, is likely ... etc ...
- Democratic party government is such a type of government, as mentioned in the first sentence, etc ...

The reasoning here is much weaker, not only because the first proposition has a narrower scope, but also, and in particular, because the reasoning may come dangerously close to being circular. But that depends, of course, on what definitions are used, on the elasticity of the regime norms, on how feelings of illegitimacy are expressed etc.

Leaving aside a number of difficulties, we can at least conclude that, according to this interpretation, the future of party government depends on its *legitimacy*. The research problem could then be stated in such a way that "legitimacy" is, as it were, the dependent variable and that we are looking for conceivable independent variables. In the working hypothesis one of those has been identified: "problem-solving capacity" (and it is taken for granted that this capacity will be used more or less).

Evidently, we are in this case asking for the instrumentality of democratic party government *as such* – well aware that any empirical studies are most likely to contain a number of "disturbing factors" in relation to the research problem stated. Hence:

- is there anything ***in the constitutive properties*** of democratic party governments which makes them score high or low on problem-solving capacity?

A line of reasoning leading to a negative conclusion could for instance take the following form:

- Frequent elections are a constitutive property of democratic government.
- Ability to conduct long-term policies is a necessary condition for high problem-solving capacity.
- Frequent elections will hamper the ability to conduct long-term policies;
- Hence: democratic government is likely to score low on 'problem-solving capacity'.

Another line of reasoning, leading to a positive conclusion, could for instance take the following form:

- High popular participation and high elite responsiveness are constitutive properties of democratic government.
- The existence of these properties is likely to lead to high system legitimacy.
- High system legitimacy is a necessary condition for high problem-solving capacity;
- Hence: democratic government is likely to have an high problem-solving capacity.

(These examples are obviously quite elliptical — and the logic in the last line of reasoning is very weak — but they may illustrate the conceivable form of answers to the research problems).

But there are different types of party government so we must proceed to a more detailed formulation of the research problem:

- Is there anything ***in the constitutive properties of a certain type of democratic party government*** which makes it score high or low on problem-solving capacity and, if so, how can different types of democratic party governments be ranked when compared in this respect?

Let us now proceed to the question of the role of institutions and political processes in the process of legitimation and start with the instrumental role, related to problem-solving.

One of the main objects of political science is of course, the study of the mutual relations between 1. institutions and political processes, 2. policies, and 3. societal outcomes. If, to simplify the reasoning, we take the desirability of some societal outcomes as given (as desired, e. g., by a majority of the citizens), then the question is:

– what types of institutions and political processes are most likely to result in policies (i. e. policy solutions) which are effective with regard to the desired societal outcomes?

In other words:

– Are some types of institutions and processes more 'rational' in this particular respect?

This way of putting the question evidently means that institutions and processes are evaluated in an highly "instrumental fashion". However, this line of reasoning is so simplified that it is misleading. We can with confidence state the following empirical generalisation:

– Political institutions and processes are not only evaluated as instruments but also assigned an intrinsic value ("*Eigenwert*") by a number of members of the political system.

Hence, political regimes are in themselves "objects of support". Presumably, this support will decline if the regime turns out to be highly ineffective from an instrumental point of view, but that relation of support/effectiveness will hardly be linear. (If a certain type of regime is assigned an "*Eigenwert*" by its citizens, or most of them, although they realise that it is not the most effective one, then we have a situation which may be analysed with the use of indifference curves).

Concerning the legitimacy of a regime a third circumstance has to be considered, viz. the regime-members' *perceptions and evaluations of regime alternatives*. Most people learn early in life that many choice situations do not involve the choice between good things but between things which are more or less bad and that the problem is to select the lesser of two (or more) evils (which may make a decisional rule like "mini-regret" applicable).

What are the alternatives to a "party government regime"? What are the benefits and costs of these alternatives as compared with those of a party government regime? How could they be ranked?

Exactly the same type of reasoning is, of course, applicable to a comparison between different types of party government within the class of "party government regimes". (I leave it open here whether these perceptions and comparisons of alternative regimes – or varieties within a type of regime – should be seen as a third separate factor, influencing legitimacy, or just as a sub-component of the "*Eigenwert*" of a regime). The reasoning so far is summed up in this figure:

A. PG regime's problem-solving capacity →
B. PG regime's "*Eigenwert*" (intrinsic value) → Legitimacy of PG regime
C. Evaluation of alternative regimes →

Or (to illustrate):

A. The higher the problem-solving capacity of the PG regime
and/or
B. The higher the *"Eigenwert"* of the GP regime
and/or
C. The lower the evaluation of alternative regimes

} The higher the legitimacy of the PG regime

— and: vice versa.

(It may be retorted, with good reason, that as the instrumental and the Eigenwert components of a PG regime have been distinguished, the same should be done for alternative regimes. This I have, however, regarded as a complication that goes "beyond necessity").

The three components ("independent variables") are conceptually distinct (it is to be hoped) but their empirical connections may vary. Some examples:

(+A, +B) seems very probable, but
(+A, −B) is quite conceivable (regime X is highly efficient but with the use of abominable means and procedures)
(+B, −A) (high popular participation in politics is to be promoted, even if it leads to decreased efficiency)
(+B, −C) (the higher the evaluation of regime X, the lower the evaluation of regime Y) but
(+B, +C) is also conceivable, e. g. in the form (the more regime X changes its means and procedures, the higher its *"Eigenwert"* ***but*** the less will the difference between regime X and Y be perceived).
Etc.

VIII. Mapping of Macro Problems — An Outline

At the beginning of the paper it was stated, that a necessary condition for understanding an individual's or a collectivity's actions and reactions is an understanding of his/her/its problem situation. Let this be represented in the following way:

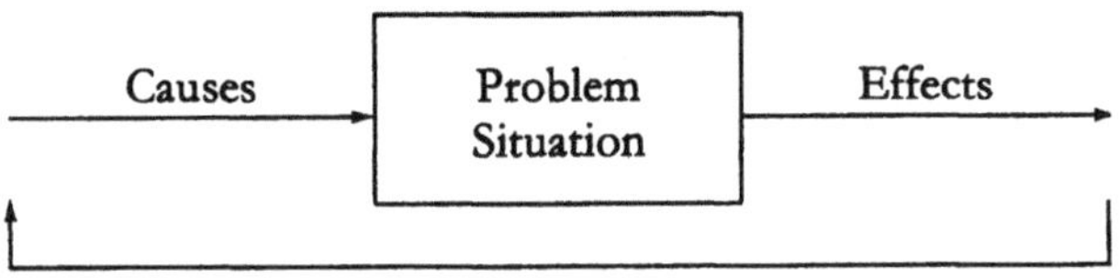

Based on this figure we can distinguish four types of research questions:

a) we can ask what are the causes that produced the problem situation at time t.
b) we can ask what are the effects of the problem situation at time t, i. e. in the form of actions taken in order to "solve" the problems.
c) we can, as it were, use the whole figure for the analysis of sequences of problem situations *ex post* (t_{+n} — t) e. g. the sequences of problem situations in country A, 1945-1983).
d) we can use the whole figure for conjectures about sequences of problems situations *ex ante* from time t to time t_{+n} (this is what happens in the writings of scenarios).

One may speculate about the relations between these types of research questions: a) may presumably be done independently; if you say that it is impossible even to describe a present problem situation (or, at least to understand it) without having at least some ideas as to its causes, then b) presupposes some form of a); a) and b) may be combined, so also a) and d); c) may be seen as a specification of a) and d) of b); c) and d) may be combined etc.

All the time we are interested in the *changes* of problem situations: the *degree of change* (small/large), the *type of change* (e. g. cumulative/"revolutionary") and the *rate of change* (slow/rapid) (some of the properties of problems as stated in Section V, are also relevant for the analysis of change — cf. e. g. Section V. C., "The 'Size' of a Problem", and V. D. "The 'Time Horizon' of Problems").

While it has always been tempting for persons to regard the epoch in which they themselves are living as very specific ("the fallacy of shortsightedness"), it seems reasonable to say, however, that the present times are characterised by an unusually high degree of change and an unusually high rate of change (cf. the catchword "future shock") (Toffler, 1970). (The assessment of the types of change may be more complicated — when will a "quantitative jump" also mean a "qualitative jump"?).

From the point of view of party governments as problem-solvers the characterisations mentioned are important: the greater the changes and the higher the rate of change, the more complicated the problem-solving. Organisational analysts have, for instance, stressed the adaptive problems for organisations in "turbulent environments" (cf., e. g., Axelson—Rosenberg, 1979).

Let us regard the public decisional machinery as an organisation of large scale (cf. Dahl—Tufte, 1974), great interdependence (cf. Alker, 1977; Gerlach—Palmer, 1981) and high complexity (cf. La Porte, ed. 1974; Nurmi, 1974). This machinery is the steering organisation of a society. The very machinery itself must be steered. Steering requires, a) some goals (value assessments must be made, otherwise it is not "steering" but "drifting") (Deutsch, 1963) and b) coordination and control. Any organisation is based on division of labour and of a certain amount of coordination between its components (cf. Mintzberg, 1979; Galbraith, 1977). To what degree can modern advanced industrial societies be steered and can even the public decisional machinery of such societies itself be steered? (cf. Lindbeck, 1973; Pollitt, 1980; Winner, 1977). And, in accordance with the theme of the research project: can they be steered by (any form of) party government?

In what follows I will try to outline — very sketchily and very tentatively, to be sure — some of the presumedly more important traits in the problem situations of present party governments.

1. The social structure has become more diversified. The meeting of most basic needs has released higher level needs (according to, say, the Maslow hierarchy). This means that demands on the public sector have increased in amount, have become more diversified and are more difficult to satisfy (they may, for instance, be presented in a "non-operational" form).

2. The public sector has grown rapidly in all advanced industrial countries and has become increasingly diversified. As a combined result of this and the diversification of the social structure (the two phenomena are partly concomitant and intermingled), a "new class" has arisen, which has strong vested interests in a large public sector (and often also in its further growth). As this sector mainly has to be financed by taxes, a new cleavage has arisen between public employees and private employees (Huntingdon, 1974) (cf. also remarks by Wildenmann, *supra*).

3. Two earlier widely held views have turned out to be wrong. The idea of "mass society" predicted that the "post-industrial society" would be characterised by increasing homogeneity, as a result of norms of equality and standardisation of living conditions[15]. While this standardisation has taken place in some areas of life, the overwhelming impression given by this society is, however, one of cultural heterogeneity and increasingly so. — The other widely held view was one of high optimism concerning social technology: societal problems were supposed to be solvable to a high degree.[16] The very high rate of policy failure, according to a number of evaluation studies, has shaken this confidence considerably[17].

Obviously, the optimism about societal technology and the idea of increased homogenisation were combined — problems were supposed to become easier and solutions to them better and more reliable. The opposite seems to be the case: societal problems turned out to be more complicated

[15] Cf. e. g. Bell, 1973; 1976; Benjamin, 1975; 1980; Crozier, 1974; Hennessey—Peters, 1976; Huntington, 1974.

[16] Typical examples are Dror, 1971; Jantsch, 1970.

[17] Cf. e. g. Campbell, 1981; van Gunsteren, 1976; Rittel—Webber, 1973; Wildavsky, 1973; Wolf Jr., 1979.

and solutions less powerful than expected – hence the policy problems have grown worse.

4. The growth of the public sector meant, by definition, that more and more of the citizens' living conditions depend on public decisions and actions. At the same time we notice a tendency toward a growing diversification of demands (cf. Easton, 1965; 1973; 1976). The result is that more and more of the political demands are only backed up by minorities, not by majorities. Now, it may well be the case that majorities have never ruled, only minorities have (cf. Dahl, 1966), but in combination with the fact that living conditions to an increasing degree are dependent on collective decisions we get a slightly paradoxical result. One of the constitutive properties of democracy is, no doubt, the majority principle – but how can majorities be formed at all in an increasingly diversified society, if the majority on each issue tends to be indifferent and/or answer "don't know". What consequences will this dilemma have for the ways in which parties try to "aggregate policies"? Is it a factor that will inevitably lead to a decrease in the relative role of political parties in the public decisional machinery? (cf. Daalder–Mair, eds., 1983).

5. Because of the increased amount and increased diversification of demands, a proportionately smaller part of them can be handled by central political authorities, who therefore have to delegate decisions to specialised bureaucratic agencies. This method of increasing channel capacity leads to a sectorised decisional machinery which is increasingly difficult to coordinate and control. The phenomenon described as "suboptimisation" is more and more common.[18]

The increased interdependence means that both the society at large and the public decisional machinery are more and more vulnerable. It also means that it is more and more difficult to structure, decompose and locate problems ("Big problems, small brains") (Lindblom, 1977). "With arithmetical changes in scale, there are geometric increases in interdependence and complexity" (De Greene, 1982:94).

I will here reproduce a long (and depressing) list of alleged properties connected with the type of organization described so far (from Elgin, 1977, as quoted in De Greene, 1982:94):

"*Characteristics of Social Systems at Extremes of Scale, Interdependence and Complexity:*

1. Diminishing relative capacity of a given person to comprehend the entire system.
2. Diminishing public participation in decision-making.
3. Declining public access to decision-makers.

[18] Cf. Deutsch, 1963; Blau, 1970; Galbraith, 1977; Olsen ed., 1978; Olsen, 1981; Lawrence-Lorsch, 1967.

4. Growing participation of experts in decision-making.
5. Disproportionately growing costs of coordination and control.
6. Increasingly rationalized person-system interactions.
7. Increasing alienation.
8. Increasing challenges to basic values.
9. Increasingly unexpected and counterexpected consequences of policy making.
10. Declining system resilience.
11. Increasing system rigidity.
12. Increasing number and uncertainty of crisis events.
13. Decreasing diversity of innovation.
14. Decreasing legitimacy of leadership.
15. Increasing system vulnerability.
16. Declining system performance.
17. Growing system deterioration that is unlikely to be perceived by most members."

The list can be regarded in different ways: as an expression of the growing doubts among policy-analysts and organisational theorists about the feasibility of large organisations and "from top to bottom" methods for solving societal problems; or as a check list of organisational maladies, including organisational and decisional costs; or, in our case, as material for speculation on what will happen to party governments if they are connected to institutions with properties of the sort analysed in the list.

6. Any regime is based on some fundamental norms[19]. Political authorities of all regimes are supposed to maintain a certain order in society. They are also supposed to create conditions for a certain degree of efficiency in the society to ensure the material living conditions of its citizens. Moreover, among the foremost (formal or informal) norms in democratic regimes are liberty and equality. Such norms function as valuational standards, against which decisions and actions are assessed. In that situation they cannot be used just as honorific terms but must be given a content; it is then evident that they may function as restraints on each other or create dilemmas. To illustrate (but side-stepping a number of definitional and operational difficulties):

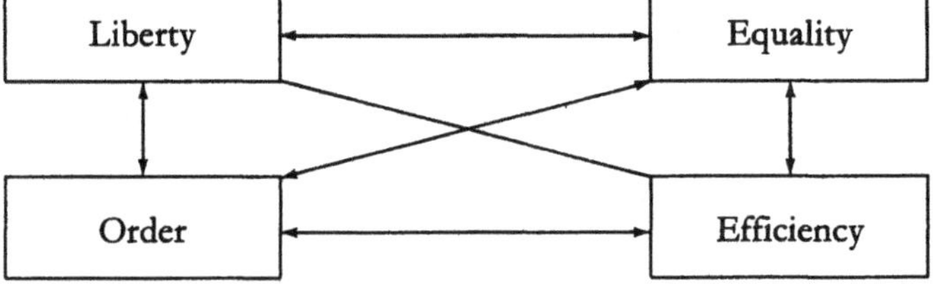

[19] Cf. e. g. Anderson, 1979; Carlsnaes, 1981; Cook, 1980; Dunn, 1978; Gibbs, 1965; Goodin, 1976; Morris, 1956.

Such potential normative conflicts belong to the fundamental problems facing public decision-makers. To what extent can individual liberties be sacrificed to maintain a certain order? How are demands for liberty and demands for equality combined? To what degree does efficiency require individual liberty and when does individual liberty decrease efficiency? How are efficiency and equality related etc.?

7. Finally, a few words will be said about one of those factors, which was supposed to influence legitimacy of the regime (Section VII.), namely the perception and *evaluation of alternative regimes*. Compare the situation in the Western democracies in this respect during the period between the wars (in particular the 1930's) and now. Then a number of persons were highly critical of democratic party government and advocated Fascist *or* Communist regimes and policies. Today only very small minorities are in favour of Fascist ideas. A great majority of citizens in Western democracies reject Communism, and even a majority of Communists in these countries seem united in their efforts to keep the existing Communist regimes at a distance. Still in the late 1960's a number of people (and not only Communists) acknowledged the Soviet Union's high degree of economic efficiency; in the early 1980's the admiration, if any, is confined to the Russian weapons industry.

This change in attitude is no doubt a major one. While people in democratic party-government-regimes often express themselves as highly critical of their own regime and their own rulers, alternative regimes are usually seen as so distant that they are not even taken into account.

IX. Epilogue

It is my hope that this essay, whatever its shortcomings, gives convincing arguments for the position that "problems" (and related notions) should be given a greater emphasis in political analysis than has usually been the case. If so, it is mandatory to investigate the preconditions and consequences of such a position. A number of theoretical, conceptual and operational issues are involved. This essay has concentrated on the conceptual issues.

It is be hoped that a number of the distinctions made should be fruitful for further analysis. While "fruitful" is a vague notion it is not empty: distinctions are fruitful *if* they allow us to come to a better understanding of the study object and *if* they permit us to formulate research problems and propositions in ways that are more nuanced and exact than in the absence of the distinctions. (Obviously, the distinctions should "make a difference", otherwise they are redundant).

In some cases I have tried to demonstrate, or at least illustrate, the fruitfulness of the distinctions, mainly by using them in the formulation of research problems. All distinctions made have not been used in this way however, due to lack of time and space (e. g. a number of the distinctions made in Section V, "Some Properties of Policy Problems"). Their fruitfulness is consequently an open question, both in general and in relation to *The Future of Party Government* project in particular.

My argument that 'problem' and related notions should be given a more prominent place in political analysis is, of course, based on my overview of the literature. As far as I know, "problems" and "problem-solving" are only prominent notions in the psychological literature often dealing with laboratory experiments. A number of social scientists have expressed their doubts about the relevance of such results for problems and problem-solving in "natural" and "collective" settings. I share these doubts, without having probed more deeply into the matter.

This essay is mainly influenced by the literature on policy-analysis and organisational theory. Not without difficulty, however, can theories, concepts and results from such literature be "translated" into party research (cf. Mohr, 1982). Most of the literature on organisational theory, for instance, deals with business firms and to some (but increasing) degree with public bureaucracies; the latter is also the case with policy analysis. Applying the treatment of "problems" and "problem-solving" from such literature to party research may require some modifications, given the special normative and institutional setting in which parties operate and given their very wide area of policy interest. I don't think such difficulties are insurmountable, but they will have to be considered very carefully.

Appendix: Some Formal Remarks

A. On Conceptual Analysis and Complications

Conceptual analyses are often met by irritation among political scientists, who curse 'les terribles complicateurs' and sometimes even believe that their exercises are made with malignant intentions, "pour épater les simplificateurs". — This is not the only reason nor the main one.

Robert K. Merton's notion of "accumulative imbalances" is useful to describe the dilemma (Merton, 1957; 1975). Any discipline is based on a division of labour: research techniques must be developed and refined, research problems stated, data collected and analysed, concepts defined, terms created, empirical generalisations provided, theoretical propositions and theories created, etc. etc. (the order of enumeration is quite arbitrary (cf. Wallace, 1971). If an empirical discipline is to advance, such different activities must keep pace, otherwise "bottlenecks" or "accumulative imbalances" exist. If a discipline is characterised, for instance, as data-rich but theory-poor, *or* vice versa, this is an example of "imbalance", so also, if it is said that we lack research techniques to handle a certain problem.

There is much to be said for the view that concept development constitutes an "imbalance" in political science; as concepts have a very strategic role in the whole research process, this has wide negative repercussions. (Among other things concepts are "containers" for data and "building-bricks" for propositions) (Sartori, 1970).

Conceptual difficulties may emerge at three different levels (at least):

1. Concepts in use may be defective (e. g. vague, clumsy, value-laden etc.).
2. Concepts in use may not be integrated but be taken from very different theoretical contexts (and hence based on very different assumptions).
3. Concepts may be too poorly developed and differentiated, making us unable to capture ("conceptualise") reality in a nuanced and exact way[20].

In the last case, when conceptual differentiations are introduced, reference is often made to Occam's "razor": "Conceptual units should not be multiplied beyond necessity". This is a very sound principle, but disagreements about the razor's applicability will be pointless until you try to assess what boundaries "necessity" sets — and you can never know what is "enough" until you know what is less than enough or more than enough.

This is not to deny that a discipline should strive for "fruitful simplifications", "parsimonious explanations" and "elegant theories", but it is assumed that it may be easier to know where to look for such simplifications once the complications are known. Awareness of complexities is of course not the same as to "solve" them but may be a necessary condition for doing so or for side-stepping them. Intelligent handling of research problems often means an ability to avoid them (observe the analogy to politics in this respect).

Another term coined by Merton (1975) may be useful in this context: "specified ignorance". If a number of problems can be formulated, about which it may be said: if these problems are solved, then we will make a breakthrough and hence progress in our discipline — then you have specified your ignorance. It should be added, that ability to specify such "strategic problems" of ignorance may require a lot of knowledge and may only be possible if a discipline has reached a fairly high level of advancement and sophistication (also including a systematic codification of existing knowledge) (Elster, 1979; Sjøblom, 1977). The more we know, the easier it may be to determine what we don't know but want to know — i. e. to formulate cognitive problems, cf. this essay, *passim* —; in other words to engage in "the mapping of ignorance". This may not only improve our overall understanding but also help us to detect unintended consequences of our research strategies, "suboptimisation" leading to "accumulative imbalances", the location of variables with high explanatory value, existing

[20] Cf. Riggs—Sartori—Teune, 1975. Good examples of conceptual analyses are: Lane, 1983; Zannoni, 1978; Zuckerman, 1975; Zwetkoff, 1977.

contradictions and incongruence between pieces of knowledge, to assess necessary and/or sufficient conditions for phenomena, to reveal hidden *ceteris-paribus*-assumptions, etc.

B. On Conjectural Reasoning

What difference for the research design of a project does it make if it is called "Party Government: Past and Present" (PGPP) or "The Future of Party Government" (FPG) – provided that the titles are seriously intended and provided that the main emphasis in both cases is positive and not normative? In both cases one has to start with definitions, limiting the range for the concept 'Party Government'. In FPG one is obliged to concentrate on predictions or conjectures about the likely persistence of party government while this is not the case with PGPP. In FPG one must, on the other hand, also take the past and present of party governments into account, both for the delimitation of the concept and in order to be able to make the predictions/conjectures. But one needs only take such past and present traits of party governments into account which presumably are relevant for an assessment of the future (and this is an important restriction for the research design).

I will take the following statements as uncontroversial:

– "Political scientists are not good at making predictions".
– "Economists are better than political scientists at making predictions".

It may be a slight consolation for political scientists that economists' reputations as prediction-makers seem to be rapidly deteriorating; it should not be forgotten, however, that poor performance by economists in this respect still evokes surprise, which would never be the case with political scientists.

There are several reasons for the relative inability of political scientists to make predictions e. g. a) the complexity of their subject, b) the relatively low theoretical standard of the discipline, c) a combination of a) and b), etc. One could also add the "problem of reflexivity", i. e. that political predictions influence actors and hence tend to be self-reinforcing or self-defeating. But that argument must also apply to economists and even more so, as they are taken more seriously by policy-makers than political scientists are. But economists also try to tackle it by building theories for such phenomena (e. g. "the theory of rational expectations" – cf., e. g. Kantor, 1979; Maddoch/Carter, 1982; Willes, 1980), something which political scientists hardly have tried to do. This last-mentioned point is, I think, something that should be seen as a serious candidate explanation for political scientists' prediction-inability: they have hardly ever tried in any systematic fashion. (That this explanation seems so very trivial makes it the more probable).

Predictions – n. b. systematic predictions, not *ad hoc* guesswork – presuppose models; stating that a change in one or several variables will be followed by a change in one or several other variables. This means "conditional predictions" of the "if...then"-type. Pertinent questions to be asked, if a model is supposed to be used for practical concerns, are then:

- Is the model applicable to a certain situation?
- How precise are its predictions?
- If it is applicable, do we have data to feed it, which are valid, reliable and up-to-date?
- What happens if a relevant decision-maker knows the model and its predictions or even uses it as an instrument in his/her policy-making?

What is the use of past and present data concerning party government for the making of conjectures about the future of that type of regime? Quite apart from the relative lack of relevant time series data, the difficulty is evidently that *only part of that which could have happened has happened.* There are, in other words, no reasons to believe that the variability of party governments seen so far, or the transformations of party government seen so far, exhaust the possibilities. Already by combining values on a limited list of conceivable central variables (e. g. of the type party system format, mechanical dispositions, etc. (cf. Sartori, 1976)) and only admitting a few values on each variable (even dichotomising them) we get a rather complicated typology, where some types may not have had any empirical counterpart – so far. The potential "repertoire", as it were, is larger than the alternatives "used" so far. Hence, we cannot only rely on past and present data.

Evidently, the ambition of the project is not confined to some general optimistic or pessimistic assessments of the future of party governments based on intensive studies of past and present party governments. The ambition is to make a diagnosis of factors favorable or unfavorable for party governments and to make as precise conjectures as possible in the form of models. Predictions will then not be expressed in the form that "party government in country X is likely to break down in the next few years" but in the form: "if conditions a, b,... n develop in such and such a way, then party government is likely to break down" (and, preferably with the addition "with such and such a probability").

It cannot be denied that the pattern of conceivable explanatory factors is highly complex, nor that political science in this field as in so many others suffers from lack of codified and (in particular) integrated knowledge. One of the virtues of model building is however, that it forces us to codify and integrate knowledge. This will, at a minimum, require a codification and systematisation of relevant "conjectures".

The difficulty with conjectures is that they may be fabricated in large numbers and that many of them, maybe most, seem to have something speaking to their advantage. But by systematic comparison a lot of them will form some pattern or disappear. Some will be incompatible with well corroborated empirical generalisations or theories; a number will turn out to be specifications or generalisations of others. Some will not be possible to combine with other conjectures into models. Others will turn out to be variations of conjectures about the same things; they will then be used as alternatives. Others may turn out to be conditional on certain social facts or institutions; they will then be subordinated, etc.

Members of the project will have to overcome the resistance towards conjectures, common among political scientists, *if* the title of the project is to be taken seriously. (Cf., e. g. Fowles ed., 1978; Sylvan—Thorsen, 1980). If it is not, the title should be changed to something like "Party Government — Past and Present".

Bibliography

ABERNETHY, D. (1978) "A Tentative Checklist of Questions to Ask when Analyzing a Government Program," 6 *Policy Studies Journal* 552.

ALKER, R. H. (1977) "A Methodology for Design Research on Interdependence Alternatives," 31 *International Organization* 29 (Winter).

ALLARDT, E. (1973) "A Welfare Model for Selecting Indicators for National Development," 4 *Policy Sciences* 63.

ANCKAR, D. (1980) "Responsivitet — am begreppet, företeelsen och forskningsomradet," 1 *Politikka* 28.

ANDERSON, C. W. (1977) "Political Design and the Representation of Interests," 10 *Comparative Political Studies* 127.

— (1979) "The Place of Principles in Policy Analysis," 73 *American Political Science Review* 711.

AXELSSON, R. and L. ROSENBERG (1979) "Decision-making and Organizational Turbulence," 22 *Acta Sociologica* 45.

BANKS, M. (1981) *Resolution of Conflict. A Manual and Theoretical Framework*. London: Pinter.

BARNES, S. and M. KAASE et al. (1979) *Political Action. Mass Participation in Western Democracies*. Beverly Hills, London: Sage Publications.

BELL, D. (1969a) "Twelve Modes of Predication — a Preliminary Sorting — of Approaches in the Social Sciences," in W. G. Bennis et al. (eds.) *The Planning of Change*. London: Holt, Rinehart and Winston.

— (1969b) *The Coming of Post-industrial Society. A Venture in Social Forecasting*. New York: Basic Books.

— (1976) *The Cultural Contradictions of Capitalism*. London: Heinemann.

BENJAMIN, R. W. (1975) "The Political Consequences of Post-industrialization," 33 *International Review of Community Development 149* (Winter).

— (1980) *The Limits of Politics. Collective Goods and Political Change in Post-industrial Societies*. Chicago, London: University of Chicago Press.

BENN, S. I. and G. W. MORTIMER (eds.) (1976) *Rationality and the Social Sciences*. London: Routledge and Kegan Paul.

BILLINGS, R. S. et al. (1980) "A Model of Crisis Perception — a Theoretical and Empirical Analysis," 25 *Administrative Science Quarterly* 300.

BLAU, P. M. (1970) "A Formal Theory of Differentiation in Organizations," 35 *American Sociological Review* 210.

BRAYBROOKE, D. (1975) "The Meaning of Participation and of Demands for it: a Preliminary Survey of the Conceptual Issues," XVI *Nomos*.

BRITTAN, S. (1975) "The Economic Contradictions of Democracy," 5 *British Journal of Political Science* 129.

CAMPBELL, T. D. (1981) "Counter-productive Welfare Laws," 11 *British Journal of Political Science* 331.

CARLSNAES, W. (1981) "Foreign Policy and the Democratic Process," 4 *Scandinavian Political Studies* 81.

COBB, R. et al. (1976) "Agenda-building as a Comparative Political Process," 70 *American Political Science Review* 126.

COLEMAN, G. S. (1966) "Foundations for a Theory of Collective Decisions," 71 *American Journal of Sociology*.

COOK, T. E. (1980) "Political Justifications – the Use of Standards in Political Appeals," 42 *Journal of Politics* 511.

CROZIER, M. (1974) *The Stalled Society*. New York: The Viking Press.

CROZIER, M., S. P. HUNTINGTON, and J. WATANUKI (1975) *The Crisis of Democracy. Report of the Governability of Democracies to the Trilateral Commission*. New York: New York University Press.

DAALDER, H. and P. MAIR (eds.) (1983) *Western European Party Systems*. London: Sage Publications.

DAHL, R. A. (1966) *A Preface to Democratic Theory*. Chicago: University of Chicago Press.

– (1982) *Dilemmas of Pluralist Democracy*. New Haven: Yale University Press.

DAHL, R. A. and E. R. TUFTE (1974) *Size and Democracy*. Stanford: Stanford University Press.

DAMGAARD, E. (1977) *Folketinget under Forandring*. København: Samfundsvidenskabeligt Forla.

DE GREENE, R. (1982) *The Adaptive Organization*. London: Wiley.

DEUTSCH, K. (1963) *The Nerves of Government. Models of Political Communication and Control*. New York: The Free Press.

– (1971) "On Political Theory and Political Action," 65 *American Political Science Review* 11.

– (1981) "The Crisis of the State," 16 *Government and Opposition* 331.

DOUGLAS, J. (1976) "Review: the Overloaded Crown," 6 *British Journal of Political Science* 483.

DOWNS, A. (1957) *An Economic Theory of Democracy*. New York: Harper and Brothers.

– (1972) "Up and down with Ecology – the Issue Attention Cycle," 28 *Public Interest* 38.

DROR, Y. (1971) *Design for Policy Sciences*. New York: Elsevier.

DUNN, W. N. (1978) "Social Values and Public Policy – a Selected Bibliography," 7 *Policy Studies Journal* 328.

EASTON, D. (1965) *A Systems Analysis of Political Life*. New York: Wiley.

– (1973) "A Reassessment of the Concept of Political Support," 5 *British Journal of Political Science*.

– (1976) "Theoretical Approaches to Political Support," 9 *Canadian Journal of Political Science*.

ECKSTEIN, H. (ed.) (1964) *Internal War. Problems and Approaches*. London: The Free Press, Collier-Macmillan.

EDMEAD, F. (1982) "Changes in Perception during the Course of Conflict," in C. Jönson (ed.), *Cognitive Dynamics and International Politics*. London: Pinter.

Edward, G. C. (1978) "Disaggregation in Policy Research," 7 *Policy Studies Journal* 675.
Elgin, D. S. (1977) *Limits to the Management of Large, Complex Systems*. California: Menlo Park.
Elster, J. (1979) *Ulysses and the Sirens*. Cambridge: Cambridge University Press.
Eulau, H., J. C. Wahlke et al. (1978) *The Politics of Representation*. London: Sage Publications.
Fowles, J. (ed.) (1978) *Handbook of Futures Research*. Westwood, Conn.: Greenwood Press.
Funkhouser, C. R. (1973) "The Issues of the Sixties. An Exploratory Study of the Dynamics of Public Opinion," 37 *Public Opinion Quarterly* 62.
Galbraith, J. (1977) *Organization Design*. Reading, Mass.: Addison-Wesley.
Gerlach, L. P., and G. B. Palmer (1981) "Adaptation through Evolving Interdependence," in P. C. Nystroem and W. H. Starbuck (eds.), *Handbook of Organizational Design*. London: Oxford University Press.
Gerwin, D. (1981) "Relationship between Structure and Technology," in P. C. Nystroem and W. H. Starbuck (eds.), *Handbook of Organizational Design*. London: Oxford University Press.
Gibbs, J. P. (1965) "Norms: the Problem of Definition and Classification," 70 *American Journal of Sociology* 586.
Goodin, R. E. (1976) *The Politics of Rational Man*. London: Wiley.
Grumm, J. G. (1975) "The Analysis of Policy Impact," in Greenstein and Polsby (eds.), *Handbook of Political Science* 6. Reading, Mass.: Addison-Wesley.
Van Gunsteren, H. R. (1976) *The Quest for Control. A Critique of the Rational-central-rule Approach in Public Affairs*. London: Wiley.
Hanf, K., and F. W. Scharpf (eds.) (1978) *Interorganizational Policy Making*. London: Sage Publications.
Hennessey, T. M., and B. G. Peters (1976) "Political Paradoxes in Postindustrialism: a Political Economy Perspective," in P. M. Gregg (ed.), *Problems of Theory in Policy Analysis*. Lexington, Mass.: Lexington Books.
Hermann, C. F. (ed.) (1972) *International Crisis: Insights from Behavioral Research*. New York: Free Press.
Hewitt, J. P., and P. M. Hall (1973) "Social Problems, Problematic Situations and Quasi-theories," 38 *American Sociological Review* 367.
Hirschman, A. O. (1970) *Exit, Voice, and Loyalty*. Cambridge, Mass.: Harvard University Press.
Huntington, S. P. (1974) "Postindustrial Society: how Benign will it be?" 6 *Comparative Politics* 163.
Jantsch, E. (1970) "From Forecasting and Planning to Policy Sciences," 1 *Policy Sciences* 31.
Kantor, E. (1979) "Rational Expectations and Economic Thought," 17 *Journal of Economic Literature* 1422.
Katz, R. S. (1980) *A Theory of Parties and Electoral Systems*. Baltimore: Johns Hopkins University Press.
Keeney, R. L. and H. Faiffa (1976) *Decisions with Multiple objectives*. New York: Wiley.
Kerr, D. R. (1976) "The Logic of 'Policy' and Successful Policies," 7 *Policy Sciences* 351.
Khandwalla, P. N. (1981) "Properties of Competing Organizations," in P. C. Nystroem and W. H. Starbuck (eds.), *Handbook of Organizational Design*. Oxford: Oxford University Press.
Kiesler, S. and L. Sproull (1981) "Managerial Response to Changing Environments: Perspectives on Problem Sensing from Social Cognition," 27 *Administrative Science Quarterly* 548.

KING, A. (1975) "Overload: Problems of Governing in the 1970's," 23 *Political Studies* 162.

LANDAU, M. (1969) "Redundancy, Rationality, and the Problem of Duplication and Overlap," 29 *Public Administration Review* 346.

LANE, J. E. (1983) "The Concept of Implementation," 1 *Statsvetenskapligtidskrift* 17.

LAPORTE, T. R. (ed.) (1975) *Organized Social Complexity*. Princeton: Princeton University Press.

LAWRENCE, P. and J. LORSCH (1967) "Differentiation and Integration in Complex Organizations," 12 *Administrative Science Quarterly* 1.

LEHNER, F. (1979) *Grenzen des Regierens. Eine Studie zur Regierungsproblematik hochindustrialisierter Demokratien*. Königstein/Ts.: Athenäum Verlag.

LINDBECK, A. (1973) *Blandekonomi i omvandling*. Stockholm: Aldus.

– (1977) *Can Pluralism Survive?* Michigan: University of Michigan Press.

LINDBLOM, C. E. (1982) "Another State of Mind," 76 *American Political Science Review* 9.

LOWI, T. S. (1972) "Four Systems of Policy, Politics and Choice," 32 *Public Administration Review* 298.

LYLES, M. A. and I. I. MITROFF (1980) "Organizational Problem Formulation: an Empirical Study," 25 *Administrative Science Quarterly* 102.

McCANN, J. and J. R. GALBRAITH (1981) "Interdepartmental Relations," in P. C. Nystroem and W. H. Starbuck (eds.), *Handbook of Organizational Design*. Oxford: Oxford University Press.

McCOMBS, M. E. (1981) "The Agenda-setting Approach," in Nimmo and Sanders (eds.), *The Handbook of Political Communication*. Beverly Hills: Sage Publications.

McGRATH, J. E. (1981) "Dilemmatics. The Study of Research Choices and Dilemmas," 25 *American Behavioral Scientist* 179.

McINTOSH, W. A. et al. (1977) "Theoretical Issues and Social Indicators: a Societal Process Approach," 8 *Policy Sciences* 245.

MAJONE, G. (1975) "On the Notion of Political Feasibility," 3 *European Journal of Political Research* 259.

MARCH, J., J. P. OLSEN et al. (1976) *Ambiguity and Choice in Organizations*. Oslo: Universitetsforlaget.

MERTON, R. K. (1957) *Social Theory and Social Structure*. Glencoe: The Free Press.

– (1959) "Notes on Problem-finding in Sociology," in R. K. Merton, Broom and Cottrell (eds.), *Sociology Today*. New York: Basic Books.

– (1975) "Structural Analysis in Sociology," in P. M. Blau (ed.), *Approaches to the Study of Social Structure*. New York: Free Press.

METCALFE, L. (1981) "Designing Precarious Partnerships," in P. C. Nystroem and W. H. Starbuck (eds.), *Handbook of Organizational Design*. Oxford: Oxford University Press.

MINTZBERG, H. et al. (1976) "The Structure of 'unstructured' decision processes," 21 *Administrative Science Quarterly* 246.

MINTZBERG, H. (1979) *The Structuring of Organizations*. Englewood Cliffs, N. J.: Prentice-Hall.

MOHR, L. B. (1973) "The Concept of Organizational Goal," 67 *American Political Science Review* 470.

– (1982) *Explaining Organizational Behavior*. San Fransisco: Jossey-Bass.

MORRIS, R. T. (1956) "A Typology of Norms," 21 *American Sociological Review* 610.

NAGEL, S. S. (1980) "The Means May be a Goal," 9 *Policy Studies Journal* 567.

NURMI, H. (1974) "On the Concept of Complexity and its Relationship to the Methodology of Policy-oriented Research," 13 *Social Science Information* 55.

NYSTROEM, P. C. and W. H. STARBUCK (eds.) (1981) *Handbook of Organizational Design*. Oxford: Oxford University Press.

Offe, C. (1979) "'Unregierbarkeit'. Zur Renaissance konservativer Krisentheorien," in J. Habermas (ed.) *Stichworte zur geistigen Situation der Zeit*. Frankfurt a. M.: Suhrkamp.
Olsen, J. P. (1972) "Public Policy-making and Theories of Organizational Choice," 7 *Scandinavian Political Studies* 45.
– (ed.) (1978) *Politisk Organisering*. Oslo: Universitetsforlagen.
– (1981) "Integrated Organizational Participation in Government," in P. C. Nystroem and W. H. Starbuck (eds.), *Handbook of Organizational Design*. Oxford: Oxford University Press.
Pace, B. I. (1976) "The Theory of Political Ambiguity," 70 *American Political Science Review* 742.
– (1977) "Elections and Social Choice: the State of the Evidence," 21 *American Journal of Political Sciences* 639.
Perrow, C. (1968) "Organization Goals," in Shills (ed.), *International Encyclopedia of the Social Science*. New York: Macmillan and the Free Press.
Pitkin, H. (1967) *The Concept of Representation*. Berkeley: California University Press.
Pollitt, C. (1980) "Rationalizing the Machinery of Government," 28 *Political Studies* 84.
Popper, K. (1976) *Unended Quest: an Intellectual Autobiography*. Glasgow: Fontana/Collins.
Quade, E. S. (1979) *Analysis for Public Decisions*. New York and London: Elsevier.
Rae, D. W., and M. Taylor (1970) *The Analysis of Political Cleavages*. New Haven: Yale University Press.
Ramos, A. G. (1976) "Theory of Social System Delimitation. A Preliminary Statement," 8 *Administration and Society* 249.
Reynolds, J. F. (1975) "Policy Science: a Conceptual and Methodological Analysis," 6 *Policy Sciences* 1.
Riggs, F., G. Sartori, and G. Teune (1975) *The Tower of Babel. On the Definition and Analysis of Concepts in the Social Sciences*. Pittsburgh: International Studies Association.
Rittel, H. W. J., and M. M. Webber (1973) "Dilemmas in a General Theory of Planning," 4 *Policy Sciences* 155.
Rokkan, S. (1970) *Citizens, Elections, Parties. Approaches to the Comparative Study of the Process of Development*. Oslo: Universitetsforlage.
Rose, R. (1978) *What is Governing? Purpose and Policy in Washington*. Englewood Cliffs: Prentice-Hall.
– (1979) "Ungovernability: Is there a Fire Behind the Smoke?" 27 *Political Studies* 351.
– (ed.) (1980) *Challenge to Governance. Studies in Overloaded Polities*. Beverly Hills and London: Sage Publications.
Sartori, G. (1970) "Concept Misinformation in Comparative Politics," 64 *American Political Science Review* 1033.
– (1976) *Parties and Party Systems*. London: Cambridge University Press.
Scharpf, F. (1977) "Public Organization and the Waning of the Welfare State: a Research Perspective," 5 *European Journal of Political Research* 339.
Schmitter, P. C. (1981) "Interest Intermediation and Regime Governability in Contemporary Western Europe and North America," in S. Berger (ed.), *Organizing Interests in Western Europe. Pluralism, Corporatism, and the Transformation of Politics*. Cambridge: Cambridge University Press.
Schumpeter, J. (1950) *Capitalism, Socialism, and Democracy*. New York: Harper and Brothers.
Simon, H. A. (1964) "On the Concept of Organizational Goal," 9 *Administrative Quarterly* 1.
– (1969) *The Sciences of the Artificial*. Cambridge, Mass.: The M.I.T. Press.
– (1977) *Models of Discovery, and Other Topics in the Methods of Science*. Dordrechts and Boston: D. Reidel Publishing Company.

Sjöblom, G. (1968) *Party Strategies in a Multiparty System*. Lund: Studentlitteratur.
– (1977) "The Cumulation Problem in Political Science. An Essay on Research Strategies," 5 *European Journal of Political Research* 1.
– (1981) "Notes on the Notion of 'Party Adaptation'." Presented at the ECPR Joint Sessions of Workshops, Lancaster (April).
– (1983) "Political Changes and Political Accountability. A Propositional Inventory of Causes and Effects," in H. Daalder and P. Mair (eds.), *Western European Party Systems*. Beverly Hills and London: Sage Publications.
Smith, B. C. (1980) "Control in British Government: a Problem of Accountability," 9 *Policy Studies Journal* 1163.
Smith, T. W. (1980) "America's Most Important Problems – a Trend Analysis," 44 *Public Opinion Quarterly* 164.
Sowell, T. (1980) *Knowledge and Decisions*. New York: Basic Books.
Starbuck, W. H. (1983) "Organizations as Action Generators," 48 *American Sociological Review* 91.
Steiner, J., and R. H. Dorff (1980) *A Theory of Political Decision Modes. Intraparty Decision making in Switzerland*. Chapel Hill: University of North Carolina Press.
Sylvan, D. A., and S. J. Thorson (1980) "Choosing Appropriate Techniques for Sociopolitical Forecasting," 12 *Policy Sciences* 265.
Tarschys, D. (1978) *Sovjetunionens Politiska Problem 1950, 1960, 1970*. Stockholm: Liber Förlag.
Taylor, D. W. (1965) "Decision making and Problem solving," in March (ed.), *Handbook of Organizations*. Chicago: Rand McNally and Company.
Tichy, N. M. (1980) "Problem Cycles in Organizations and the Management of Change," in Kimberly, Miles et al. (eds.), *The Organizational Life Cycle*. San Francisco: Jossey Bass.
Toffler, A. (1970) *Future Shock*. New York: Random House.
Walker, J. L. (1977) "Setting the Agenda in the U.S. Senate: a Theory of Problem Selection," 7 *British Journal of Political Science* 423.
Wallace, W. L. (1971) *The Logic of Science in Sociology*. Chicago: Aldine – Atherton.
White, L. G. (1976) "Rational Theories of Participation. An Exercise in Definitions," 20 *Journal of Conflict Resolution* 255.
Wholey, J. S., et al. (1975) "If you don't care where you get to, then it doesn't matter which way you go," in M. Lyons (ed.), *Social Research and Public Policies*. Hannover, N. H.: Dartmouth University Press.
Wildavsky, A. (1973) "If planning is everything, maybe it's nothing," 4 *Policy Sciences* 127.
Willes, M. H. (1980) "'Rational Expectations' as a Counterrevolution," *The Public Interest* 81 (Special Issue on "The Crisis in Economic Theory").
Winner, L. (1977) *Autonomous Technology, Technics-out-of-control as a Theme in Political Thought*. Cambridge, Mass.: The M.I.T. Press.
Wiseman, C. (1978) "Selection of Major Planning Issues," 9 *Policy Sciences* 71.
Wolf Jr., C. (1979) "A Theory of Non-market Failures," 55 *The Public Interest* 114 (Spring).
Zannoni, P. (1978) "The Concept of Elite," 6 *European Journal of Political Research* 1.
Zimmermann, E. (1979) "Crises and Crises Outcomes: Towards a New Synthetic Approach," 7 *European Journal of Political Research* 67.
Zuckermann, A. (1975) "Political Cleavage. A Conceptual and Terminological Analysis," 5 *British Journal of Political Science* 231.
Zwetkoff, C. (1977) "On the Adequacy of the Concept of Alienation in Empirical Research," 5 *European Journal of Political Research* 433.

Chapter IV

The Impact of Institutions on Party Government: Tentative Hypotheses*

GIANFRANCO PASQUINO

Contents

This paper is to a large extent an exercise in the impossible and for the remainder an attempt to go beyond simple generalisations. It is an exercise in the impossible because in analysing and specifying the institutional structures and mechanisms leading to party government it takes into account many variables, perhaps, but inevitably, too many. It is an attempt to go beyond simple generalisations, because it tries to combine together in a meaningful but complicated set of hypotheses the relationships existing among electoral systems, forms of government, party systems and types of party government.

"The problem of party government is a problem of institutions." Following this very precise statement, Richard Rose (1974:1) provides a wide ranging analysis of the experience, practice, obstacles, and difficulties of party government in Great Britain, but offers no reflection on the nature of the institutional setting facilitating the emergence of party government and allowing its continuation. However, one gets the impression that for Rose the "problem of institutions" has mainly to do with the organisation of

* The final version of this paper was written and revised while I was Visiting Professor of Political Science at the School of Advanced International Studies of the Johns Hopkins University, Washington, D. C. I want to thank Richard Katz for his extensive and very helpful comments on a previous version.

parties and their relationship with the bureaucracy. Unknowingly, therefore, Rose touches on one of the most difficult topics to be faced in analysing party government, that is the nature of the institutional setting in which party government appears and succeeds in flourishing.

Briefly stated, the topic of this paper is the identification of that complex set of relationships which exists between institutional structures and mechanisms and party government.[1] While it is obvious that party government appears and functions in diversified institutional settings, we are interested specifically in the nature of the electoral system and in the form of government as they impinge upon the possibility of creating and maintaining party government. However, it is possible that in trying to account for the changes in and the difficulties of party government today one might feel the need to look at other "institutions," more or less properly defined, such as the bureaucracy and the media. Only brief reference will be made to them here. Finally, an attempt will be made to suggest what are the institutional changes which would need to be introduced in order to strengthen party government.

I. The Problem of Party Government: A Developmental Perspective

It is important to define specifically what party government is. However, let me stress that attention has more often been addressed to the nature of the party organisation taking over the government than to the institutional setting in which this takes place and the factors facilitating or hindering such a development. Richard Katz's conditions are very clear: "The party government model makes government accountable to the general public by entrusting it to individuals organised into parties that owe their positions to electoral approbation." Therefore, what is needed for party government to exist is a set of loyal party politicians, who operate in a cohesive way, are accountable to the electorate, and occupy a powerful position vis-à-vis other socio-political actors (that is, are central in the *Herrschaftsorganisation* of the overall society).

It is most important that we realize that there may be effective and ineffective types of party government. Katz defines this as the problem of capacity and identifies four elements: 1) the capacity to get a specific policy implemented; 2) the ability to frame policies that will produce the desired

[1] Overly preoccupied with functions and behaviour, contemporary political science, even in its best formulations, has not given enough attention to structural-institutional problems and their impact on the dynamics of the political system. For attempts to provide more balanced explanations, see, for example, Apter (1968); Blondel (1969); Finer (1970); and LaPalombara (1974).

(by the policy-maker) results; 3) the ability to choose the "right" aims or policies; and 4) the will of party leaders to expand the resources and bear the costs involved in formulating and implementing policies.

In theory, then, one might identify four (pure) cases. On the basis of the existence of party government, as defined with reference to the criteria provided by Katz, there may be types of effective and ineffective party governments and types of effective and ineffective non-party governments. However, it might be better to think in terms of range of "partyness of government" and of the capacity of party government. This approach would allow a developmental analysis and would afford the possibility of suggesting which reforms might be introduced to strengthen or weaken the hold of parties over institutions and to increase the capacity of some types of party governments.

If this is so, then our central question becomes: Which are the institutional structures and mechanisms most conducive to the creation of party government? That is, which structures and mechanisms operate in such a way as to encourage, or compel, party members and leaders to behave in a loyal and cohesive way, to remain accountable to the electorate (and to take this obligation into consideration in their decisions), and allow parties to acquire and to continue to occupy an important position in the *Herrschaftsorganisation* of society? Subordinately, which are the structures and the mechanisms which increase or decrease the overall capacity of party government and which are the types of relationships between parties and the other institutions which lead to the emergence and persistence of party government or prevent its existence and lead to its demise?

There are various, understandable difficulties in this type of broad developmental approach. The first one is immediately visible: there are many different varieties of party government, though they all share to a large degree the conditions and the criteria set out by Katz; indeed, at first sight it appears that the range of variations and variability is rather wide. A second difficulty, which is the central focus of this paper, is that different institutional structures and mechanisms might be responsible for the creation of different types of party government, even though perhaps differentiated on the basis of their capacity. (If that is so, then, explanation will require some attention to the nature of the parties and the party systems insofar as they are conditioned by the very institutional structures and mechanisms we have taken into account). This is why this exercise, the analysis of the impact of institutional structures and mechanisms on party government, has not been attempted in a comparative way so far. And, of course, this is why this paper will only offer tentative generalisations to be refined in the various case studies to appear in a subsequent volume.

Two different approaches are feasible. One might look at the evolution of party government as conditioned by institutional structures and mechanisms over a certain period of time. This approach could be applied to one or more countries on a comparative basis and yield interesting results and variations as to the rate of success in respect of each of the four above-mentioned variables, and therefore suggest which institutional structures and mechanisms are most conducive to party government. This evolutionary or strictly developmental approach would also allow meaningful speculation on those institutional transformations which might strengthen or weaken party government and which might make it more effective in retaining its "policy capacity."

Another approach is possible: a synchronic and comparative analysis of the variations in party government associated with variations in institutional structures and mechanisms. A broad overview of the existing situation in contemporary governments might be useful, but it appears less promising than the developmental approach in explanatory terms. It can tell us which institutional arrangements accommodate party government, but not if party government has been facilitated in its emergence and strengthened in its consolidation by those specific institutional arrangements.

Once we select the developmental approach, however, we must make a clear choice as to the type of variables which will be taken into account. Since we want to discover the type of relationships which exist between institutional structures and mechanisms and party government, the choice is relatively simple. The three most important institutions which impinge upon party government are: the nature of the electoral system, the type of national elected assemblies, and the form of the Executive. To some extent, these three institutions might also be considered as stages. At each of them some conditions appear or are created which influence the evolution of party government in a more or less favourable way. Obviously, a certain solution given to an institutional problem will have an impact on other subsequent problems, and possible solutions. Therefore, a satisfactory analysis ought not to lose sight at any stage of the various linkages among the different institutions and the four conditions of party government. Those conditions and party government itself remain therefore as the dependent variable, while parties, in their organisation and in their dynamics, constitute intervening variables.[2]

Stage 1: The Electoral System

The type of electoral system adopted and utilised is so important that many authors consider the possibility of the emergence of party government as being directly and substantially, if not totally, influenced by the selection of a specific electoral system (namely, and favorably, by the plurality or first-past-the post formula: Hermens, 1941; 1958 and 1963). This conclusion

[2] Only tangentially have party systems been studied from this perspective. See for instance Sartori (1966) and for a recent example, with bibliographic references, Pasquino (1980).

is controversial and has been disputed. However, the very fact that an excellent example of party government, that is Great Britain, utilises a first-past-the post formula has lent substance to that conclusion, and the fact that most countries utilising that formula qualify for the party government category has strengthened it. However, a major exception exists: the United States where the first-past-the post formula has not produced party government (according to any strict use of the definition) and not even a cohesive team of party representatives. (But, of course, the overall institutional arrangement is different in the USA as we shall see later on). Therefore, in itself the first-past-the-post formula cannot be considered a sufficient condition for the emergence of party government. Since, as we shall see, party government might be said to exist in countries utilising different electoral systems, then the first-past-the post formula cannot either be considered a necessary condition for the emergence of party government.

This said, however, it is still interesting to speculate on some of its effects, real and potential. At least three deserve some mention: the impact of the first-past-the-post formula on the voter, on individual parties, and on the party system. A wealth of analyses exist (Rokkan, 1970; Rae, 1971), but rarely have they been conducted in such a way as to account for the way in which the organisation as well as the strategy of individual parties are shaped by the electoral formula.[3] Much of the attention, instead, has been devoted to the relationship between the electoral formula and the party system. Whether it is simply a well-established, strong correlation or a cause-and-effect relationship, plurality formulae are associated with two-party systems (if we count parties according to their coalitional or blackmail potential, as does Sartori, 1976). And, overall, two-party systems (with the exception of the United States) present cases of party government.

This need not be the case, though, and perhaps the relationship is much more complex, complex enough to deserve more attention. At this point the behaviour and the expectations of the voters come into the picture together with the organisation of individual parties. The question is whether voters' expectations are reasonably satisfied by an electoral system which sharply constrains their choices or whether a greater or lesser number of them express dissatisfaction with the existing choices by opting for third parties and/or for abstention (Finer, 1980). Here the well-known trade-off between governmental stability (and perhaps effectiveness) and representation of voters' preferences appears (even though there might be a perfect fit or a total disjunction, setting aside the problem of trading-off systemic qualities against individual actors' expectations).

As to party organisations, while it is conceivable that they might be strong at the local level and tightly tied in with control of the national

[3] The excerpts from Hermens (1963) do exactly this in a very powerful and passionate way.

Executive, this is not necessarily the case, as the U.S. case once more shows. The loyalty of party representatives and the cohesiveness of the party organisation, therefore, are not (solely or essentially) a product of the electoral system but, as we will see, of another institutional feature. What might be lost then in single-member constituencies in terms of the necessary party loyalty and discipline, may be reacquired at the parliamentary level.

While plurality formulae exercise a constraining influence on the voters, if they do not want to "waste" their ballot, as well as a constraining impact on the number of political parties, proportional representation formulae are, in contrast, "weak" electoral systems (Sartori, 1968). Even though they do not necessarily multiply parties, they photograph the existing situation in terms of party alignments, and even though they might not be considered responsible for promoting the fragmentation of the party system, they allow it to take place. They counterpose a very weak barrier to this fragmentation. However, some of them (more specifically those which have percentage thresholds (*Sperrklauseln*) to representation, as in the Federal Republic of Germany and in Sweden, for instance), have been rather successful in preventing the fragmentation of the party system.

As to individual parties, at least theoretically, proportional representation formulae applied in large constituencies compel parties to get organised on a national scale and to penetrate deeply into the local areas (Katz, 1980). Their electoral success is also a function of their ability to be present and organised in most and possibly all constituencies. Therefore, PR formulae have at the same time negative and positive consequences for party government. The negative consequence is of course represented by the fact that PR is usually associated with a relatively large number of parties (and therefore with bargaining and coalitional difficulties at the parliamentary level, sometimes having serious implications for internal cohesion); the positive consequence is that PR formulae encourage the formation of national parties, well structured and centrally organised and therefore create one of the necessary premises leading to and sustaining party government.

Being a weak electoral formula, PR does not exercise a constraining influence on the voters either. Although the representation of their preferences, old and new, is often easily assured, the price is then paid at the parliamentary level when it comes to the problem of coalition formation. This is not the place to discuss which came first:[4] the diversification of preferences which required PR or PR which allowed the electoral and political diversification of preferences. (Rokkan, 1970). Suffice is to say that while PR does not facilitate the creation of party government, it does

[4] Rokkan (1970) and Duverger (1964) seem to hold opposite, polarised views on the subject. Of course, it is possible that the two motivations appeared more or less at the same time and had a combined impact.

not prevent it in a decisive way. However, it is not true, as has often been maintained, that a representational formula applied in one national constituency will make it very hard for a cohesive, stable, and accountable party coalition to emerge and operate in the form of party government. While the Dutch case may lend support to such a view, the Israeli case manifests instances of party government first by the Mapai and recently by the Likud. This, of course, is intended only to stress the point that in itself PR does not preclude party government.

The run-off majority formula provides empirical evidence coming from the French case only, though in two different instances: during the Third Republic and during the Fifth Republic. It is to be remembered that we are analysing the impact of the electoral system on the election of the legislature. However, a comparison of the Third and the Fifth republics demonstrates such wide divergence in the resulting types of party government, that the variance has to be attributed to two other variables (therefore indicating that the electoral system, per se, is never a sufficient condition for the emergence of party government). The two other variables are: the nature of the party system and the selection of the Executive and its powers.

The run-off majority formula is certainly a strong electoral formula in the sense that it exercises a constraining effect on individual parties. Indeed, it has been largely responsible (together with de Gaulle's appeal and with the constitutionally implied need parties have to collaborate in the election of the President) for the realignment of the French Right and Center and for the renewal of the French Socialists. It has also had a major impact on the party system, reducing its fragmentation and encouraging coalitional agreements at the electoral level, which are then reproduced at the parliamentary level. This has moved the French political system away from the *système d'assemblée* which characterised the Fourth Republic and towards the present form of party government. However, the formation of four large parties and two adversary alliances is also the product of the type of parties which came into being and of their previous organisational resources. In this context, it should be recalled that the peculiar positioning and nature of the Radical Party in the Third Republic was responsible for a different outcome and for a much lower degree of party government.

It might be that the French run-off majority cannot be fully understood in its impact in isolation from the contest for the Presidency (and that the two arrangements have a reinforcing effect). But it seems important to underline that the outcome of the French institutional reforms of the Fifth Republic has been a complete overhaul of the dynamics of the French party system and the introduction of many necessary components of (an effective) party government. While not all of these favourable developments can be ascribed to the electoral system, there is much to be learned from the French experience because it is one of the very few cases in which a weak electoral system (proportional representation) has been replaced by a strong one, with manifest restraining consequences on the party system and positive consequences for party government (Bartolini, for 1981; Reif, 1982).

The alternative vote utilised for the election of the Lower House in Australia comes rather close in its effect to the run-off majority system and, indeed, under the 'normal' circumstances of Australian politics, it appears to have maintained a situation where partyness of government is the characterising feature of the political system. However, circumstances are not always normal, and Australian politics is complicated by the enduring strength of bicameralism in the context of a federal system of politics (see next section), leading sometimes to quite flagrant departures from the conduct assumed by the party government model (viz. the dismissal of the Whitlam government with a Lower House majority in 1975). Despite this, one might argue, on the basis of simulations and projections of the electoral system alone, that the Australian alternative vote might appear an attractive solution to those seeking ways to strengthen the party system and prevent its fragmentation, thereby creating some of the conditions conducive to party government.

Analysed in isolation, the nature of electoral systems cannot provide the entire explanation for the emergence or otherwise of party government. However, if one conceives of party government as a continuum, then it seems plausible and appropriate to stress that plurality and majority formulae are associated with higher levels of party government, at least in terms of the greater likelihood for the creation of a more cohesive team, which is oriented towards a stricter control of elected positions and which can more successfully and credibly claim legitimacy on the basis of electoral success (applying once more Katz's criteria).

Finally, while plurality and majority formulae are relatively precise and undifferentiated in their clauses, there exist many variations in the types of proportional representation formulae. They differ not simply in terms of clauses for access to the distribution of seats, but also in the formulae applied to the allocation of seats, size of constituency, and, last but not least, in terms of whether the voter can or cannot cast a preference vote, that is choose among the candidates. In all likelihood, this latter element weakens the possibility for the creation of a cohesive team of party leaders. Party government might still emerge, as for instance in Italy but its effectiveness may well be hindered by inter- and intra-factional struggles.

All this said, however, any electoral system is but one stage, one threshold in the process through which party government emerges or is prevented from appearing, with specific features which reflect not only the electoral system, but also the total impact of political institutions in the context of a particular historical and cultural matrix. The electoral system impinges upon the cohesiveness of the parliamentary representatives and their behaviour in the elected assemblies. However, a more precise identification of variables is needed to push the analysis one step further.

Stage 2: Elected Assemblies

To a large extent, stage one is really the beginning of the process and shows therefore an independent impact specifically on the nature of the parties and the party systems which emerge out of the process and which will condition the type and quality of party government. Stage two, the type of elected assemblies, is largely, but not totally, conditioned by stage one. It is not totally conditioned by stage one because much depends on the institutional arrangements a political system has devised for its elected assemblies and on the kind of dispersion/concentration of power that has been achieved and sanctioned by custom and by the Constitution.

If party government is the product of a successful effort at controlling those who are elected to governing positions, and if effective party government is characterised by the ability of the party(ies) in power to frame and implement desired policies, then the relevant questions are: which kind of parliamentary arrangements have been conducive to this situation in the past, which kind of arrangements have parties pressed for, which kind of arrangements are associated with party government in its different manifestations and specifically with effective party government?

The major distinction runs between unicameral and bicameral Parliaments. From a developmental perspective, it is plausible to assert that in their drive towards party government, the parties attempted to get rid of the Upper House, often controlled by interests in opposition to those of "purely" party politicians. Therefore, we would expect that, both in the process of creation of party government and under present circumstances, party government would be associated with unicameral assemblies. Alternatively, the Upper House might effectively have been stripped of its powers and therefore no longer represent a threat to party government.

As a rule the more party government, the less truly bicameral a Parliament. All systems which have streamlined their decision-making process, either by severely curtailing the powers and the functions of the Upper House or by doing away with it altogether, have actually had experiences of party government, have moved in that direction, or have ongoing forms of party government. One can jump to the conclusion that when the decision-making process in the elected assemblies or, more precisely, in the Lower House, acquires the characteristic of being transparent and decisive, because it cannot be made fuzzy and amended by being sent to a second forum of debate and decision, then the responsibility of the government will be heightened. This phenomenon increases the likelihood of party government: in terms of discipline, cohesiveness, accountability, and even power vis-à-vis other socio-political actors.

On the other hand, it might be exactly because ruling parties wanted to obtain this transparency, which obliges their members to be loyal and disciplined and allows them to present their programme and policies in an accountable way to the electorate, that the transition to a unicameral assembly was accomplished and/or that the powers of the Upper House were curtailed. That the opposition has accepted this transition should not surprise us, at least under circumstances where it has the expectation of taking advantage sooner or later of the same institutional arrangements or because those very arrangements make it easier to call the government to task.

Where the transition has not been made, there may be different motivations: particularly historical factors such as protection of state rights (federalism), or, as in Italy, *garantismo* (broadly speaking, protection of minority rights and an attempt to create political balance – see later chapter by Di Palma). One would expect all these systems, *ceteris paribus*, to be characterised by less effective forms of party government. On the other hand, it might be worthwhile to explore if and when any type of bicameral Parliament creates a *need* for party government. In a developmental perspective, the persistence of a bicameral Parliament is less conducive to party government. However, if the parties are strong and cohesive, they might be in the position of providing the necessary "glue" between the two Houses. Even so the main hypothesis should stand: the result will be and remains a relatively less effective form of party government (specifically in terms of problem-solving capacity).

The structure of elected assemblies is then very relevant to the problem of party government; the adoption of a specific variant is probably related to the desire and inclination to increase the strength of party government or at least to improve one of its important components. Still, the structure of the elected assembly(ies) might be less important, according to many authors (Loewenberg and Patterson, 1979; Blondel, 1973), than their internal distribution of power. That is, even a unicameral assembly may well be relatively inefficient in its decision-making process and highly opaque, if it is fragmented into different coalitions and has loosely organised factions.

An analysis of the internal distribution of power (that is, in the first instance, seats) within an elected assembly cannot be rooted but in an assessment of the way the electoral system translates votes into seats. Assemblies elected through a plurality formula have, generally speaking, less parties or less relevant parties than assemblies elected through a run-off majority formula, which, in their turn, have less parties than assemblies elected through proportional representation formulae. Indeed, with due allowance made for some exceptions, a continuum could be created going from highly cohesive to highly fragmented elected assemblies and related to the variant of the electoral formula which has been utilised. But not even this would tell the whole story in a significant way.[5]

[5] A very useful array of data and interpretations is presented in Butler, Penniman, Ranney (1981).

Indeed, even though plurality formulae are associated with few parties and most of the time with a majority party, in recent years this has always not invariably been the case as, for instance, it used to be in Great Britain and Canada. And even though proportional representation formulae are usually associated with fragmented elected assemblies, this is not always the case and the fragmentation (as in Sweden or in Israel, for instance) may be inconsequential from the point of view of the existence of a relatively comfortable, and anyway cohesive, majority party (the Social Democrats up to 1976, and again after 1982, and Likud respectively) capable of exerting a fair amount of attraction on other parties.

At this point, the very complex problem of coalition-formation, coalitional propensities, and behaviour enters into the picture. The literature is indeed quite abundant on this subject (de Swann, 1973; Browne, 1962; Budge, 1982), but it has not been exactly focused on the requirements and the consequences of coalition-formation (and dissolution) for party government. Instead, the focus has been on the size of the various coalitions and their lasting capability (less often on their policy-making activities and performance).

A useful starting point might be the identification of and the differentiation among the way representatives have been elected. Schematically, one can say that in any Parliament there are, in different proportions to be sure, three main types of representatives. First, those who have succeeded in being elected thanks to their own personal resources and efforts. Presumably, therefore, they will remain in the position of obtaining re-election irrespective of their parliamentary discipline in respect of their party. They enjoy a large amount of independence and can vote their conscience (or their constituency). If such "notables" exist in large numbers, they counterpose an obstacle to the creation and the effectiveness of party government. Second, there are those who do belong to a party, but owe their election to organised groups have, in one word, *factional* backing. They are, therefore, likely to follow the wishes of their external supporters on at least some key policy votes. This is often the case of representatives elected through some form of preference voting for ideologically heterogeneous parties in large constituencies.

Finally, there are those representatives who are totally dependent on their parties for nomination to office, election, re-nomination, and re-election. In the past such an ideal type has been used to describe British representatives and parties. However, generally speaking, it may refer and be extended to almost all leftist parties in Western Europe (Social Democrats, Socialists, and Communists alike) in proportional representation systems where the candidates rarely have the resources to challenge their party's decisions and are unable to appeal to inner or outer constituencies.

The way representatives are elected, then, is very likely to make an important difference to the way they behave in Parliament[6] in respect

[6] An excellent discussion of the organisation of Italian parties in Parliament is to be found in Cotta (1979), though, perhaps, the relative "parliamentarisation" of the

of all issues concerning the formation, functioning, transformation, and dissolution of governing coalitions. This is all the more so since "the disciplined support of a parliamentary majority is a *sine qua non* of Cabinet government as we know it." (Rose, 1974:133.) And of course this disciplined support, important for all forms of party government, is more easily acquired when the government is made up of one party only or, if it is made up of more than one party, when the representatives of governing parties are aware that their electoral destiny is substantially determined by their parliamentary behaviour.

An additional variable may be introduced into the analysis. The existence of alternative and equally viable coalitions in Parliament may, of course, relax the discipline among party representatives and therefore weaken any variant of party government. Paradoxically, the very existence of alternatives may also in some cases solidify minority governments and minority coalitions. It certainly constitutes a major incentive for parties governing alone to stay cohesive, loyal to the office-holders, disciplined, and responsive to popular preferences. Once again the analysis of governmental coalitions and their behaviour cannot go very far without taking into account variables related to party organisation and the working of the electoral system. The need to preserve a viable party organisation and, at the same time, to retain and, if possible, enhance electoral opportunities are powerful considerations in the implementation of coalitional strategies and therefore in the creation of some form of party government.

Stage 3: The Legislative – Executive Relationship

The previous two stages have set the conditions for the emergence of party government and have circumscribed the likelihood of its effectiveness. The stage of legislative-executive relationships is crucial for the functioning (and reproduction) of any form of party government. Specifically, according to Walter Bagehot, and still just as true today, the most important function of a Parliament is to elect a government.[7]

There are different ways one can tackle the issue of legislative-executive relationships (King, 1976). As a first approximation, one might want to start from the well-known tripartite distinction, presidential, semi-presidential, and parliamentary systems. Two elements are relevant to our discussion: the way the Executive is selected and the kind of powers the Executive is allotted. Presidential systems are characterised by direct election of the Chief Executive by the population and there is a total overlap between the office of Head of State and that of Chief Executive. This

Communist party ought to be imputed more to the desires of the party and its representatives to keep in touch with the voters and their idea of the overall "Communist" constituency than to control by the party leadership.

[7] A useful discussion is to be found in Crick (1970).

system characterises the US form of government and has been widely imitated through Latin America; it presupposes a total separation between the executive and the legislative branch. It must be kept distinct from those cases in which the Executive is elected by the Houses, but retains all the prerogatives of Head of State and of the government (as in Brazil under the military regime) and from the cases in which the Head of State is elected by some form of popular vote, but does not have full executive powers (as in Finland, which belongs therefore to the category of parliamentary systems, although exceptional circumstances have so far strengthened the role of the President, without altering the system's basically parliamentary features).

The only case of a semi-presidential system is represented by the French Fifth Republic. Its distinguishing features are: direct election of the President by the population; the President is the Head of State, but also enjoys a number of executive prerogatives; he appoints the Prime Minister who is responsible to the National Assembly, but has, in consultation with the Prime Minister, the power to dissolve the Assembly. The overlap of power, this potential duarchy, has not been tested in practice, although it is likely that the President might be on the winning side.[8]

Parliamentary systems are characterised by a clear-cut distinction between the Head of State, who may be hereditary (as in the case of the many monarchies existing in Europe), or, most often, indirectly elected (that is, by the two Houses), and the Head of Government. Perhaps, the most important distinctions are those running through different forms of parliamentary systems. There are those in which the leader of the majority party is automatically appointed Prime Minister and those in which interparty (and intra-party) bargaining determines who will become Prime Minister. In the first case, one can state that it is the voters who select the Prime Minister; in the other cases, this assumption cannot be made and the relationship between voters' preferences and government formation is, at best, rather tenuous.

Indeed, the formal and substantive procedures through which the Heads of the Executive branch are selected can tell us a lot about the likelihood of party government as well as about its solidity and effectiveness. In presidential systems, (and not only in the United States) not only does the President represent a different constituency from the elected representatives, but can also effectively claim a wider legitimacy. Rarely does he depend for election and re-election on the organised support of one party, because his own "machine" will take over a party for its endorsement. Furthermore,

[8] Of course a more refined analysis of this peculiar case would be highly recommended. There are many juridical texts in French which provide the background information. Among them, I recommend the analysis by Quermonne (1980), who bridges law and political science.

as is frequently the case in the U.S., he may not necessarily be the head of the majority party in the elected assemblies. The President enjoys stability in his office and cannot be replaced until the end of his term. However, deprived of dissolution powers he cannot create his own majority. Thus, often his stability amounts to a decision-making paralysis, unless the President succeeds in mobilising either party support or appealing to outside constituencies capable of putting pressure on the representatives. In the first case, there might be an approximation to party government; but the first case is precisely the least frequent, and in recent times only too often presidential government has bordered on sheer paralysis.

The French President too can claim a wider legitimacy than individual deputies. But increasingly he has become a party leader (Reif, 1982). One could still envisage a situation in which a presidential candidate might appeal to the voters without having the official nomination of one party; but it is more difficult to believe that he might be able to win office without the official support of a major party. Certainly, unless he is able to shape a parliamentary coalition of a relatively tight and disciplined kind, he will definitely fail in his governing efforts. A Constitution designed to weaken the political and policy impact of parties has, in the end, strengthened the parties both as organisations and as policy-makers. (Reif, 1982.)

In parliamentary systems, Prime Ministers (and their executive teams) claiming a wider legitimacy than the legislative branch (and therefore than the other members of Parliament) may always be challenged. They are not insulated against parliamentary challenges because they are thoroughly dependent on constant parliamentary support and, constitutionally, must resign following a vote of no-confidence (or, in the German case only, a "constructive vote of no-confidence" providing for the election by the same Parliament of a new Chancellor). Therefore, in parliamentary systems the Executive finds itself at the same time in a weaker and in a stronger position than in presidential and, probably, in semi-presidential systems. It is in a weaker position because it may be ousted at any time; it is in a stronger position because it is more likely that it will command a majority, at least a working majority. Presidents may once have been able to reign and rule, but increasingly they seem to have lost their capacity to rule. Prime Ministers must rule if they want to reign at all, and to survive.

In other words, while presidential systems seem to diffuse political and governing responsibilities; parliamentary systems, particularly when there is a majority party, but in all cases of cohesive coalitions as well, seem to require the existence of a sense of collective responsibility and to encourage its appearance. Moreover, while presidential systems used to be extolled for their propensity to create strong leadership, leadership qualities, visible and "implementable," are no longer absent from many parliamentary systems. This marks a major extension in the overall scope of partyness of government (even though other recent socio-political transformations analysed by Rudolf Wildenmann might point in the direction of erosion of party government).

When it comes to legislative-executive relationships, an important factor is not so much the reliance of the Executive on the Legislature in terms of votes of confidence, but the power of dissolution available to the government. While often underestimated, the power of dissolution gives the Executive in parliamentary systems a weapon which can be used to discipline the majority and, to some extent, to "threaten" the opposition. In a different vein, it might be pointed out that the power of dissolution can be used to break a deadlock and to form a new majority. It is at the same time a weapon for strengthening majority party discipline and provides an opportunity for acquiring renewed (electoral) legitimacy.

The lack of these powers in presidential systems is a serious disadvantage for the Executive, while semi-presidential systems such as the French one are similar to parliamentary systems in this respect. By threatening (and actually practicing, within limits) dissolution of the House, the French semi-presidential system has acquired an additional element which has worked in favor of the emergence, maintenance, and consolidation of party government.

One final factor to be taken into consideration has to do with the accountability of the Legislature, the Executive, the parties, and their elected representatives to the voters. Since electoral accountability is a very important characteristic of party government, the identification of the manner and timing of its exercise may reveal something relevant to the analysis of the impact of institutional structures and mechanisms on the creation and the persistence (and, perhaps, the effectiveness) of party government.

The most important preliminary generalisation is that staggered electoral terms are not conducive to collective accountability and somewhat hinder the likelihood that the voters may express a precise evaluation of the government and its policies. Staggered electoral terms may be considered useful from the point of view of gauging the state of public opinion and its preferences and of verifying changes and moods. They might, however, prevent a government from implementing a programme consistently. From this point of view, the US practice while emphasising the democratic value of electoral choice, has increasingly shown the tendency to evade the attribution of clearcut responsibilities (Fiorina, 1980). This is, of course, also due to the lack of national, cohesive parties, but has been shaped and strengthened by a system of government that has been aptly defined in terms of "separate institutions sharing powers" (Neustadt, 1960).

In the French case (the President elected for a seven year term, the Assembly for a five year term), the problem has been dodged, when necessary, by holding elections for both offices very close to each other in time, (for instance, in 1981 after Mitterrand's election, the Assembly was dissolved and its composition renewed). In the American system, due to the absence of this kind of flexibility, the blame can be easily shifted, in different periods of time, from one institution to the other. Thus, since confusion prevails as to the locus of power (Congressional Government, Imperial Presidency, the Federal Bureaucracy), the very issue of accountability may be either evaded or raised in vain.

The situation is quite different in parliamentary systems, even though there are variations according to the type of party systems and to the pattern of competition which prevails in each of them. Generally speaking, however, the government and the opposition (be they formed by a single party each or by coalitions) are easily identified as the targets of satisfaction or dissatisfaction by the voters. And even though the majority of the voters might not necessarily vote simply on the basis of their satisfaction or dissatisfaction, the minority which does so provides a judgment which tends to reinforce the belief that governments are indeed accountable, or, at least, ought to be.

Insofar as I have been successful in disentangling some of the complexities of the relationships between institutional structures and mechanisms and party government, I have only provided very partial snapshots of the different "stages" and the different arrangements at each "stage". These snapshots do not tell the entire story and they have to be supplemented by additional information and further considerations. To these we now turn.

II. Drawing the Threads Together

The reader might suggest two reasons for objecting to the over-simplification of this analysis. The first one is that I have been dealing only with the most visible institutional structures and mechanisms — the electoral system, the type of elected assemblies, legislative-executive relationships, the form of government — and I have left out others: for instance, the bureaucracy, whose nature and activities certainly influence the way party government works and is maintained, and the media.

This is not, obviously, the place for a detailed treatment of the impact of the bureaucracy and the media on party government. Suffice it to say that, in a developmental perspective, what is of interest to us is the ability of the bureaucracy to maintain its independence from parties and therefore to circumscribe the influence of party government, to set clear limits to the partyness of government. Indeed, the problem here is that there may be too much or too little partyness of government with reference to the bureaucracy; that is, there will be situations in which the bureaucracy is totally penetrated, dependent on and colonised by the parties and situations in which the bureaucracy escapes the control of the parties (cannot be steered) representing a serious and insurmountable obstacle to the creation and perhaps the maintenance of party government (the strong autonomy acquired by such bodies as central banks might be a case in point). (Many of these considerations are discussed in detail in the subsequent chapter by Freddi.)

Insofar as the media challenge the political parties in performing the functions of political communication and in breaking the monopoly long held by mass parties over their expressive and symbolic functions and over the political discourse within the party organisations themselves, they do represent a threat to party government. It is, however, a "mediated" threat, since what the media are doing is not simply circumscribing the area of influence of party government, but impinging upon "party governmentess": the nerves of government are no longer solidly in the hands of party leaders. This threat is common to all political systems and no differentiation is useful or desirable on the basis of the distinctions made between electoral formulae or executive-legislative relationships. However, the type of electoral competition and the nature of party organisations at the time when the impact of the media was first being felt might go a long way towards providing an explanation of past events and a forecast of forthcoming changes.

I share the second reason for objecting to the oversimplicity of the analysis. Party government is actually a complex mixture of party *and* government. To a large extent I have skipped both. Little attention has been devoted to issues related to the actual performance of government (but a subsequent volume will specifically address that question), and only passing remarks have been made in respect to party. It is now time to combine some or possibly all those threads together.

A first way of doing so might be to create profiles of the various countries on the basis of the existence or lack of some of the attributes which seem conducive to party government. A score could be given for instance, to a certain electoral formula, to the types of elected assemblies, to the form of government and so on. The difficulty with this attempt at quantification of complex phenomena is that we would need weighted measures. It seems in fact likely that the weight of a specific electoral formula in facilitating the emergence and the persistence of party government should be greater than the impact of a specific parliamentary arrangement. Since we are not dealing with the presence or absence of specific elements, but with differences, variations, degrees, then a weighted index would be absolutely necessary. The difficulty then would lie in finding the appropriate weights.

A second difficulty is also immediately evident. At no point is it possible to speak of party government, and of the influence of constitutional structures and mechanisms on party government, without giving some consideration to individual parties and to the party system. Indeed, it might easily be that the most important institutional structure leading to party government is the party system itself. Even though one might agree with this statement, our original purpose was to evaluate the independent impact of the above-defined institutional structures and mechanisms on party government, leaving aside temporarily the party system (itself anyway conditioned, if not shaped, by institutional factors). A more appropriate answer would seem to be that individual parties and the party system are crucial intervening variables in the process that leads to the establishment and consolidation of party government. This pushes the analysis forwards towards the identification of the necessary steps to be undertaken in order to initiate and sustain party government.

I would claim that there are two important conclusions to be drawn from the preceding exploratory hypotheses and that there is a practical lesson to be learned too. The first important conclusion is that there are, to be sure, many different institutional arrangements under which party government comes into being and flourishes. However, a thorough evaluation of the constraining power of these arrangements and of the effectiveness of these different types of party government remains appropriate.

Let us identify the most relevant problem of party government as that of manufacturing a majority on the basis of the party criteria proposed by Katz. Different electoral formulae might be associated with this outcome. However, plurality formulae make it easier, while proportional representation formulae make it more difficult. To some extent because they combine a wider spectrum of political preferences, proportional representation formulae may create forms of party government which seem to be more legitimate. The trade-off for plurality formulae is that their party governments might seem less legitimate because less "representative," but being more cohesive are potentially more effective in terms of problem-solving capacity.

Both categories of party government, if effective, will enter into a positive spiral whereby their legitimacy will be bolstered by their effectiveness in solving problems. If ineffective, the opposite will be the result. Of course, crystal-clear situations and non-controversial assessments will rarely appear. If they do, they signal the need for and open the door to meaningful changes, i. e. to institutional reforms.

Presidential forms of government represent an altogether different conception and an almost opposite structural arrangement from party government. They may indeed be irreducible to it, since they are based on the predominance of the governing machinery over the party organisation. Still, the semi-presidential system of the Fifth Republic in France has rapidly and successfully moved in the direction of party government and, although this is probably the product of the overall configuration of the constitutional structure and the party system and of their peculiar combination and interaction, this allows us to suggest that presidential systems might not be immune from structural changes leading towards some form of party government. Finally, and most significantly, party government seems very frequently to be associated with monocameral Parliaments or with Parliaments where one House is clearly dominant over the other. Perhaps, this could be phrased differently and more incisively: dispersion of legislative powers and confusion of functions is not conducive to party government; indeed, it is one of the major obstacles on the road to it.

Summing up, the best institutional setting for both the establishment and the persistence of party government is a political system characterised by a parliamentary form of government, a unicameral elected assembly, and a plurality electoral formula. At the opposite extreme, one finds the most difficult setting for party government is offered by a presidential form of government, a bicameral Parliament with the two Houses sharing similar powers and functions, or having independent and autonomous powers and functions, and with a proportional representation formula unmitigated by any threshold or *Sperrklausel.* Since party government has to be conceived as a range of variations, in between lie many other possibilities.

In particular, one must search for the conditions and the constraints which reward party unity and impinge upon the cohesiveness and loyalty of the members of the majority, be it a single party majority or a coalition. From the point of view of "institutional engineering", manifold factors might be worthy of attention: from party financing to media advertising, to take two elements left out from the previous discussion.

The second important conclusion flows to a large extent from the first one. Since there are different institutional arrangements under which party government can be accommodated and made to flourish, it is also likely that there are different paths to party government. Therefore, Richard Katz may be correct in stating that "the strongest conditioning factor for party government at the present is to have had party government in the past" (see above p. 55), but from an institutional and developmental perspective it is desirable and possible to be more precise. It is desirable and possible, both for those who want to strengthen party government and those who want to weaken it to identify some of the conditions and some of the steps which have led to party government and contribute to its maintenance.

A change in the form of government only takes place when dramatic events exercise an intolerable pressure on the previous constitutional arrangements. On the other hand, if a parliamentary form of government is an appropriate setting for party government, that form is already quite widespread. It might be difficult, but not impossible, to reform the electoral system, although most reforms have traditionally gone in the direction of easier access to the distribution of seats and more proportionality; that is away from a condition leading to party government (witness the debate in Europe: Finer, 1975; and on Great Britain: Finer, 1980; but a contrary case is offered by Italy: Bartolini, 1982; Pasquino, 1982).

It has to be stressed that apparently minor changes, such as the introduction of *Sperrklauseln*, the reduction in the size of the constituencies, or the elimination of preferential voting, are likely to have important consequences for voters' behaviour and on parties' organisation. It might be less difficult to conceive of and implement a reform of elected assemblies, that is to move towards a sharply differentiated allocation of political functions and/or a monocameral Parliament. Out of reform of this latter type judging from the available evidence, a major incentive might follow for the streamlining of both the governing team's policies and the opposition's team's proposals. Moreover, a strong unicameral Parliament would certainly become more of a match for those powerful socio-economic actors now increasingly challenging the role of parties in the *Herrschaftsorganisation* of society.

III. An Inconclusive Conclusion

Party government is one historical answer to the problems of mass politics and class confrontation. It was meant to produce governments based on organisations accountable to the electorate. These organisations, the political parties, in time shifted from the channeling function (social demands and preferences brought to the consideration of policy-makers) to the steering function (their own ability to guide the socio-political process of allocation of resources – their problem-solving capacity – however hypothetical that might on occasions seem). Various institutional choices were made in this long term historical evolution mostly intended too strengthen the role of the parties and the partyness of government.

Though difficult to identify and too complex to be measured, each institutional structure and mechanism has had an impact on the appearance, maintenance, and dynamics of party government. Only detailed country studies will be in a position to specify better and in a more satisfactory way some of the hypotheses which have emerged in this synthetic overview of many diverse factors. The most important finding is that even strong institutions, that is those having a high constraining power on the behaviour of political parties, must come to terms with well entrenched, pervasive, highly organised political parties. On the other hand, institutional structures and mechanisms do provide the environment in which political parties come to operate, and diverse opportunities for party government will correspond to different environments.

The practical lesson to be learned from the preceding analysis is a complex one. Due to a vast array of socio-economic changes, the power of political parties has slowly been eroded and their problem-solving capacity weakened. With the decline in effectiveness, the very legitimacy of party government becomes affected in a negative way. Parties are seen as having too much power and too little ability to produce meaningful decisions and coherent policies. The paradox, however, is that changes in the institutions which weaken individual parties and party systems automatically and negatively impinge upon the possibility of the appearance and persistence of party government. These changes, though, have not, as yet, signalled how to replace party government with a more effective political arrangement. If this is correct, then institutional reforms might be devised and analysed from this specific point of view: their projected impact on the organisation of political parties. The power of the parties in the *Herrschaftsorganisation* of society may be reduced (indeed, in some cases, it is desirable to do so in order to reach a new and better balance among the various political actors), but their organisational presence ought not to be curtailed by those who want to retain some form of party government.

Parties and party organisations may be revived through institutional reforms, though unexpectedly and inadvertently, as in the case of the Fifth Republic in France, or may be further weakened, as in the case of the "democratisation" of a series of processes concerning the nomination of candidates in the United States. But, perhaps, the most damaging reforms of all are those which "contain and encapsulate the role of parties at different levels in the political system, which prevent parties from playing a unifying role throughout the system." The "disjointedness" of party activities and their disorganisation are the most serious blows to party government. While this disjointedness might be the product of changes in the environment of political parties — with the mass media taking over the communication function, the unions expropriating some of the socialisation and recruitment functions, the bureaucracy and other technical bodies entering into the decision-making function, new single-issue movements appearing to articulate interests and demands and making it difficult to pursue the aggregation of interests in coherent packages of proposals in priority-setting programmes — it might be aggravated by the nature of institutional reforms. Even minor changes, if not seen in the light of the "whole" system and from the perspective of strengthening "responsible" government, might have far-reaching consequences.

"When party government is diminished, other institutions may act in its stead, but they cannot fully replace parties in the government of a modern state" (Rose, 1974: 380). We might then find ourselves in the situation described by Otto Kirchheimer vis-à-vis the disappearance of the class-mass party and the denominational party,[9] both important elements in the

[9] Whose dominance in some countries might explain the political resistance, at the doctrinal level of some scholars against the creation of party government.

creation and persistence of party government. We will regret their passing – even if it was inevitable (Kirchheimer, 1966: 200). Perhaps, we might prepare for that event by devising institutional frameworks capable of accommodating new forms of responsible government and of slowing down the process of change.

At this point, however, the impossible exercise of tracing and combining the many variables related to institutional structures and mechanisms with forms and variants of party government rightly comes to an end. And politics take over.

Bibliography

APTER, D. E. (1968) "Government," in *International Encyclopedia of the Social Sciences*. New York: Crowell Collier and Macmillan.

BARTOLINI, S. (1981) "Il mutamento del sistema partitico," 30 *Il Mulino* 169.

– (1982) "The Politics of Institutional Reform in Italy," 5 *West European Politics* 203.

BLONDEL, J. (1969) *An Introduction to Comparative Government*. New York: Praeger.

– (1973) *Comparative Legislatures*. Englewood Cliffs: Prentice-Hall.

BROWNE, E. C. and J. DREIJMANIS (eds.) (1982) *Government Coalitions in Western Democracies*, London: Longman.

BUDGE, I. (1982) "Democratic Party Government. Formation and Functioning in Twenty-one Countries." Presented at the Workshop on The Future of Party Government, European University Institute, Florence (June 8–15).

BUTLER, D., H. R. PENNIMAN and A. RANNEY (eds.), (1981) *Democracy at the Polls. A Comparative Study of Competitive National Elections*. Washington, D.C.: American Enterprise Institute.

COTTA, M. (1979) *Classe politica e parlamento in Italia, 1946-1979*. Bologna: Il Mulino.

CRICK, B. (1970) "Parliament in the British Political System," in A. Kornbery and L. D. Musolf (eds.), *Legislatures in Developmental Perspective*. Durham, N. C.: Duke University Press.

DE SWANN, A. (1973) *Coalition Theories and Cabinet Formations. A Study of Formal Theories of Coalition Formation Applied to Nine European Parliaments after 1918*. Amsterdam: Elsevier.

DUVERGER, M. (1964) *Political Parties*. London: Methuen.

FINER, S. E. (ed.), (1975) *Adversary Politics and Electoral Reform*. London: Anthony Wigram.

– (1970) *Comparative Government*. London: Allen Lane.

– (1980) *The Changing British Party System, 1945-1979*. Washington, D.C.: American Enterprise Institute.

FIORINA, M. (1977) *Congress. Keystone of the Washington Establishment*. New Haven-London: Yale University Press.

– (1980) "The Decline of Collective Responsibility in American Politics," 109 *Daedalus* 25.

– (1981) *Retrospective Voting in American National Elections*. New Haven–London: Yale University Press.

HERMENS, F. A. (1941) *Democracy or Anarchy? A Study of Proportional Representation*. Notre Dame: University of Notre Dame Press.

– (1958) *The Representative Republic*. Notre Dame: University of Notre Dame Press.

– (1963) "The Dynamics of Proportional Representation," in H. Eckstein and D. E. Apter (eds.), *Comparative Politics. A Reader.* New York: Free Press.

KATZ, R. S. (1980) *A Theory of Parties and Electoral Systems.* Baltimore: Johns Hopkins University Press.

– (1982) "Party Government: A Rationalistic Conception." Presented at the Workshop on The Future of Party Government, European University Institute, Florence (June 8–15).

KING, A. (1975) "Executives," in F. I. Greenstein and N. W. Polsby (eds.), *Handbook of Political Science.* Reading, Massachusetts: Addison-Wesley, vol. 4.

– (1976) "Modes of Executive-Legislative Relations," *Legislative Studies Quarterly.*

KIRCHHEIMER, O. (1966) "The Transformation of the Western European Party System," in J. LaPalombara, and M. Weiner (eds.), *Political Parties and Political Development.* Princeton: Princeton University Press.

LAPALOMBARA, J. (1974) *Politics Within Nations.* Englewood Cliffs: Prentice-Hall.

LEHMBRUCH, G. (1979) "Liberal Corporatism and Party Government," in P. Schmitter and G. Lehmbruch (eds.), *Trends Toward Corporatist Intermediation.* Beverly Hills-London: Sage Publications.

LOEWENBERG, G., and S. C. PATTERSON (1979) *Comparing Legislatures.* Boston: Little, Brown, and Co.

NEUSTADT, R. E. (1960) *Presidential Power. The Politics of Leadership.* New York: Wiley.

PASQUINO, G. (1980) *Crisi dei partiti e governabilità.* Bologna: Il Mulino.

– (1982) *Degenerazioni dei partiti e riforme istituzionali.* Bari: Laterza.

QUERMONNE, J. L. (1980) *Le Gouvernement de la France sous la Ve République.* Paris: Dalloz.

RAE, D. W. (1971) *The Political Consequences of Electoral Laws.* New Haven: Yale University Press.

REIF, K. H. (1982) "Parteienregierung in Frankreich. Die Transformation des Parteiensystems durch die Institutionen der V. Republik," Mannheim: Habilitationsschrift.

ROKKAN, S. (1970) *Citizens, Elections, Parties.* Oslo: Universitetsforlaget.

ROSE, R. (1974) *The Problem of Party Government.* New York: Free Press.

ROSE, R., and E. SULEIMAN (eds.) (1980) *Presidents and Prime Ministers,* Washington, D. C.: American Enterprise Institute.

SARTORI, G. (1966) "European Political Parties: The Case of Polarized Pluralism," in J. LaPalombara and M. Weiner (eds.), *Political Parties and Political Development.* Princeton: Princeton University Press.

– (1968) "Political Development and Political Engineering," in A. O. Hirschman and D. Montgomery (eds.), *Public Policy.* Cambridge, Mass.: Harvard University Press, vol. XVII.

– (1976) *Parties and Party Systems.* New York: Cambridge University Press.

SMITH, G. (1982) "The Futures of Party Government." Presented at the Workshop on The Future of Party Government, European University Institute, Florence (June 8–15).

Chapter V

Bureaucratic Rationalities and the Prospect for Party Government

GIORGIO FREDDI

Contents

This essay is characterised by manifold perspectives and interests. It has, however, a unifying theme that may be summarily denoted as "politics and administration revisited". As is well known, the relationship between politics and administration has been, and is, one of the constant concerns of political science: this essay is largely constructed as an analysis and an evaluation of how the ways in which that relationship operates affect both the viability of party government and the governability of the complex polities of today.

The approach adopted here, then, is meant to broaden the scope of most discussions about politics and administration which, with a few exceptions, have been the province of specialists in the discipline of political science: by this I mean that such discussions have been concerned with the analysis of an admittedly important segment of the political system, but seldom have tried to explore its implications for the performance of the whole system. On the other hand, studies centered on the issues of either party government or governability, while taking into consideration a host of societal and cultural factors to account for variance in, and problems of, performance, give marginal, if not scanty, attention to the administrative instruments of governance.

Granted, then, that a large number of factors condition the performance of political parties and affect governability, public administration is here singled out as one, and crucially important, among such factors. As was pointed out at the outset, doing so involves tackling the traditional issue of the relationship between politics and administration: the conceptualisation of this relationship, however, has undergone many a revision in a literature that spans a very long period. I am going to show that even the most recent revisions do not succeed in satisfactorily explaining the complex interplay of policy-making activities undertaken by political parties and elected personnel on the one hand, and professional administrators on the other.

In order to arrive at a more satisfactory and comprehensive approach, a critical survey of existing conceptualisations and of the empirical circumstances that have prompted their formation is needed. This endeavor, as will be seen, entails the development of both analytical and historical arguments: in the following section an effort is made to present alternative definitions of the problem in as orderly a fashion as possible, with the aim of developing a new, more complete and explanatory conceptual framework. However, as doing so involves the exploration of empirical situations that — being historical — are sequentially arranged, some redundancies will be inevitable.

I. Bureaucracy and Party Government

In the Western liberal and scholarly traditions, bureaucracy and democracy are perceived as being antithetic, antagonistic, and mutually exclusive or, to put it less bluntly, bureaucracy and bureaucratisation are perceived as being inimical to democracy. The Weberian scenario, whereby the modern world and its social and economic life will be dominated and controlled by large and impersonal bureaucracies, stifling individual enterprise and imperilling freedom, has been with us for a long time.

Thus, it is not surprising that, according to democratic theory, the making of politically relevant authoritative decisions ought to be the exclusive province of elected officials and no decisional discretion ought to be left to professional and institutionalised administrative agencies, which, as a consequence, ought to devote themselves to the mere execution of those decisions. During the 19th Century the Western world developed two radically different — indeed alternative and mutually exclusive —

doctrinal and operational approaches to the problem of how to control the bureaucracy.

In the United States, political agencies were to control the bureaucracy by negating that administration could be kept separate from politics, by making public administration conterminuous with elective political organs and by affirming the political nature of administrative action. In other words, by instituting the spoils system.

In Continental Europe, where the liberal-representative regimes that had emerged at mid-century had inherited solidly articulated professional bureaucracies from the *ancien régime,* a normative theory was developed introducing the principle of separation between politics and administration. As is well known, the functional correlates of that theory were and are the twin principles of the political neutrality of the civil service and the purely executive (non-decisional) role of public administration. These principles, which were treated as validated empirical propositions by European doctrine, that is as correct descriptions of reality, were adopted in America too at the turn of the century, when the merit system began its course, after the dismal administrative record of the spoils system had begun to imperil the very legitimacy of democratic government. They were, however, treated not so much as empirically tested propositions but, rather, as moral imperatives which, if adequately pursued, would have made administration a truly neutral and "scientific" technique (Goodnow, 1900; Wilson, 1887).

We know that things have not quite worked in this way. In fact, modern political science has disowned the conception that has been just summarised as formalistic and axiological: administrative action is no longer defined as politically neutral, nor are bureaucratic agencies any longer maintained to be the passive and docile instruments of elective institutions. The position now generally accepted is that professional civil servants share in policy-making and, in doing so, start from ideological and/or political value-premises which might, or might not, coincide with those adhered to by the personnel of elective institutions.

If, then, the theory positing the separation between politics and administration has been so thoroughly abandoned, why do we continue to consider as relevant analyses and discussions revolving around the twin concepts of "bureaucracy and democracy"? Because, obviously, this is a central part of democratic theory, and plays a fundamental role in those political cultures which have accepted and absorbed the values and institutions of constitutional and representative government. The idea of a separation between politics and administration is culture-bound; it is a relevant issue in some political systems (constitutional and representative), and a negligible and marginal one in others (authoritarian and traditional). Even though the political neutrality and the merely executive role of public administration have been invalidated as descriptive statements, as *is* propositions, and shown to be formalistic myths, they however retain much strength and appeal as normative statements, as *ought to* propositions. They, in sum, represent permanent values, desirable and essential objectives in democratic and constitutional polities.

The crucial role played by such values is made even more apparent as we turn our attention to the party government model (taken here as the one which is ideally fitted to articulate democratic theory in the context of mass democracy). Even though one finds many a shade of opinion in the literature, there seems to be a general agreement on the point, as Sartori puts it, (1976: ix) that "Parties are the central intermediate and intermediary structures between society and government". Descriptively, the functions that political parties perform can be divided into two main categories: those that can be characterised as inputs, such as mobilisation and channelling of support, formulation of alternatives, recruitment and replacement of leadership (with which this essay is not concerned). And those functions having to do with outputs, performed by political parties when in power, such as formation and implementation of policy and control over public administration (which are the main concern here).

What has been said so far implies that party government is strongly associated with a view of democracy whereby the political system is made democratic by the electoral and decisional roles of parties (Ranney, 1962). As the events and the literature of the approximately last twenty-five years have made clear, however, this normative idealisation of the role of parties has been called into discussion: the governability of industrial and post-industrial societies and, therefore, the ability of parties and party governments to cope with contemporary problems have become the subject of serious concern (Crozier et al., 1975). For instance, the observation that bureaucrats frequently act as independent decision makers or in concert with organised interests, has cast doubts on whether parties are actually in control of policy. This train of reasoning has quite logically led many an observer to ask the question whether political parties have the capacity to perform the functions that both normatively and descriptively have been assigned to them.

At this point, the following question arises: having focussed our attention, both descriptively as well as normatively, on functions performed by political parties such as policy formation and execution, which conditions must obtain if we are to speak of party government? Two seem to stand out: the first is that all significant policy decisions are made by people chosen in partisan elections or else by those whom they appoint. In other words, "the party government model requires that party based leaders be able effectively to control the bureaucracy and other public or semi-public agencies." (Katz, *supra*: p. 43).

That political parties effectively control public administration, however, is not a sufficient condition. Party government, if it wants to retain legitimacy, must also exhibit some "problem-solving capacity", consisting of several elements, among which one enumerates "*the capacity to get a specific policy implemented*", "the ability to frame policies that will produce the desired (by the policy maker) results", and "the ability to choose the 'right' aims or policies". (Katz, *supra*: pp. 46–47. Emphasis added). In this volume, the essay which is specifically concerned with problem solving in politics, drives the point home even more forcefully. In fact, "democratic party government is likely to persist if, and only if: (a) the more important societal problems are put on the agenda, i. e. turned into policy problems, and (b) *the more important policy problems are solved in an acceptable way* and, (c) the more important governance problems are solved in an acceptable way". (Sjöblom, *supra*: p. 101. Emphasis added).

Now, the second condition of party government that has been just presented (and particularly that, among its components, identified by Katz as policy implementation, and by Sjöblom as acceptable solution of policy problems) can be met in the complex polities of today only by resorting to the professional know-how and technical expertise usually associated with an institutionalised and permanent civil service. This latter condition, however, is at least partially incompatible with the former, which calls for direct control by parties over administration for, as it has been stated tersely, "recognising that a permanent bureaucracy is an essential feature of all modern governments, this [the first] condition is violated to the extent that bureaucrats exercise independent policy making authority". (Katz, *supra*: p. 43).

This contradiction leads us back to the two basic patterns of administrative organisation which have emerged from the historical experience of Western political systems: on the one hand, the spoils system, with its attendant inefficiency, corruption and potential for delegitimation, which, nevertheless, maximises the probability that elected personnel control the bureaucracy. On the other hand, the continental bureaucratic model which, while fostering expertise and technical know-how, has frequently seen its allegedly neutral cadres exercising independent policy making authority.

To recapitulate: in the context of the modernised and complex polities of the present time, the idea of separation between politics and administration, (as formulated in the 19th century) and the correlative principles of the neutrality and instrumentality of administrative action are neither descriptively valid nor empirically tenable. In all Western political systems, bureaucracies loom large over the political arena and have been exerting a more and more pervasive influence on decision-making. And yet, in polities where party government is conceived as the sole, or main, policy-making agency, those ideas and principles are taken to be the central prerequisites for the correct performance of the political system.

Apparently, we are faced here with what looks like an intractable problem of the either-or kind. In short compass: (a) party government must have direct control over policy making; (b) effective policy making can take place only when a problem-solving capacity exists; (c) such capacity may be obtained only by resorting to a permanent professional bureaucracy, whose controllability by political parties should be insured *via* a neat and rigid separation between policy and administration; (d) the theory of separation has been invalidated by the empirical observation that bureaucrats tend to act as independent decision makers.

I am going to argue that the apparent intractability of the problem depends largely on the fact that the theory of separation between policy and administration has been dismissed too lightly, as being both heuristically invalid and operationally impracticable. The policy-administration dichotomy, in other words, is treated in the modern literature of political science as being false, and *as always having been false*. This happens because the theory has been tackled from a static perspective, that is without paying attention to the circumstances that prompted its original formulation. But, as such circumstances are historical, the analytical approach that one wants to adopt must be sensitive to the diachronic dimension.

In summary, the case that will be made is that the theory was not false when first enunciated, and this will be demonstrated by calling attention to the social, economic, and political conditions prevailing when and where the theory was originally formulated. Further, it will be shown that, much later, the theory was empirically invalidated when the conditions which prompted its formulation no longer existed. Finally, by means of an analytical investigation of the organisational properties of contemporary administrative structures, and of the rational requisites for different types of decisional processes, it will be argued that given the appropriate circumstances, the old theory can be valid today. Put differently, what I am doing here can be seen as an effort to rehabilitate the policy-administration dichotomy.[1]

The relationship between politics and administration (and, more specifically, the constraints that this relationship imposes on the realisability of party government) is here treated as our dependent variable. Our independent variables will be more precisely identified as our argument unfolds in the following pages: they are constituted by a set of factors — cultural, structural, and behavioral — that either maximise or minimise the probability that the two conditions for party government which we have stipulated (party control over administration and problem-solving capacity) are actually met. For the time being, they can be expressed as questions: (a) which factors help in explaining the degree to which a *bureaucratic system exerts an autonomous power* uncontrolled and/or uncontrollable by elected

1 Aaron Wildavsky (1972), in discussing some organisational trends which have recently surfaced in several Western political systems, has also suggested that we might be moving toward a rehabilitation of the policy-administration dichotomy.

officials? (b) which factors explain whether a *bureaucratic system has the capacity for effective policy performance?*

In the following sections, approaches to, and conceptions of the policy-administration dichotomy are critically reviewed; a number of theoretical relationships among historical, structural, and heuristic dimensions having to do with policy performance are outlined; and hypotheses (that might be tested in future research) about which factors maximise the probability of party government are formulated.

II. The Performance of Western Political Systems: The Bureaucratic Factor

After the Second World War, a disquieting syndrome — whose intensity has been growing with the passing of time — has become apparent in modernised and constitutional Western political systems, even though to different degrees in different countries: the inability of political parties and party systems, and of the public institutions that they are supposed to activate and operate, both to adapt to the challenges posed by rapid socio-economic-political change and to govern effectively. Numerous conditions have been pinpointed and offered as hypotheses potentially capable of explaining that syndrome, mainly focussed on the relationship between party system and society. Thus, attention has been directed to whether the party system is competitive or not, to whether parties operate in a homogenous or fragmented cultural context, and to the way in which this affects modes of mobilisation and the functions of interest articulation and interest aggregation. Frequently, the malfunctioning of institutions charged with policy-making and policy-execution is treated as a dependent variable, to be seen as a consequence of the failure of the party system adequately to process diverse and conflictful demands. In other words, governability, or the lack of it, would be a function of largely cultural factors.

The point of view taken in the present discussion leads to an approach somewhat divergent from the one just outlined; while the influence of political culture on the performance of institutions is taken for granted, one should also take into account that institutions have properties of their own which affect policy-making and policy-execution pretty much independently. As Richard Rose aptly puts it "the discussion about 'un-governability' is concerned with the ability of government to influence the larger environment of which it is a part as well as its citizens. While compliance follows logically from popular support for a regime, the effectiveness of a government in controlling the environment does not necessarily follow" (Rose, 1977: 5).

The thrust behind this argument is that political systems may be encountering problems in performing effectively regardless of their prevailing ideological and/or cultural composition and that, therefore, some light may be thrown on these problems by focussing on institutional functioning. This is made the more plausible by the circumstance that the current debate about governability tends to include all the modernised Western political systems, which are thus depicted as sharing commom problems and characteristics in the area of governmental performance. For instance, in a recent discussion of the problems of party government, Wildenmann sets forth an extensive catalogue of constraints, conditions and challenges that, in the course of recent decades, have made governing a difficult and frustrating endeavor in Western Europe; some are societal, or economic, or international, but others are definitely structural and institutional, as the following quotations make clear:

> "there is a diversification... creating a division of responsibility not in conformity with traditional models of government".
> "...the task of government, including the implementation of policies, seems to be confronted with almost unsolvable problems" "...There seems to be a loss of control over governmental and administrative decision-making bodies, and a growing inability of party government to carry out organised and...legitimised policies..."
> "The ability of decision making bodies to solve fundamental policy questions has to be assessed" (Wildenmann, 1981: 7,10,16).

Our attention is here directed to a familiar picture: "old" governmental systems are forced to adapt to new requirements, that is those requirements largely generated by "the well-known increased intervention of governments in the allocation and/or redistribution of the G. N. P. in connection with the evolution of the welfare state" (Wildenmann, 1981: 9) as well as by the new economic, managerial and industrial functions performed by the modern state. More specifically, our attention is directed to those phenomena that the literature frequently labels as "overload" and "overcomplexity".

These two terms should be denoted more precisely at this point. When we say that governments are overloaded, we do not imply a merely quantitative question, *i. e.*, the functional load of governments is greater but, also, and preeminently, a qualitative question, *i. e.*, the load is not only greater, but different from what it used to be, thus burdening and straining policy-making structures with task-domains that they were not meant to tackle originally.

The concept of overcomplexity can be denoted similarly: in the words of Richard Rose, "Because organizations 'institutionalize' decisions from the past, they do not ...adapt well to changing...conditions. The relative rigidity of government institutions intensifies overcomplexity, for some activities of government will reflect decisions made in circumstances no longer appropriate. Yet government agencies continue to move forward, propelled by inertia commitments" (Rose, 1977: 8).

What, in other words, the notions of overload and overcomplexity both suggest can be succinctly described as follows; first, poor policy performance is a function of the growing *incongruence* between the governmental institutional machinery (notably public administration) and the new tasks (of intervention into the economy and society) being undertaken by the political system; second, poor policy performance is not so much a question of inefficiency, that is of an unsatisfactory ratio between inputs and outputs but, rather, a question of *ineffectiveness*, that is of an unsatisfactory ratio of expected outcomes to actual outcomes; third, structural-bureaucratic arrangements are among the most important factors leading to poor policy-performance, both *per se* (because of an inadequate fit between structures and functions) and as premises for decision-making (because different structures designed to pursue the same goals may do so with different decisional styles leading to more or less satisfactory outcomes).

These last three points are taken here as working assumptions: they have the nature of hypotheses which need to be tested empirically in a systematic fashion, but since some empirical and historical data are available, as hypotheses they exhibit some *prima facie* plausibility.

III. Structural vs. Attitudinal Conditions of Policy-Performance

The central assumption of this essay is that the performance of the political-administrative system can and must be explained chiefly in the light of structural variables and modes of decision-making. However, as will be seen, this is still a moot question in the political science literature. A compressed summary of this issue is in order at this point.

In recent decades, constitutionally and economically advanced political systems have been developing a set of largely common features: a) governments have been acquiring a larger and larger number of functions to perform in their societies and economies; b) concomitantly, public bureaucracies have increased in size and have expanded their participation in policy-making; c) at the same time, the performance of the political and administrative system has become less than satisfactory; in any event, it has proved to be inferior *vis-à-vis* rising expectations, and incapable of processing the diverse and growing demands articulated by social and economic groups.

An issue which looms large in this area is well summed up by the following question: to what extent are policy decisions (as formulated in elective organs and political parties) influenced by professional administrators?

For a long time, political science has accepted conceptions, originated from legal axiology, and most specifically set forth by such scholars as Wilson and Goodnow, which define administrative action as politically neutral, and maintain that bureaucratic agencies are the docile instruments of elected bodies. This point of view has been taken for granted until comparatively recently. This has been the case, interestingly enough, regardless of the ideological propensities of individual scholars; just to cite some classics, the positions of progressive writers like F. Neumann and C. Wright Mills, and those of conservative thinkers like L. von Mises and F. von Hayek, are virtually identical concerning the negligible impact of bureaucracies on policy-making.

Now the situation is totally different; after the pioneering work of authors like Appleby, Kingsley and Lipset, there is now a vast body of literature the position of which – generally accepted and validated empirically – is that higher civil servants take part in policy-making and, in so doing, start from value-premises which might, or might not, coincide with those adhered to by the nation's elected representatives and inherent in the party system.

The view that professional administrators conduct their business sustained by coherent and explicit systems of ideological beliefs has been empirically demonstrated beyond doubt. In a recent and monumental work, which applies sophisticated behavioural procedures to opinion data from seven Western political systems, important analogies and similarities between the ideological positions of politicians and bureaucrats have been identified: "...both types of policymaker typically express ideologically consistent points of view on the basic issues of social change and government activism that have structured politics in the West during this century. Bureaucrats may display a more inductive, less philosophical approach to public affairs than politicians...but this does not mean that their positions on fundamental ideological issues are any less coherent", (Aberbach et al., 1981: 130).

In the literature which pursues this line of inquiry a common trend can be discerned: it consists in a position whereby a strong relationship exists between the overall performance of the administrative system and the political attitudes of professional bureaucrats (as well as those demographic factors that more directly influence political socialisation).

A conclusion frequently arrived at from this position is that where we observe a high degree of congruence between the values prevailing in the political system and the attitudes of the higher civil service, the performance of the administrative system is satisfactory, whereas the opposite is true when the values of the political system and the attitudes of the civil service are incongruent, antagonistic and/or incompatible. (Putnam, 1973). An implication of this is that effective party government (as was defined at the outset) would be largely a function of the political attitudes and ideological profiles of higher civil servants.

The assumption behind the approach being discussed (*i.e.*, that the political attitudes of the bureaucracy as a social group explain and/or predict their professional and institutional behavior) revolves around a central concept, that of the *responsiveness* of the civil service as contrasted with the traditional and legalistic concept of *impartiality* or *political neutrality* of the professional administrator. As J. D. Kingsley wrote: "...the essence of bureaucratic responsibility in the modern State is to be sought, not in the presumed and largely fictitious impartiality of the officials, but in the strength of their commitment to the purposes that State is undertaking to serve" (Kingsley, 1944: 274).

In a more recent discussion, Putnam has defined responsiveness as the ability of a bureaucracy to react positively, with readiness, faithfulness and efficacy, to the needs and demands of society and of its political representatives, and to show, at the same time, more concern with programmes and problems than with procedure and rules; and the same author points out that the political opinions and values upheld by bureaucrats are a most important indicator of their proclivity to act responsively.

That behavioural studies of administrative action emphasise responsiveness as a central concept makes, of course, perfectly sound sense in methodological terms, as responsiveness may be gauged quite effectively on the basis of attitudinal data. The substantive results obtained by such studies are extremely valuable, moreover, as they increase and systematise knowledge about elites and their relationship to the values of the political system. A different appraisal must be made, however, when, either implicitly or explicitly, a relationship between responsiveness and effectiveness is postulated; the empirical evidence made available so far does not warrant such a conclusion. More specifically, I contend that the relationship between the political *responsiveness* of civil servants and the *effectiveness* of administrative action is far from being unilinear. The political attitudes of higher civil servants constitute a set of variables which — of great interest *per se* — explain only a part of the performance of the administrative system. More precisely, while such attitudes are crucially important in interpreting crisis-situations bordering on or leading to regime-transitions, they do not explain much (taken alone), if we are interested in understanding administrative action and policy performance in more or less stable contexts.

On the contrary, a different kind of variable is centrally relevant in the latter connection, which is usually neglected or underplayed by studies investigating the relationship between politics and administration and the decisional role of professional bureaucrats. I define this kind of variable as the *organisational properties* of administrative structures *qua* structures.

An analysis and interpretation of policy-performance[2] centered on the study of organisational properties implies that administrative behaviour and processes should be considered in the light of structural determinants (Thompson, 1961: 6–9). The concept of structural determinants as utilized in this discussion is defined quite broadly: it includes not only the formal features of administrative organisation, but also factors of a cultural and/or ideological nature, such as the values which, deeply implanted in formal structures and procedures, act as decision-premises and affect thoroughly the processes of institutional socialisation of bureaucratic actors (Blau, 1964: 224–331).

An analytical treatment of organisational properties as conditions of policy-performance, and a discussion of the conceptual arguments supporting the approach suggested here are developed in Sections IV. and V., which may be outlined as follows.

The administrative institutions of Western Europe emerged as professional organisations a very long time ago (Armstrong, 1973). Their formation took place simultaneously with – and partly antedated – the consolidation of the modern state, that is during the period of mature absolutism and enlightened despotism and, to a larger degree, during the age of oligarchic liberalism. A tenable assumption, then, is that such dimensions as organisational format, division of work, professional socialisation, institutional ideology, and so on, are still guided by the original historical matrix.

When the bureaucracies under discussion were organisationally rationalised and assumed the formal structure that, to a large extent, they still exhibit (late 19th Century), their functional load was relatively light and not very diversified. Basically, administrative activities were aimed at preserving law and order and regulating minor areas of social and economic life. As was noted previously, a massive load of functions bearing upon direct socio-economic intervention has been assigned to the public sector in recent decades. This has caused administrative agencies to undergo a crisis of adaption of old organisational models to new functional tasks and exerts important consequences on the performance of both the bureaucratic and the political systems. The main argument advanced here is that this crisis only partially and marginally depends on the political attitudes of top-bureaucrats, allegedly – and sometimes demonstrably – opposed to the socio-economic activities that mass-democracies have assigned to the

[2] This essay is not concerned with a discussion and an evaluation of the problems encountered when defining and analysing the concept of political performance, but only with a particular moment or dimension of it; namely policy performance which, in the structural approach adopted here, is relatively simple to isolate. For a discussion of the multifaceted problems and dimensions one encounters in defining political performance, cf. Eckstein (1971).

public sector. Rather, the most important conditions explaining the crisis of adaption being discussed are represented by the organisational properties of the legal-rational model of bureaucracy (especially as observed in the administrative law systems, which emerged and consolidated in the 19th Century), whose principles are largely incompatible with an effective intervention in the social and economic sectors.

As was observed previously, mass-democracies whose governments are directly concerned with social welfare and the management of the economy have altered radically the context of administrative action. And yet, the performance of the political system has grown more and more dependent upon the ability of the 19th Century bureaucracies to cope successfully with such a new task domain. As a rule, and in varying degrees, this adaptive effort has not been satisfactory: the main reason for this must be found in the fact that the administrative rationality of those bureaucracies, and the organisational and normative structures supporting it, were never meant to deal with social welfare and with managing the economy in a democratic, participatory, and pluralistic environment.

IV. Diachronic Conditions of Bureaucratic Performance

In the preceding section attention has been called to the fact that a professional public administration emerged and was consolidated in Continental Europe in a period which antedates both the industrial and the liberal revolutions. This fact sets Continental political systems apart from other Western systems such as the English one – where a professional civil service was instituted toward the end of the 19th Century when both economic modernisation and the constitutionalisation of the polity had been accomplished – as well as the United States – where the merit system became a widespread phenomenon in a context of mass democracy and advanced industrialisation.

This makes Continental bureaucracies much older than their Anglo-Saxon counterparts and, as a consequence, the task of analysing their structures and pinpointing their organisational properties is particularly complex. In fact, organisational forms and types have a history and this history determines some aspects of the structure and values of present organisations. In particular, careful attention should be paid to the notion that "the organisational 'inventions' that can be made at a particular time in history depend on the social technology available at the time" (Stinchcombe, 1964: 155), as well as to the cultural values and models definable as authoritative at that same time, and that all tend to be perpetuated even in the face of radical changes in the environment. To sum up, the main thrust of the argument developed here is that present behaviour and performance of public bureaucracies are affected by historically emergent structural and value-determinants.

What has been suggested so far does not, of course, imply a static rigidity of organisational models through time but, rather, as periodic reorganisations have occurred, the survival of older structural and value-features on which newer ones have been superimposed, so that a given concrete administrative structure or apparatus ends up by being characterised by a series of chronologically successive and organisationally overlapping features. The older an administrative system, the more numerous are these strata, and the more intermittent, latent, and difficult to pinpoint is their influence on present behaviour and performance.

The structural evolution of Continental administration spans three such strata: the preliberal and preindustrial period (late absolutism) when the basic structure of professional administration was laid out; the liberal period (19th Century) when the rationalisation of those structures was effected; and the post-liberal period (that of the welfare state and of public management of the economy) when these older structures have had to face an entirely new task domain (Freddi, 1982). This section is intended as an analytical attempt to isolate and characterise those organisational properties of Continental administration which respectively proceed from the preliberal and liberal periods. Only the conclusions immediately relevant to the argument unfolded here are set forth in this section.[3]

A. The Constraints of the Preindustrial Period: Hierarchy and Generalism

A term coined by those writers who tried to apply scientific management to public administration best summarises the organisational properties of hierarchy and centralisation as consolidated in absolutist administration and perpetuated to the present day: "generalism". Its ideal type can be outlined here, by stressing those structural traits of the classic continental bureaucracies of today which were already clearly observable in the administrative apparatus of mature absolutism and enlightened despotism.

Candidates for administrative positions are selected on the basis of educational qualifications at a relatively young age, no previous practical training or work-experience being required of them. Entrance tests are largely designed to ascertain a certain degree of "cultural literacy" rather than to assess and predict future performance along specialist lines. Normally, organisational participants are expected to spend their entire working lives in the public service, nearly always beginning at the bottom of the organisational ladder. Professional training is acquired within public

[3] For a more articulated and detailed discussion cf. Freddi (1982).

administration; the relevant skills are learned on the job, after the selection process has taken place, and generationally transmitted to the newcomers, who are thus slowly and safely coopted to higher and higher positions. This peculiar form of recruitment is possibly the most fool-proof mechanism for institutionalised resistance against change ever conceived.

Organisational subunits, or offices, are ordered according to the principle of hierarchy; in the same fashion, incumbents of organisational roles are ordered according to a hierarchy of ranks to which differential degrees of material and psychological gratification are attached. Advancement along the career-ladder is competitive, and promotions are granted according to criteria which combine seniority, merit, and political "savvy"; in more general terms, what we observe is a system of extrinsic rewards administered by the hierarchy of authority (Thompson, 1961: 5).

This approach to work-performance and role-assignment best demonstrates the inherent properties of generalism; by this I mean that the European central administrative structures are staffed by individuals whose training, qualifications, aptitudes and, in general, professional orientation are assumed to be homogenous. Participants, then are supposed to be capable of playing all organisational roles that are formally associated with a certain rank. The organisational logic of such a structure does not allow for individual specialisation for assignments that permanently require functional specificity. On the contrary, the system works on the assumption that participants are *omnicompetent vis-à-vis* the different functional spheres that can be distinguished within the whole compass of governmental activity. Personnel policies, in fact, are oriented toward individual rotations among several functional alternatives, and toward role interchangeability.

There is, however, another important structural characteristic: differentiation among participants takes place only along the vertical dimension. This implies the assumption that although all functions performed by a preoccupation with the monistic ideal (Barnard, 1946); administration are, at the same time, characterised by increasing degrees of difficulty, and call for more expert and refined handling as one goes up the hierarchical ladder. Generalism — that is, the assumption of functional omnicompetence — geared to the vertical dimension of hierarchy, leads to a second assumption: that of hierarchical *omniscience* (Thompson, 1961: 40—82; Crozier, 1963: 213—269). In sum, these administrative institutions are characterised by a preoccupation with the monistic ideal (Barnard, 1946); administration is a monocratic institution articulated on the basis of a vertical sequence of superior — subordinate relationships in which the superior is the source of legitimate influence upon the subordinate. The cultural definition of roles is autocratic and authoritarian. The nexus between higher and lower participants is not mediated by considerations of functional or specific competence; on the contrary, it is based on a system of rights and duties.

There is, then, a confusion between the notion of right and that of ability, so that purely formal responsibility for something and competence to do something are assumed to coincide. It frequently follows that the greatest importance is attributed to suppressing conflict, to avoiding a pluralistic orientation, and to preventing innovation.

As can be readily observed, many of the features of Max Weber's ideal type of bureaucracy are recognisable in this discussion, but not all. Notably, those that are missing concern the normative stance of legal-rational bureaucracy. This is so because, while the structural features of absolutist administration already incorporate, to a very large extent, the formal set-up of contemporary Continental administration, the conception and management of authority-relationships is radically different. And the difference can be explained by the modifications introduced into or, better, layered over the administrative apparatus during the period of constitutional liberalism.

B. The Constraints of the *Rechtsstaat*: Legal Rationality

Continental European constitutional liberalism, speaking in a very general way, took the form of the *Rechtsstaat:* order, certainty, predictability, equality before the judge and the tax collector were the goals pursued by a bourgeoisie that was aiming to avoid capriciousness, arbitrariness, and unreliability in political rule. By and large, the liberal regimes of Europe tackled their tasks retaining the administrative apparatus of the preliberal period practically unchanged in its organisational structure: centralisation, hierarchy, authoritarianism, and unresponsiveness remained its dominant characters.

Yet, against this largely unchanged set of structural features and value-premises, a set of new guiding principles, characterised by properties of their own, emerged to fit the old administrative machinery. The single most important such innovation was a meticulous, detailed, systematic, and explicit regulation of the administrative apparatus, extended to the relationships obtaining within such apparatus, to those between the apparatus and its political environment, and to those between administrative agencies and individual citizens. This complex regulation assumed the form and status of positive law and developed into a self-contained legislation, guided by rules of its own. A peculiarly European institution was thus born, *i.e.*, the system of public and administrative law, regulating the skewed and hierarchical relationships taking place within the compass of sovereignty, and sharply distinguished from the body of civil law, which regulates relationships entered into by legal equals.

The system of public and administrative law thus emerged elaborated some central principles which define the relationship between bureaucracy and its socio-political environment — principles that characterise, so to speak, the external "slope" of public administration. The more detailed principles that guide administrative action – that characterise its internal "slope" – be they value-premises, standards of behavior, organisational charts, rules of procedure (the combined impact of which results in what I call the organisational properties of the bureaucratic structure), can be seen as practical and operational applications of those central principles.

In the following paragraphs an attempt is made succintly to characterise the central principles of legal-rational administration. Then a brief analysis of its more detailed and operational traits is presented.

a) *Administrative impartiality, i.e.*, the idea that administrative action *is* politically neutral (Gerber, 1880; Laband, 1894). The principle has exhibited, and still exhibits, great vitality: legal doctrine still treats it as an *is* proposition; public opinion treats it at least as an *ought* proposition; bureaucrats on the whole deem it to be relevantly descriptive of their role. Historically, this principle has been crucial in supporting legislation introducing job-security for civil servants, and in arguing that a professional bureaucracy can alternately serve with equanimity political parties supporting different ideologies and sponsoring different programmes and policies.

b) *The purely executive role of public administration i.e.*, the idea that the law – the authoritative decisions formulated by political parties and the elective agencies expressed by political parties – embodies *per se* the substance of administrative action. Bureaucrats merely need apply logical deductions to the law, and administrative decisions will ensue from it automatically. In other words, we have here the hypostatisation of public administration as a passive machine, as an instrument in the hands of its political master.

As we pointed out at the outset, modern political science has shown both principles to be empirically untenable. Now there is consensus in the literature on the fact that civil servants are active in policy-making, enjoy a quasi-monopolistic control over information, act to strengthen their already strong position by exercising discretionary controls over policy-execution, and engage in all these actions either representing their own values or siding with fractional groups and views. Elsewhere I have discussed at some length the historical and epistemological conditions that explain why the two principles emerged in 19th Century Continental Europe (Freddi, 1982). Here, it will be sufficient to outline them succinctly pointing out how, due to those conditions, the twin principles of administrative neutrality and instrumentality constituted valid and realistic descriptions of what was actually taking place; that is, public administration *was*, in fact, both neutral and instrumental. The Continental legal theorists who first formulated the theory of separation did so by abstracting and conceptualising the basic trends of the administrative state that was then consolidating.

The (now mythical and then factual) principle of neutrality was a consequence the following factors: (a) a political suffrage limited to the upper middle classes; (b) a representative assembly seating well-to-do politicians basically agreed on fundamentals and free from head-on ideological combat; (c) a higher civil service recruited from the same social strata from which those members of parliament who formed the ruling elite had also come (indeed, there was much horizontal mobility between the political establishment and the higher civil service). It should not be surprising then, that such conditions of social, economic, and cultural homogeneity engendered a happy propensity to agree, and an excellent rapport between politics and administration that could correctly be described as administrative impartiality or neutrality.

The factors behind the principle of administrative instrumentality are equally compelling: the period analysed by the legal theorists was that of the *laissez faire* economy. The state did not interfere in the workings of society and of the economy. It was a state of regulation, and not of intervention; a guarantor of order and a referee, not an activist agency. No wonder again that, to a large extent, the functions performed by public administration could correctly be described in logical-deductive terms, as a form of syllogism not dissimilar from that observed in the work of a judge acting as the interpreter of a codified system of law.

Thus, professional administrators performed their functions neutrally and instrumentally not because the law ordered them to do so, but thanks to the socio-political and economic circumstances that denoted the 19th Century administrative state. The bureaucracy of that state had acquired the nature of a servo-mechanism: it behaved, to use a metaphor coined by Herbert Kaufman, like an 'internalized gyroscope'. *Political parties and elected officials, in sum, could avail themselves of an administrative apparatus comparable to an efficient automaton completely identified with the public goals then being pursued*; as a consequence, our conditions for party government — control over administration and problem-solving capacity — were essentially met.

As was pointed out in Section II, basic features of contemporary political systems, notably mass democracy and the welfare state, have practically obliterated those conditions. On the one hand, no longer does one observe cultural, social and ideological homogeneity between civil servants and political personnel, and thus no longer can one maintain that bureaucracies are naturally representative of the political class (Kingsley, 1944; Subramaniam, 1967; Meier, 1975) and hence, led to behave in a neutral fashion. On the other hand, the task domains which characterise the bureaucracy of the welfare state and of economic intervention cannot be satisfactorily performed *via* the deductive processes of legal-rational administration.

We should, nevertheless, take note that the twin principles of neutrality and instrumentality still hold much currency and continue to be the backbone of the institutional ideology of legal-rational administration, with important operational implications. Indeed, the organisational design and the procedural rules of legal-rational bureaucracy should be interpreted as structures that give body and concreteness to those central principles.

The key-words used so far in characterising the systematic goals of the *Rechtsstaat* are: certainty, predictability, reliability. Moderate liberalism was bent on erecting a state where the abuses, the capriciousness, and the corruption of despotic rule should not occur. Public administration is that component of the *Rechtsstaat* where this preoccupation is best in evidence; it is a system designed to insure maximum controllability. The socio-economic stance of 19th Century regimes greatly reinforced the systemic values of the polity: "The best government is the government which governs least". The paramount goal is the avoidance of undesirable events — such as waste and abuse — not the furtherance of positive objectives. In sum, we have what has been called the "limited" or "negative" state.

The standard legal doctrine definition of control is verification of whether a function has been performed according to preestablished rules. Keeping in mind this definition as well as the basic value-premise whereby the government pursues negative and/or limited goals, the structural and functional characteristics of 19th Century legal-rational bureaucracy fall into place very neatly. Very sketchily, such characteristics can be outlined thus:

a) the administrative process — that series of decisions and executions which begins with the identification of a policy objective (the law) and eventuates in the accomplishment of the same objective — is segmented according to a sequence of acts, issued individually by the several administrative subunits (ministries, boards, agencies, departments) which, on the basis of their precisely defined competences, participate in the realisation of the final goal.

b) each such subunit performs its task as if it were, so to speak, a monad. It guards jealously its own area of competence, and it is not expected, in the performance of its task, to take into consideration the interests and sub-objectives which constitute the competence of other subunits. In other words, the institutional objective aimed for here can be characterised as the pursuit of accountability *via* the avoidance of organisational redundancy and the accentuation of formal controls.

c) the assumption is that administration is a self-propelling and self-contained machine. The logic of legal rationality calls for "each role to be perfected, each bureau to be exactly delimited, each linkage to articulate unfailingly, and to produce one interlocking system, one means-ends chain which possesses the absolutely minimum number of links, and which culminates at a central point" (Landau, 1969: 354).

d) all these characteristics and traits are reinforced by the judicial and formalistic bent of mind of the civil servants, whose professional socialisation is largely in the field of legal interpretation (*Juristen Monopol*).

To sum up: the impressive work of administrative rationalisation carried out in 19th Century Continental Europe ended up by fusing and enmeshing two fundamental organisational properties. The first — which, as we have seen, has both a preindustrial and preliberal matrix — is hierarchic centralisation; superiors provide exact value premises to their subordinates who, accordingly, do the same for their subordinates, and so forth. The result is a "transitive and asymmetrical structure giving rise to the chain of command and compliance" (Landau and Stout, 1979: 159).

The second has reemphasised the drive for centralising authority in order to anchor the legal-rational notion of accountability: it is based on the assumption that it is possible to formulate unambiguous value premises and precise goals which, in turn, lead to a "formal deductive system, synoptic in character, and entirely consistent". (Landau and Stout, 1979: 153).

Self-consistency, then, is the paramount value in legal-rational bureaucracy, the core of its institutional ideology. This engenders a circular process causing immobility in decision modes — what Crozier (1963) has called the "bureaucratic vicious circle" — for the performance standards and norms of behaviour enforced by the formal organization derive from the values crystallized in the bureaucratic ideology.

This circular process not only induces decisional immobility, but also stability of performance criteria through time, regardless of external stimuli. As Blau has argued cogently (1964: 270—331), organisational ideology is supported by two factors: legitimating values and the process of institutionalisation. Legitimating values buttress authority, functioning as media of organisation and thus extending the scope of organised control; they are enforced through the socialisation of participants. Institutionalisation, in turn, through a set of formalised procedures, perpetuates organising principles and internalised cultural values which, again, are transmitted *via* processes of organisational socialisation.

These are the reasons which prompt and reinforce the suggestion that studies of the political attitudes of bureaucrats (the end-result of political socialisation) are not likely to shed much light on decision modes and policy performance. More insight can be gained by concentrating on institutional, organisational, and professional socialisation. And this is exactly why so much attention is here devoted to structural constraints.

V. Synchronic Conditions of Bureaucratic Performance: Administrative Rationality or Administrative Rationalities?

What has been said so far points indirectly to the fact that the task of public administration is now not only quantitatively much larger, but qualitatively different. A formalistic, logical-deductive orientation to administrative decision-making was tenable in a context exclusively concerned with the maintenance of law and order. Now it has become a fiction. A managerial aptitude rather than a judicial bent of mind is needed. When public agencies are concerned with social welfare, managing the economy, actually running large industrial concerns, top civil servants are daily confronted with decision-situations of a pragmatic-inductive nature. Cost-benefit considerations, choices between technically alternative solutions, nearly always leading to different political consequences, bargaining with clienteles and special constituencies are but a few examples of situations likely to occur in the normal course of administrative activity. No matter how detailed, well framed, and up-to-the-point legislation may be, it certainly cannot provide concrete guidance for solving such complex problems.

Two immediate consequences can briefly be indicated here. On the one hand, the more "modern" functions of the state have made it inevitable that higher civil servants play a central role in actual policy making. On the other hand, the persistence through time of the fiction whereby what the civil service does is merely instrumental execution of what political parties and elected officials, chosen according to partisan criteria, have decided creates a smoke-screen which keeps the level of awareness of what actually happens very low, and hence reduces the probability that relevant and indispensable controls be effectively exercised.

The search for a streamlined predictability and reliability of administrative processes had been prompted by essentially negative considerations; in other words, they can be construed as an expedient contrived to prevent abuses, waste, and corruption. Legality, not flexibility, systemic maintenance, not operational effectiveness, had been the objectives. Within these limitations, the design had been successful.

Under modern conditions, however, the reverse is true. The series of bottlenecks designed in the 19th Century have now become strangleholds on the 20th Century functions. Delays, inability to adapt, failure to spend allocated moneys before the planned deadlines, ritualism, buck-passing, and displacement of goals are some of the results.

The conclusion of all this is then obvious: legal-rational bureaucracies are incompatible with the functions of the welfare state and of governments concerned with managing the economy. Both administrative value-premises and organisational techniques must be radically overhauled if a new compatibility between administrative structure and policy-functions is to be engendered.

In order to put in perspective the requirements of an interventionist administration operating in a democratic context, and so to augment the possibility that the party government model and its prerequisites be realised, an investigation of the organisational properties that such an administration ought to possess is indispensable. This is best done by contrasting them with the properties of legal-rational bureaucracy. At the outset, and painting with a broad brush, one should note that the limited, negative state of the 19th Century performed authoritative functions mediated by the attributes of *certainty* and predictability, whilst the contemporary interventionist and pluralist state deals with *uncertain* and *problematical* situations and it does so allegedly guided by criteria of effectiveness and responsiveness.

Now, if the functional load of contemporary Western European governments is characterised by situations that are both uncertain and problematical, it follows that all policies, by their nature, lie in the future tense and are, therefore, *hypothetical* (Landau, 1973; and Landau and Stout, 1979).[4] Their results then, can be defined as outcomes on a test of adequacy of policy, which is like saying that policies are solutions to problems. If a policy fails to produce the specified outcome, this may arise because:

a) it is simply an incorrect hypothesis
b) it has not been executed properly – i. e., its implementation is weak, which means that in its initial formulation it was incomplete –
c) it was misinterpreted, which means that those charged with its execution, changed it, either unintentionally or willfully.

In almost every area of the governmental scope of action, therefore, we observe a competition of solutions with respect to a given situational problem. This is why we quite often observe heated and vigorous debates on all sorts of policy issues. In only one area of policy do we rarely, if ever, have explicit discussion; in the area of organisational policy. It would seem that, in most cases, the heroic assumption of Taylorism is made the *one best way* to organise is already known.

That there can be, or must be, different organisational structures for different types of problem situations, escapes notice. The basic form (as emergent in absolutist Europe and explicitly rationalised and politically tamed in the 19th Century) remains virtually universal: the hierarchic pyramid, generalism, the twin myths of functional omnicompetence and of hierarchic omniscience, the search for predictability and certainty. There are variations on the theme, but they are usually minor. The fundamental (legal-rational, Weberian) assumption remains that all we need in order to make a correct decision in the single case is logical deduction from the law.

Since, as was affirmed above, policies are hypotheses, organisations which either make and/or administer policy must be sensitive and must

[4] For the arguments developed in this section I am much indebted to Martin Landau: not only to his published work, but also to the great stimulation received in discussion with him. However, I apply or develop some of his concepts to situations and according to criteria that are quite different from those encountered in his work, and that he might not approve of. Thus, the responsibility for such applications and developments is solely mine.

respond to error. A central concept must be emphasised here: that contemporary bureaucracies deal in knowledge, that their work is empirical and experimental, and that it has been made thus by governmental intervention in the economy and in society. Administrative activities are not any longer simply matters of law; they are also, and predominantly, matters of fact. If bureaucracies are not organically aware of this, and are then organised so as to preclude appreciation of fact, they are, as a consequence, incapable of detecting error (Landau, 1973; Landau and Stout, 1979; Wildavsky, 1972).

Let us go back to the notion whereby all organisations are systems of knowledge. Presumptively, the knowledge necessary (i. e., of technical instrumentation and cause-effect relations) is contained in an organisational structure: in the law which "structures" it, and in its rules and regulations which, according to the perspective developed here must be viewed as decision rules – rules which provide solutions to problems. An organisation design is therefore an empirical claim, namely that its structure contains the knowledge necessary to accomplish its tasks.

If we conceive of the organisational structure as a body of knowledge, then its operational outcomes are a function of that knowledge. If an organisation had been constituted with perfect knowledge, it would mean that it would never be surprised: save for the equivalent of measurement errors, everything would proceed as expected, and nothing would be problematical. Thus, surprise, deviation from expectation and anomaly mean that the organisation has less than perfect knowledge (Landau, 1973), and that, as a consequence, an error has been made.

In a well-run organisation, the appearance of error signals an organisational (that is, structural) inadequacy. Steps are then taken to find a correction. Constant corrections mean that an organisation is continually modifying structure so as to reduce the probability of error. When this occurs over long periods of time, the organisation takes on the properties of its task environment and ceases to resemble its original structure. If, in fact, an organisation system created a very long time ago (as in the case of many branches of Continental administration) retains its basic original structural features, it either has had perfect knowledge (which is impossible) or it has not learned very much from experience.

Returning to a quotation from Landau and Stout (1979: 154) "a perfect knowledge system takes the form of an abstract calculus. As in classical mechanics, it is hierarchical and pyramidal, asymmetrical and transitive". Through processes of logical deduction, one moves down the logical chain. If the system is purely formal, it has no empirical content: therefore, a perfection can be attained. It is, however, a formal or logical perfection. If, on the contrary, it has empirical content, then deductions must be tested – verified or falsified. The greater the power of the system, the less the probability of surprise; the less the probability of surprise, the less the error. In other words, events occur as predicted. If outcomes occur that are unexpected, the system is immediately re-examined for error and save for measurement or test error, they are corrected.

As was shown in the previous sections, virtually all classical bureaucracies exhibit the form of this kind of knowledge system: they are pyramidal, hierarchical, and therefore asymmetrical and transitive. A structure distinguished by such attributes is naturally led to assume that near perfect knowledge is available and, universally, this is a case of ***institutionalized self-deception*** (Landau and Stout, 1979: 155). Bureaucracies in general, bureaucracies involved in social and economic intervention in particular, simply cannot be characterised by such a type of knowledge. So long as they maintain this fiction, then their procedures, rules, and regulations are purely formal, devoid of empirical power, and problem solving capacity. Consistency – as was noted in section IV.B. – becomes their modal pattern of operations, regardless of stimulus, and thus we observe mechnical rule following and displacement of goals.

All that has been said in the last few paragraphs impinges on the notion of administrative rationality, and it leads to a conclusion: in the same way that it is incorrect to assume the existence of one best way to organise, so it is equally incorrect to assume that there is one best administrative rationality.

It is, therefore, important to distinguish among types of rationality, so as to avoid the risk of concentrating all the attention on just one definition, such as that of legal rationality, or on that close relative, the rationality of efficiency, as defined by economists of the neo-classical persuasion, and generally cast in terms of input-output ratios (Buchanan and Tollison, 1972; Downs, 1967; Niskanen, 1971; Bréton, 1974; Tullock, 1963; Peacock, 1979). As we shall see shortly, we may as well speak of the rationality of effectiveness, defined as the ratio of expected outcome to actual outcome. Or we may, under conditions of conflict, speak of the rationality of acceptability. (Lindblom, 1959; March and Olsen, 1976; Wildavsky, 1966). What is necessary at this point is to make clear that rationality is a systemically bounded concept: what is rational under one set of circumstances is irrational under others.

The importance of this fact has particularly to do with the concept of legal rationality cast mostly in terms of certainty, consistency, predictability, reliability, syllogistic logicality (and which, as we have seen, is frequently assumed to be the only type of modern rationality). Now, legal rationality must be understood in terms of a two-fold perspective. Following Max Weber, legal rationality is first to be understood in contrast to tradition and charisma: it refers to a set of behavioural constraints that differ from the latter. And its main point is not just directed (as the ideology of the ***Rechtsstaat*** would have us believe) against arbitrary action by governmental authorities, for there is little that is arbitrary in traditional, percedentbound systems. Rather, and most importantly, legal rationality has to be understood in terms of providing an objective basis or standard of justification for actions taken by bureaucrats. Hence the establishment of sets of rules and regulations that are technically warranted. However, what is technically warranted is not synonymous with efficiacy and certainty (the objectives predominantly pursued by legal rational administration). It can also be based on criteria of effectiveness and criteria of acceptability.

Distinguishing rationalities relates directly to distinguishing decisions. In raising the question of organisational policy, the point is that different situations are different precisely because their modal patterns of decision differ. Hence, for different types of situations, we need organisational structures that permit the most "rational" types of decisions. What is required now is to establish a typology of decisions as clearly as we can so that each subset is easily identifiable.

The seminal contributions of Simon (1947; 1960) are, of course, crucially important in this respect. As is well known, Simon characterises an administrative decision in a modernised and secularised context as a function of both fact and value. In traditional and sacred contexts, one can find examples of decisional situations which do not admit of fact as a legitimating basis for decisions. There, a factual challenge is perceived as deviation from dogma, and as deserving suppression and sanction.

This peculiarity, however, is not limited to traditional and presecular societies only. In fact – as we have seen – Western bureaucracies too can take on this property, when, *e.g.*, they root themselves in decision-rules which have become a dogma (certainty, legality) and, therefore, guard against challenges of fact. Needless to say, organisations which exhibit these modes of decision are incapable of detecting error and of effecting corrections, and thus are ill-fitted to cope with the task domains introduced by public intervention into society and in the economy.

A modern, technically based organisation should exhibit quite different characteristics: it should not preclude value judgments while simultaneously employing factual warrants in establishing and justifying its decisions. Dogma should have no place in such an administrative system,[5] only error. Error would signal the need for correction and an organisation built on this principle should devote considerable amounts of its resources to the task of correction.

Keeping in mind that three types of administrative rationality have been distinguished (efficiency and/or certainty, effectiveness, and acceptability), and using Simon's basic formulation, we can now establish a decision matrix, which further clarifies decision types:

[5] Probably, it is not a coincidence that in the technical jargon of Continental jurists, legal doctrine is sometimes referred to as "dogmatics".

F \ V	+	−
+	A Syllogistic Programmed Synoptic Computational Algorithimic ↓ *Authoritative decisions*	B Bargaining Negotiation Trade-off ↓ *Responsive or acceptable decisions*
−	C Pragmatic Experimental Heuristic Incremental ↓ *Effective decisions*	

On the F axis, Facts are to be understood in terms of knowledge of cause-effect relations, of instrumentation, of process laws; in a more directly administrative language, they refer to organisational means. Where a + appears, the knowledge necessary to achieve a goal exists. Otherwise, it does not; organisational means are inadequate to the tests.

On the V axis, Values are to be understood as motivational, as setting up drive-states or predispositions which give rise to organisational goals. A + means the goal consensus exists; there is agreement and organisational goals have been unambiguously defined. A − means lack of agreement and/or ambiguously defined goals.

This discussion of alternative operational definitions of administrative rationality can be concluded with a few interpretative comments concerning the figure presented above. Cell A accommodates legal-rational bureaucracy as well as the rationality of efficiency[6]: it is the locus where decisions of a

[6] Placing these two concepts (legal rationality and the rationality of efficiency) under the same label might cause some surprise in view of their largely separate histories in the literature. The impression, though, is likely to vanish if we concentrate our

logical-deductive nature are made, whose validity is a function of the system of norms and/or parameters from which they issue. Their cornerstone is codified law. When quite some time after the administrative structures having these properties had been erected, governments began to intervene in the social and economic sectors, an important phenomenon became evident.

Many of the new task-domains and decisional situations which were thus assigned to public administration are characterised by internal logics of their own, be they those of economics, of technology, of social welfare. What they have in common is a high empirical content, which means that satisfactory decisions can be made only after careful experimentation and repeated testing (cf. cell C). The point is well illustrated, from different angles, by such authors as Lindblom, Allison, March & Olsen. In sum, policies have acquired here the nature of hypotheses and the bureaucrats who had been trained to think of themselves as deductive logicians have had to tackle problems usually faced by empirical technicians.

At the same time, governments began more and more frequently to act as brokers, mediators, articulators, trying to process the diverse and contradictory demands issuing from pluralistic and mass-democratic societies. (This is the case in cell B). The degree of authoritativeness of governmental action decreased markedly). Traditional *überparteilich* civil servants were faced with the task of advocacy, calling for political responsiveness and an aptitude for compromise.

In some political systems new structures, both administrative and normative, were erected to deal with these new functions. In other political systems, notably those with entrenched and powerful legal-rational bureaucracies, the opposite trend has been observed: the new functions were forced into the old structures. The decisional situations located in cells B and C, were treated according to the criteria postulated in cell A.

Management — that is the approach to decision-making that best sums up the contents of cells B and C — was equated with control, an approach perfectly suited to the decisional situations described in cell A. Unfortunately, management and control are terms inversely related to each other. If a situation *can be controlled*, it means that it is not problematical. The assumption that problematical situations can be controlled has led to the lamentable situations that have been illustrated in our discussion of legal rationality: management problems that are overwhelmed by premature programming and premature control systems (Landau and Stout, 1979: 149).

attention on the organisational properties which are associated with the types of rationality being discussed. For pioneering remarks about the close relationship between Weberian legal rationality and the underpinnings of the Scientific Management school, cf. March, Simon, and Guetzkow, 1958).

To sum up: administrative institutions cast in the legal-rational mould "tend (statistically speaking) to commit Type II errors: accepting as true hypotheses that are false". (Landau and Stout, 1979: 216).

VI. Party Government and Bureaucratic Effectiveness and Responsiveness: A Framework for Comparative Analysis

As was stated at the outset, two conditions must exist for the model of party government to be realised: control over the bureaucracy by elected officials and an administration capable of a satisfactory or, at least acceptable policy performance.

The discussion developed thus far has shown that in order for these conditions to obtain, bureaucracy must be denoted by the two characteristics of responsiveness (defined as readiness to pursue policy-goals in accord with the values prevailing in the political system), and of effectiveness (defined as a satisfactory or acceptable ratio of expected outcomes to actual outcomes).

Historically, two alternative strategies have been employed to bring about those desirable characteristics: on the one hand, the American spoils system which, while bestowing on elected officials a capacity of total control over the bureaucracy, led to disastrous consequences in terms of effectiveness — let alone graft and corruption — and prompted Wilson to suggest that the American system of government, if it wanted to become effective, would have needed to create an administrative system modeled after that of the Emperor of Germany. On the other hand, a politically neutral and technically competent civil service, that is legal-rational bureaucracy (by and large, the above mentioned administration of the Emperor of Germany).

In the preceding sections, a good deal of attention has been devoted both to the socio-political characteristics of European civil servants of the late 19th and very early 20th centuries, and to the organisational properties of European bureaucracies during the same period.

So far as the socio-political characteristics of the civil service are concerned, we have seen that, for reasons both cultural and sociological, higher civil servants tended to be attitudinally homogeneous *vis-à-vis* elected officials. This happy coincidence made for continuous decisional processes between the political and administrative classes, so that the latter performed rather like an automatic servo-mechanism (hence the idea of neutrality).

At the same time, the organisational properties of the bureaucratic apparatus proved to be admirably fitted to the task domains of the administration of the limited or negative state of law and order and of the *laissez faire* economy. They were made obsolete and/or insufficient when the task domain of the bureaucracy came to include interventionist policies. Here the central point concerns modes of decision-making. More specifically, the argument was developed in the following manner: a) administrative rationality, that is the mould of decision-making, is the function and product of organisational structure and procedural norms; b) different functional task domains call for different decision modes, which will obtain only in the context of an appropriate administrative rationality; c) satisfactory performance is a function of a positive correlation between task domains and administrative rationalities, of which three can be distinguished:

1) legal rationality, conducive to synoptic, syllogistic and deductive processes leading to *authoritative* decisions in a context where goals are unambiguously defined and means are fully adequate;
2) the rationality of intervention, involving incremental and pragmatic processes, leading to *effective* decisions, (provided that the adequacy of organisational means is constantly tested empirically);
3) the rationality of advocacy of, and/or intermediation among interests, involving processes of bargaining and negotiation, conducive to *acceptable* decisions whose main objective is the clarification of ambiguous and uncertain goals.

It was then argued that the unsatisfactory policy performance plaguing contemporary political systems stems from the fact that both the functions of intervention and those of intermediation have been forced into the mould of legal rationality – assumed as the only and one best way to make decisions – while the task of erecting administrative structures capable of accommodating alternative rationalities has frequently been neglected, though to varying degrees in different political systems. The consequences of this situation have been described: ritualism, rule-following, formalism, premature planning, all leading to the conclusion that "a bureaucratic organisation cannot correct its behaviour by learning from its errors" (Crozier, 1963: 187); an organisation, in other words, not only ineffective, but unresponsive as well, for the relevant knowledge to run it has become a monopoly of its participants, less and less controllable by its alleged political masters.

The argument developed in this essay, and particularly in section V., is that the task domain of the modern state has caused accepted notions of bureaucratic responsiveness and policy performance (derived from the 19th century conceptions of neutrality and instrumentality) to become obsolete; and that they can be rendered adequate to the complex task domains of our times by incorporating and appropriately structuring the forms of rationality outlined in our decision matrix. The main hypothesis here is that to the extent that an administrative structure is capable of incorporating the "modern" rationalities, the probability will increase that the basic conditions of party government will be approximated.

How could one propose to test this hypothesis? By starting from the observation that the structural features of the bureaucracies of different political systems are different and by investigating which structural features are more likely either to incorporate those forms of administrative rationality that are associated with an effective policy performance, or to facilitate those processes of socialisation that are associated with bureaucratic responsiveness.

As was noted previously, responsiveness and effectiveness, though they are closely linked, are not in a unilinear relationship: neither could be predicted from the other. Responsiveness is, to a sometimes large extent, a function of attitudes and sociological factors which are antecedent to processes of institutional socialisation, whereas effectiveness is mostly a function of structural variables and organisational socialisation. Thus, responsiveness ought to be gauged with indicators sensitive not only to structural variables, but also to attitudinal and exo-organisational variables.

On the basis, then, of the argument developed so far, a framework for comparative classification and analysis can be constructed. Its aim is the assessment of the extent to which two dependent variables (the conditions of realisability of the party government model) are affected by a set of independent variables. The two dependent variables are: effectiveness of policy performance (or problem-solving capacity) and bureaucratic responsiveness (which obtains when the bureaucracy exerts a power which is neither independent from nor uncontrolled by elected officials).

A tentative checklist of independent variables is presented here. Some are of a structural nature, and some are attitudinal. They are displayed as *continua*. The hypothesis formulated here is that the trends implicit in the captions itemised in the left hand column are associated with both low effectiveness and low responsiveness, pointing to modes of decision of oligarchic legal-rational bureaucracies, whereas the captions that can be read in the right hand column indicate trends associated with high effectiveness (the first four) and high responsiveness (the last three), pointing to modes of decision that incorporate the "modern" rationalities.

Party Government

1. Hierarchic centralisation	Decentralisation
2. Structural diffuseness	Differentiation
3. Generalism	Functional specificity
4. Monopoly of knowledge (e. g., adm. law)	Pluralistic knowledge
5. Bureaucratic ethos (localism)	Outside reference groups (cosmopolitanism)

6. Socio-political particularism	Representativeness
7. Attitudes incongruent with political system's values	Congruent

A few concluding comments will, it is hoped, clarify the implications of this framework for comparative analysis. Hierarchic centralisation typifies those administrations where nearly all decisions, both substantive and instrumental, are made by small and highly cohesive groups of officials, with no leeway left to intermediate executives. Here the possibility of experimental and pragmatic feedbacks is minimal, and self-corrections are slow and rarely resorted to, as in the French case (Crozier, 1963) and, as was pointed out by the Fulton Report, in the British case as well. In such situations, moreover, the probability is high that an unsatisfactory distinction is made between policy-making and policy-execution, with negative consequences both on efficiency and on the ability of cabinet ministers effectively to control administrative action. Both the American situation, where one sees ample decisional powers granted to the men on the spot (Corson and Paul, 1966) and the West German experience (Mayntz and Scharpf, 1975; Mayntz, 1978), where the *Länder* do over 90 per cent of the administrative work, with the central government departments engaged with the larger questions of policy, illustrate the opposite trend.

The notions of structural diffusion and generalism (as contrasted with structural differentiation and functional specificity) were discussed in detail in Section III. Among the largest Western political systems, Italy and Britain seem to score lowest on these dimensions with, however, an important difference; Italian officials, being nearly all trained in the law, *exacerbate* ritualism and premature programming, while the members of the administrative class are much more flexible and adaptable, moving frequently, as they do, among the great departments and having been chosen for qualities of intellect that enable them to understand policy (Fry, 1969). The American and the French cases exemplify, even though in different ways, the opposite tendency: in both systems, administrative leaders are the carriers of diversified types of relevant talents. They are professional specialists and thus are capable of bringing different and necessary perspectives to bear upon decision-making (Corson and Paul, 1966; Suleiman, 1978).

The next two variables (monopoly of knowledge vs. pluralistic knowledge, and bureaucratic ethos vs. outside reference groups) illustrate mutually reinforcing dimensions. The potential of a monopolistic control over the relevant knowledge to run the bureaucracy is typical — as Weber observed — of legal-rational administration. In the Italian case and, to a somewhat lesser extent, in the German case, higher civil servants are the stern custodians and the formalistic interpreters of legal rules used as standards for decision and evaluation, practically reducing to nil the possibility of intelligent scrutiny by outsiders. The opposite applies where different technical and professional outlooks are observed: there, as in the American case (Aberbach *et al.*, 1981) and, to a less intense degree, in France (Suleiman, 1974), one looks at a veritable market place of options and counteroptions, where decisions are reached *via* confrontation of alternative policy solutions. In turn, where a monopoly of knowledge obtains, we tend to observe also the particular form of secrecy and social cohesion referred to as bureaucratic ethos, characterised by localism, or unilateral identification with the traditional values of the institution (Merton, 1957; Gouldner, 1957). Where, on the contrary, civil servants are prevalently guided by professional values, active not only in bureaucracy, but also in the societal environment; where, in other words, we have cosmopolitanism (Merton, 1957; Gouldner, 1957), whose reference groups operate outside the bureaucracy, the probability will be higher that effective controls be exercised and access to the administration be granted more easily to concerned individuals and interest groups.

The last two variables (socio-political particularism vs. representativeness, and attitudes incongruent vs. congruent with the political system's values) are those which have constituted, so far, the main concern of behavioural studies investigating the motivational factors of administrative action. Where the bureaucracy as a social group is incapable of representing either society or the political class — the notable case here is France (Suleiman, 1978) and, to a lesser degree Italy (Aberbach et al., 1981; Putnam, 1973) — the likelihood is great that the higher civil service is a semiautonomous and unresponsive (to party government) political agency (Suleiman, 1974), whereas the opposite is true where a good fit exists between administrators and politicians, as in Britain (Kingsley, 1944) or between bureaucracy and society as in the United States (Bendix, 1949; Aberbach et al., 1981).[7]

In conclusion, the dimensions listed in the left hand column constitute the main headings of an ideal type of bureaucracy which is both incapable of tackling the task domains of contemporary political systems, and undermines the possibility of effective party government. By contrast, those dimensions that are listed in the right hand column illustrate a totally alternative ideal type. *Mutatis mutandis*, an administration thus characterised would recreate the conditions that we have seen to have obtained in 19th Century Europe: the bureaucracy would act largely like an automatic servomechanism, like a gyroscope entirely identified with both its task domains

[7] This framework is partially grounded on a conceptualisation presented in my earlier work (Freddi, 1968), developed, however, solely on the basis of an analysis of structural traits of bureaucratic institutions, and not of historically explained organisational properties.

and the values prevailing in the political environment. Party government would be in effective, not nominal, control and, in the context of this updated version of the policy-administration dichotomy, could count on an instrument capable of producing acceptable solutions to policy problems.[8]

Bibliography

ABERBACH, J. D., R. D. PUTNAM and B. A. ROCKMAN (1981) *Bureaucrats and Politicians in Western Democracies*. Cambridge, Mass.: Harvard University Press.

ALLISON, G. (1971) *Essence of Decision*. Boston: Little Brown.

APPLEBY, P. H. (1949) *Policy and Administration*. Alabama: University of Alabama Press.

ARMSTRONG, J. A. (1973) *The European Administrative Elite*. Princeton: Princeton University Press.

BARNARD, C. (1946) "Functions and Pathology of Status Systems in Formal Organizations," in W. F. Whyte, (ed.) *Industry and Society*. New York: McGraw Hill.

BENDIX, R. (1949) *Higher Civil Servants in American Society*. Boulder, Colo.: University of Colorado Press.

BLAU, P. (1964) *Exchange and Power in Social Life*. New York: Wiley.

BRAYBROOKE, D. and C. E. LINDBLOM (1963) *A Strategy for Decision*. New York: The Free Press.

BRETON, A. (1974) *The Economic Theory of Representative Government*. Chicago: University of Chicago Press.

BUCHANAN, J. and R. TOLLISON (1972) *Theory of Public Choice*. Ann Arbor, Mich.: University of Michigan Press.

CORSON, J. J. and R. S. PAUL (1966) *Men at the Top: Filling Key Posts in the Federal Service*. Baltimore: Johns Hopkins University Press.

CROZIER, M. (1963) *Le Phénomène Bureaucratique*. Paris: Editions du Seuil.

CROZIER, M., S. P. HUNTINGTON and J. WATANUKI (1975) *The Crisis of Democracy*. New York: New York University Press.

[8] The comments briefly developed here are impressionistic and merely exemplify possible lines of research. Neither the empirical referents that have been mentioned nor the literature that has been cited could be described as even remotely comprehensive. Continuing in the same tentative and sketchy vein, a classification of the bureaucracies operating in the largest Western political systems might look as follows: the Italian bureaucracy would score low (or lowest) on all seven variables, whereas American administration would be located at the opposite end. The French system would score low on variables 1, 5, 6 and 7 and rather high on the others. The German system would score high on 1, 2, 6 and 7, low on 3, 4 and 5. The British system would score low on 1 and 3, somewhere in the middle on 4 and 5, and high on the others. In conclusion, the American bureaucracy would come out as the one most approximating the conditions of control by elected officials and of acceptable problem solution capacity. It is the most fragile bureaucracy in terms of its probability of enjoying autonomous power and, at the same time, the most flexible and adaptable from an institutional point of view, having been capable of incorporating the professional talents and technical properties that continuously emerge in societal and organisational development.

Downs, A. (1967) *Inside Bureaucracy*. Boston: Little Brown.

Eckstein, H. (1971) "The Evaluation of Political Performance: Problems and Dimensions," 2 *Sage Professional Papers in Comparative Politics* 1.

Freddi, G. (1968) *L'Analisi Comparata di Sistemi Burocratici Pubblici*. Milan: Giuffrè.

— (1982) *Historical Constraints on Administrative Performance in Legal-rational Bureaucracies*. Berkely: Studies in Public Organization, Institute of Governmental Studies.

— (1982) "Vincoli Storico-Strutturali sulla Prestazione delle Burocrazie Legali-Razionali," 2 *Rivista Italiana di Scienza della Politica*, 2: 183–212.

Fry, G. K. (1969) *Statesmen in Disguise: The Changing Role of the Administrative Class of the British Home Service 1853-1966*. London: Macmillan.

Gerber, von C. (1880) *Grundzüge des Deutschen Staatsrechts*. Aalen: Scientia Verlag.

Goodnow, F. J. (1900) *Politics and Administration*. New York: Russell & Russell.

Gouldner, A. W. (1957) "Cosmopolitans and Locals: Toward an Analysis of Latent Social Roles," 2 *Administrative Science Quarterly* 284.

Hayek, von F. (1944) *The Road to Serfdom*. Chicago: Chicago University Press.

Kaufman, H. (1967) *The Forest Ranger: A Study in Administrative Behavior*. Baltimore: Johns Hopkins University Press.

Kingsley, J. D. (1944) *Representative Bureaucracy*. Yellow Springs, Ohio: The Antioch Press.

Laband, P. (1894) *Das Staatsrecht des Deutschen Reiches*. Leipzig: Mohr.

Landau, M. (1969) "Redundancy, Rationality, and the Problem of Duplication and Overlap," 4 *Public Administration Review* 345.

Landau, M. (1973) "On the Concept of a Self-Correcting Organization," 6 *Public Administration Review* 533.

Landau, M. and R. Stout, Jr. (1979) "To Manage is not to Control: Or the Folly of Type II Errors," 1 *Public Administration Review* 148.

Lindblom, C. (1959) "The Science of Muddling Through," 1 *Public Administration Review* 29.

Lipset, S. M. (1950) *Agrarian Socialism*. Berkeley & Los Angeles: University of California Press.

March, J. G. and J. P. Olsen (1976) *Ambiguity and Choice in Organizations*. Bergen: Universitetsforlaget.

March, J. G., H. A. Simon and H. Guetzkow (1958) *Organizations*. New York: Wiley.

Mayntz, R. and F. W. Scharpf (1975) *Policy-Making in the German Federal Republic*. Amsterdam: Elsevier.

Mayntz, R. (1978) *Soziologie der Öffentlichen Verwaltung*. Heidelberg: C. F. Müller Juristischer Verlag.

Meier, K. J. (1975) "Representative Bureaucracy: An Empirical Analysis," 3 *American Political Science Review* 526.

Merton, R. K. (1957) "Patterns of Influence: Local and Cosmopolitan Influentials," in R. K. Merton (ed.), *Social Theory and Social Structure*. Glencoe, Ill.: Free Press.

Mises, von L. (1944) *Bureaucracy*. New Haven, Conn.: Yale University Press.

Neumann, F. L. (1942) *Behemoth*. New York: Oxford University Press.

Niskanen, W. (1971) *Bureaucracy and Representative Government*. Chicago: Aldine.

Peacock, A. (1979) *The Economic Analysis of Government*. London: St. Martin.

Putnam, R. D. (1973) "The Political Attitudes of Senior Civil Servants in Western Europe," 3 *British Journal of Political Science* 257.

Ranney, A. (1962) *The Doctrine of Responsible Party Government*. Urbana Ill.: University of Illinois Press.

Rose, R. (1977) *Governing and 'Ungovernability'. A Sceptical Inquiry*. Glasgow: Centre for the Study of Public Policy, University of Strathclyde.

SARTORI, G. (1976) *Parties and Party Systems.* Cambridge: Cambridge University Press.
SIMON, H. A. (1947) *Administrative Behavior.* New York: Macmillan.
– (1960) *The New Science of Management Decision.* New York: Harper.
STINCHCOMBE, A. L. (1964) "Social Structure and Organizations," in March, J. G. (ed.) *Handbook of Organizations.* Chicago: Rand McNally.
SUBRAMANIAM, V. (1967) "Representative Bureaucracy: A Reassessment," 4 *American Political Science Review* 1010.
SULEIMAN, E. N. (1974) *Politics, Power and Bureaucracy in France.* Princeton: Princeton University Press.
– (1978) *Elites in French Society.* Princeton: Princeton University Press.
THOMPSON, V. A. (1961) *Modern Organization.* New York: Knopf.
TULLOCK, G. (1963) *The Politics of Bureaucracy.* Chapel Hill, North Ca.: University of North Carolina Press.
WILDAVSKY, A. (1966) "The Political Economy of Efficiency," 4 *Public Administration Review* 302.
– (1972) The Self-Evaluating Organization. Presented at the National Conference of the American Society for Public Administration, New York (March 24).
WILDENMANN, R. (1981) *The Future of Party Government: A Research Project.* Florence: European University Institute, Department of Political and Social Science.
WILSON, W. T. (1887) "The Study of Administration," II *Political Science Quarterly* 197.
WRIGHT MILLS, C. (1956) *The Power Elite.* New York: Oxford University Press.

Chapter VI

Party Government and Democratic Reproducibility: The Dilemma of New Democracies

Giuseppe Di Palma

Contents

To quote myself, "ultimately, political parties are for governing."[1] Or are they? Under a minimal definition of parties the claim holds. What else are parties if not the quintessential mechanism for legal access to public office under conditions of mass democracy? But let us take a more ambitous definition of parties: one that looks at them as the main force affecting and therefore changing, when in power, what governments *latu sensu* do. It takes little to see that the definition no longer holds. What we have is no longer a definition but a hypothesis that admits variance: the fact of parties *in* government does not secure party government (not in the ambitious sense above).[2] I would venture further, and suggest that even when held as an ideal state, approached only in varying degrees by concrete parties, party government, unless scaled down to sense variation, holds little discriminant value.

Consider the following. If party government must entail no less than clear party preeminence over the affairs of the state, then Richard Rose is right in asserting that "only in a totalitarian society would one expect party government to reign absolutely" (Rose, 1969: 414). It takes a party that

[1] This is the opening line of Di Palma (1980b: 162).

[2] The distinction between parties in government and party government is in Sartori (1976:19). For the notion of variability in party government see Rose (1969).

incorporates the whole, in fact, a party that coincides with the state itself ... to run the state. If on the other hand, parties are parts – components of a plural system of parties, itself formally distinct from decisional institutions – then Rose is again right in pointing out how factually absurd (and normatively dangerous) it is to expect that a change in the governing parties will unilaterally achieve what party government *strictu sensu* ultimately implies: a full undoing of what the previous government did (Rose, 1980: 156). No democracy that intends to reproduce itself can and does tolerate such a level of uncertainty. The only fairly sure thing that a governing party changes is party-appointed government personnel. Almost unheard of is the case in which parties regularly replacing each other in government routinely change significant facets of the political or socioeconomic structure. Though there are and have been a few democracies whose parties do not see eye-to-eye on many constitutional and structural matters, there have been fewer still that have witnessed and none that has long withstood repeated rotations among such parties. More likely and tolerable is the case of parties coming into government with alternative sets of specific policies.[3] Yet, even here the distinctiveness of party platforms, the ability of governing parties to fulfill their pledges, as well as their ability to leave a significant partisan imprint over and above that of various state institutions and organised societal interests, are more often than not below the expectations of the party government model. And if we go by expectations, even the British party system, long considered the model's prototype, would not strictly fit it.[4]

To rescue the concept of party government for comparative purposes we must relax its most onerous requirements and expectations; something which, for the purposes of this essay, I can do by a mere sleight of hand: by advancing the banal truth that parties do make "some" difference after all, and in some cases more than others. The question I am now in a position to address in this essay is how much of a difference parties can make. As the discussion in the previous paragraph implies, there are two sides to the question: how much party government any particular system is capable of mustering and how much it can actually afford? The first side of the question is about instrumentalities. It takes part goverment as the proper arrangement for processing popular demands and holding government to accountability, and only inspects the ways and means to secure it. It is a side of party government which appears at first of the greatest relevance nowadays, when an alleged loss of party control over public

[3] The distinction between changes in personnel, policies and structures and its implications for patterns of government and opposition are discussed by Dahl (1966:332–47).

[4] This is Rose's conclusion (1969). For a less stringent assessment of the English case see Rose (1980).

policies in favor of other bureaucratic or societal agencies raises issues in many minds about democratic representativeness.

But the more intriguing side of the party government question, also in light of the alleged crisis, is in reality the second: if there are limits beyond which party government may threaten instead of assisting democratic *reproducibility* (I will dwell on that term in the next section) – if, that is, the ultimate value is not party government but democratic reproducibility – exploring those normative-behavioural upper limits is a task integral to and in fact preliminary to the study of the instrumentalities for party government. There have been democracies that have sacrificed the latter for the sake of reproducibility; others, on the contrary, have sought to enforce party government at great costs; and still other and luckier ones have reconciled party government with reproducibility without much of a serious problem. Why the difference? Why have some democracies been able to afford party government more than others? Thinking in terms of and understanding the reasons for the difference serves to touch upon questions of democratic theory and practice which a narrower focus on party government as the proper result of instrumental arrangements tends to miss. It serves in particular to address the very question of when and how instrumentalities for party government come into being, and to what extent they can be put to legitimate use.

My essay begins with a section devoted to the concept of democratic reproducibility. To stress its market and exchange features, and hence its delicate nature, I will contrast it to reproducibility in nondemocratic systems. A second and longer section follows in which I analyse the difficulties encountered by new democracies in reconciling party government with democratic reproducibility, as well as their responses to the predicament. I will employ a few scenarios of transition to democracy to demonstrate the most exemplary types of difficulties and responses. The scenarios – inspired by postwar transitions in Europe – look at the parties of a new democracy as only part of a larger and still forming *Herrschaftsorganisation* (to use the term employed by Rudolf Wildenmann, Richard Katz, and others in this volume). They therefore see the rise of party government as involving the ability of prospective governing parties to achieve legitimately a central position in society's emerging *Herrschaftsorganisation.*[5] Hence, finally, the scenarios prove to be a useful methodological tool to show that such an achievement is neither the simple product of free-willed institutional engineering, nor the product of objective and historically-given sociostructural preconditions, but is rather the product of a political contest requiring a constrained and time-bound political calculus. Why this is so I begin to explain in the coming section.

[5] Richard Katz, in this volume, speaks in this regard of "party governmentness," and defines it as a characteristic of the *Herrschaftsorganisation* of the wider society.

I. Reproducing Consent: Democracies and Nondemocracies

Democracy is a matter of consent and consent, though often durable, does not come free. It must be reproduced. That is why, above, I have spoken of reproducibility rather than simply consent, legitimacy, consensus, or some similar term. Reproducibility begins to convey what it takes; the operational side of consent. Let me add that the key to reproducibility is the political party, or better, the system of parties. Their plurality; the plurality of opinions and interests they variously transmit, mediate, package, and even deflect or label; their institutional separation from and yet their collective/competitive hold on government – these are the factors that explain why consent is required, why it does not come free, and why at the same time it is parties that *ultimately* reproduce consent (thus reproducing themselves) or arrest it.

By contrast, in a totalitarian or authoritarian regime the key agent of reproducibility is the state itself, or the party-state where it exists. This does not mean that matters of consent are irrelevant. But it does mean that since consent does not depend on the uncertainties of the political market (the survival or revival of such market would in fact threaten consent) reproducibility is less of a problem. It also means that, where consent fails and a political market begins to stir, force is strictly speaking still sufficient to preserve a nondemocratic order[6] – as well as being justifiable in the light of some principle of organic unity inherent in that order. A democracy, however, extracts consent from a competitive political market – a more aleatory process requiring replication. If consent fails, a democracy cannot live on force alone without eventually putting into question its own authenticity; it can justify force only as an emergency. It is finally less likely to muster force anyway, since ultimately support and sanction for its use must again come from a political market, which is however naturally prone to fall further apart on the issue.

Besides, what is democratic consent about? To answer the question is to underscore once more the calculus that is behind it. For consent is about the political market itself or nothing else. More precisely it is about what Przeworski (1980b) calls uncertainty – the uncertainty of political outcomes which naturally results from a competitive market with multiple arenas. Outcomes depend on both politico/institutional and socioeconomic positions, and the adoption of a competitive political market allows a democracy to prevent fixed and repetitive outcomes from such positions: winners always winning, losers always losing. Thus, by preventing a monopoly of politico/institutional positions and by institutional dispersion, democracy avoids two institutional sources of certainty about outcomes and winners which are typical of totalitarian/authoritarian regimes. At the same time,

[6] An elegant demonstration is in Przeworski (1980b).

by legalising equal access to institutional positions, and by deploying them to countervail socioeconomic positions, democracy also corrects the unequal effects of social and economic privilege. It is in sum the essence of political democracy that no single social or institutional formation should determine outcomes by monopolising and fusing institutions (a class-party state) or by its sheer social position (a *laissez-faire* capitalist class). But why should any group prefer the uncertainty of democracy — more precisely, why should it consent to be at times a loser? One answer often advanced by liberal-democratic thinkers is that consenting to lose is a condition for winning at other times (Dahl, 1970: 3-58).

However, the answer requires elaboration, for it is not the simple, rock-bottom, all-explaining answer that it sounds. To say that accepting to lose is a condition for winning is not to say that democracy is only the residual option, entered into by any collective actor if chances of winning all the time, that is under a different political order, are limited. First of all, there are political actors today who enter into democracy's bargain implicitly; i. e., without a calculus of the feasibility and personal advantages of other alternatives. They look at it as a multicentered positive-sum game, capable of producing and distributing surplus to all competitors, but more importantly they take its superiority with respect to other games as a matter that needs no self-interested demonstration. For them the democratic bargain is a natural and appropriate bias.[7] Second, even those political actors who may seem to us to be compelled toward democracy as a residual option may not always find or perceive the option as equally residual, unpalatable, and conditional: hence, the range and consistency of consent will vary. To give flesh to this point it is sufficient to reflect on concrete cases of democratic inauguration, following a prolonged period of dictatorship, and the response by former members of dictatorial coalitions. They suggest that, given certain conditions, even its inner core may find dictatorship expendable and democracy something more than a temporary retrenchment.[8]

There have been cases in which democracy materialised almost as an afterthought (the Second Spanish Republic), and cases in which it was inescapable (post-Nazi West Germany); cases in which the dictatorship remained largely cohesive to the bitter end (World War II Japan), and cases in which, by splitting, it put in motion democratisation (post-Salazar Portugal); cases in which entering into the democratic bargain was necessary

[7] This does not mean that such actors, once they enter into the bargain, may not engage in a contest over the exact definition of the bargain. But the contest will be time-bound. It will not be resumed unless, as indicated in the text, a tolerable range of expected outcomes is violated.

[8] We like to think of democracy as fragile. It is time to reflect on the internal fragility of nondemocratic orders as well. Along these lines see recently Schmitter (1980).

for the recognition, in some reformed way, of old interests and formations connected with the dictatorship (the Italian monarchy after Fascism), and cases in which those interests and formations might have survived at least in part without full democratisation (Greece under the colonels); cases in which entering into the democratic bargain was sufficient (large sectors of the right after Franco), and cases in which it was not (the right after Primo de Rivera). If we combine these various possibilities we find therefore instances as disparate as the Second Spanish Republic and Spain after Franco. In the former, the old right – having survived and regrouped after Primo de Rivera's uneventful fall – looked at democracy as a residual option, and not even that compelling and unavoidable. It also looked at it as progressively unpalatable or at least conditional (*incidentalismo* described the attitude at the time), as the republican left moved to undercut the right's share in the democratic bargain beyond limits which the right considered crucial for its survial. In post-Franco Spain, on the contrary, the process of democratisation was initiated by forces inside the Franco coalition itself; and while the move was probably necessary to secure the recognition of old interests on new competitive grounds, it was also sufficient.

The implications of the two cases for the transfer of consent from one political order to another are rather simple: transfer, though by no means easy, is at times possible. The fact of previous consent to a nondemocratic order is no necessary impediment. And though we may fear mental reservations in the attitude of social formations that turn toward democracy, the only thing we can firmly observe – and the only that counts for democratic reproducibility – are repetitive deeds: playing by the adopted rules, hence sharing a probable amount of wins and losses, and advocating no other order.

Democracies, as Dankwart Rustow aptly reminds us in a seminal paper, have historically been born as only the by-product, conscious and intended though it may have been, of some further aim: usually, to terminate or forestall a prolonged and inconclusive struggle. This implies that genuine democrats need not preexist democracy. Further, being a means for reconciliation, the democratic compromise must have seemed second-best to all concerned parties; and this implies that the rules of the democratic game are more a matter of a working agreement, concurrence or assent than one of *a priori* consensus on fundamentals. In sum, "what matters at the decision stage is not what values the leaders hold dear in the abstract, but what concrete steps they are willing to take" (Rustow, 1970: 357). True, if the passage to democracy occurs abruptly, thus demanding a quick transfer of allegiance, those who are called to change the object of their allegiance, being accustomed to the starker certainty of the nondemocratic game and unaccustomed to risk-taking, may be initially predisposed toward a hard-nosed, zero-sum and indeed conservative calculus of gains and losses.

Under this calculus, any prospective win by a democratic opponent in any arena would reciprocally appear as a net loss and the transfer of allegiance would occur only if the old game is no longer playable. Taken by themselves, these strike one as rather unpromising circumstances. Yet, whether allegiance will indeed be transferred and how reliable and stable the transfer will be does not depend on these initial circumstances alone. It also and in fact mainly depends on the structure of opportunities offered by the unfolding transition and by the actions of other political actors. It depends for instance on whether the democratic game can be structured as a positive game, in which old interests can find satisfaction, in some reformed way, next to new ones. *If* this is possible, then the transfer of allegiance becomes easier, the calculus becomes more relaxed, and even the double question of whether the old order is preferable and preservable becomes ambiguous and muted – leaving only a hard-core to mourn the past no matter what.[9]

Still, joining the democratic bargain remains a complex and delicate matter: there is a whole range of possibilities about being a winner, or a loser, "some" of the time: how often is that? It is clear that in setting up a political market this is a matter of great contention among collective political actors. It is equally clear that in an open and competitive democracy the matter is not settled by deciding ahead of time exactly how often, how much and when each actor will win or lose. Rather, compromise is upon a set of rules of the game: norms, procedures, and institutions whose operation will probabilistically and therefore uncertainly effect a fair balance of winning and losing.[10] If rule agreement is reached, its institutional nature and the acceptance of the fact that institutions are only probabilistically and each partially related to outcomes mean that the agreement can have a span of endurance. Still, the agreement is instrumental, a means to an end; and political actors, even when they consent outright to sharing losses and victories or they are reassured that the sum-total of the game is positive, will try as far as possible to bend both means and ends in their favour. Therefore, agreement on rules is continuously, though implicitly, tested against performance and may at times require renegotiation if, for reasons having to do with the rules' actual operation or their changing environment, performance falls eventually outside a tolerable range of expected outcomes.

It seems, then, that when political parties are centrally involved in the inauguration of democracy, they have quite a task to attend to.[11] The

[9] In other words, whether loyalty to the old regime is a matter of values and ideology or of interests, these motives are not always as deep-seated as to render them invariably impermeable to a changing reality. After all, it takes all sorts to make up a nondemocratic regime.

[10] On democracy as an institutional compromise see Przeworski (1980a).

[11] There are also cases in which parties are not centrally or initially involved in the

demanding nature of the task is stressed by the fact that it is at this juncture that the issue of how much a democracy can afford in the way of party government typically arises.

II. Successor Democracies and the Limits of Party Government[12]

Let us imagine, to start with, a set of parties which – by any number of acceptable criteria we employ – are committed unreservedly to the democratic bargain.[13] Their commitment means that their first objective is to build the institutional and, through them, material conditions for reproducing consent on the broadest basis. At the same time, as parties prospectively competing for government, it is also their objective to try and carve the best possible deal for themselves and their followers. I have already pointed out the difficulties inherent in principle in reconciling the two objectives: both objectives are pursued through institutional manipulation; but the latter points ideally toward the directness and purposefulness of party government and is therefore focused on victory and policy delivery; the former points toward a balance of wins and losses and therefore puts an upper limit to the pursuit of unilateral victory. But successor democracies are likely to have special difficulties, which serve well to highlight the general problem: what does reconciliation entail and how do you get there?

The key source of difficulty stems from the probability that next to parties unreservedly committed to the democratic bargain (I will call them for short democratic parties), a set of forces will appear, possibly rallied around their own parties, whose commitment to the bargain – owing to their past allegiance to the old regime – is *or seems* to the democratic parties less than certain and unconditional (I will call them nostalgic forces or parties). In other words, if the democratic parties were alone in the transition to democracy they would find it much easier to reconcile party

inauguration of democracy, because democracy is mainly imposed by an occupying power or by a monarch, a military dictator, or similar. And there are cases when democracy is not inaugurated following the sudden collapse of an old regime but evolves by less compressed though not necessarily smooth and unplanned transformation. I do not rule out a future extension of my analysis to such cases, but I prefer not to consider them in this paper. This will make my point about the affordability of party government more incisive and straightforward.

12 By successor democracies I mean democracies that follow an authoritarian or totalitarian regime.

13 One easy criterion – though possibly too narrow – is that these parties opposed the dictatorship during its life, and opposed it in the name of democracy and no other order.

government with the notion that wins and losses should be fairly shared. Each party would agree that institutional arrangements favoring party government should not violate the capacity of prospective oppositions to maintain their identity and their interests as they themselves define them. Further, mutual trust in democratic commitment and awareness that institutional arrangements influence outcomes only probabilistically and each only in part would leave the door open for a wide range of tolerable arrangements, including those strongly favoring party government and alternance.

But as soon as nostalgic forces and parties are involved in the transition the reconciliation above meets a harder test. It is still possible to come out of the test successfully; but it is also possible that – as already indicated in the opening pages – either party government or reproducibility will be sacrificed to some extent. The best way to appreciate the internal dynamic of any of these outcomes is by playing out hypothetically a number of scenarios which *per se* appear to be otherwise "reasonable" (not too easy but not too difficult either) for the prospects of democratic transition.[14]

The presence of nostalgic forces has, first, the effect of confronting the democratic parties with the issue of how much space those forces should have in the share of wins and losses. More precisely, what confronts the democratic parties is not just a choice between a set of tolerable options shading into each other. What confronts them is a principled dilemma: should the democratic bargain make special room for nostalgic forces in order to render them safe for democracy, or should it cut them off totally in order to make democracy safe from its "enemies?"

True, in concrete cases the dilemma may not be that difficult to resolve. But even assuming a "reasonable" scenario – i. e., the democratic parties show restraint in the treatment of nostalgic forces, they ultimately favour national reconciliation, they find the nostalgic forces available for such a solution – the scenario still implies some troubling complications. One complication of special interest from our viewpoint has to do with the nature of the trade-off that nostalgic forces are likely to seek for agreeing to democracy. Since these forces include institutions with a central role in the old regime (typical examples are the monarchy, the military, the church) they are likely to interpret the democratic bargain in a way that may thwart or distort its authentic meaning. What they intend to bargain on is neither a probabilistic and uncertain share of wins and losses (something more

[14] In other words, easy and difficult scenarios hold no special interest in that they overdetermine outcomes: either a successful democracy with no problems stemming from its inauguration, or a short-lived democracy, if any. Reasonable scenarios, instead, are much more open and uncertain in their outcomes. Therefore they illustrate better what it takes to reach (or miss) that delicate balance which the democratic bargain implies.

appropriate when the allocation of material resources is at stake), nor a competitive access to institutions, but the immediate preservation in no uncertain terms of "some" of their exclusive institutional roles. It is clear that, beyond a certain point, similar demands make the new regime into a hybrid – a guided democracy of a sort; a political market that tolerates corporate monopolies of institutions and hence outcomes. It is also clear that the democratic parties – even if they recognise that institutions such as a monarchy, a military, or a church are not inherently incapable of consenting to democracy – find it difficult to subscribe to some of their institutional demands.

To complicate matters (but still remaining in the realm of the "reasonable"), there is the fact that, as well as nostalgic force, other putatively nondemocratic forces may appear in the transition. I am speaking of forces or parties of the extreme left. Let us again overlook the obviously difficult scenarios: the extreme left pushes for a pitched battle against nostalgic residues or even resists a conventional democratic outcome.[15] Let us instead assume that the extreme left accepts, and is indeed instrumental in achieving the democratic bargain, and let us also assume that it takes a less than nastily punitive view of how nostalgic forces should or could be handled. Even so, the democratic parties should still reasonably expect that the extreme left will never quite rid itself of an ambiguous or critical stance toward the actual versus expected accomplishments of the democratic transition and will recurrently denounce creeping institutional *continuismo*. And since the extreme left is likely to point to *continuismo* as one major stumbling block in reaching a distribution of wins and losses more equitable toward the lower classes, this buttressing of economic with civic-institutional criticism may even succeed in rubbing onto at least the democratic left. It may variously blackmail it or attract it toward forms of political action in common with the extreme left (the more so if the democratic left already had its own reservations about the leniency toward the nostalgic forces). The important point to make here is that such common action cannot and at any rate will not be considered by other democratic parties (typically a large conservative or moderate party) as a readily acceptable policy option. Rather, it will be considered a symptom, if not a cause of, an early and recurrent weakness in the institutional bases and therefore in the reproducibility of consent.

The reader should notice that I have spoken of common action between democratic and extreme left; I have not spoken of formal and stable government coalitions, for the reason that – as I will detail later – such coalitions do not constitute likely (and reasonable) scenarios. Too many

[15] The difficulty is not just in the fact that the extreme left favours something quite different from the other political forces, but in the fact that it does this against other forces which are by no means insignificant.

things usually divide the two branches of the left, even when the extreme has been behind the democratic transition, to allow for more than emergency government alliances.[16] Yet, if this suggests that government coalitions will typically be limited to democratic parties, much of what I have said so far also suggests that such a limitation does not guarantee effective and stable partnership either.

But reasonable complications do not stop here. If the extreme left shows suspicion of the nostalgic right, the latter is almost certain to reciprocate by escalating its demands beyond the preservation of some of its institutional roles. Fearful of the extreme left's resistance to *continuismo* – muted as that resistance may be – it may in turn demand constraints on the extreme left's competitive access to institutions. Even without pushing for outright banning of its parties, it may insist on party licensing based on ideological-organisational criteria which the extreme left may not easily meet; or it may insist on the decoupling of party-union ties, controls on unions themselves and constraints on bargaining powers and job action – all of which would have particularly negative effects on the extreme left. And even if the right formulates no specific demands against the extreme left – even if it accepts that the same constitutional guarantees be extended to the extreme left as to all other political forces – the least we can expect is that the presence of the extreme left will heighten the right's circumspection toward the whole process of transition. It will for instance heighten suspicion toward institutional guarantees that, by favoring emerging interests in particular, would make democracy a "free-for-all." Either way, just as the extreme left will at least try to get on its side the left of the democratic parties, so the nostalgic right will try to attract the democratic right. This too must be seen as a symptom if not a cause of an early and recurrent weakness in the institutional bases of consent; those bases are likely to be questioned and to be checked against material outcomes more often.

True, we are far from a scenario in which the extremes engage not simply in protecting their place in the democratic bargain, but also in arresting the bargain itself. Also true, since the democratic parties have an implicit commitment to the bargain, and as long as initially the extremes are not unconditionally opposed to the same, it is unlikely that – barring special and unusual circumstances – the pressure exercised by the extremes on the democratic parties will in short order spell doom for the democratic experiment. It is unlikely, in other words, that starting from an original attitude of circumspection the extremes will naturally and progressively move toward a more unconditional resistance to democracy, attracting, hegemonising or coercing in the process the democratic parties them-

[16] This is even truer when the alliance is between the extreme left and all the democratic parties.

selves.[17] On the contrary, given the initial scenario I have just depicted, time (even in the sheer sense of gaining time) should eventually favor a democratic outcome. The democratic mobilisation of large sectors of society that almost inevitably and spontaneously accompanies the crisis of dictatorship, the desire for normalisation that follows the initial and more turbulent period of transition, and the hard reality of prolonged negotiations on the terms of the democratic bargain should all work in the same direction: bolstering the democratic compromise and in fact inducing the extremes to comply with initially feared and unthinkable sacrifices. As Rustow puts it, citing Leon Festinger's theory of cognitive dissonance, "a distasteful decision once made, is likely to seem more palatable as one is forced to live with it" (Rustow, 1970: 358; Festinger, 1957). Moreover, democracy being a competitive process, competition gives an edge to those who believe in it or can at least rationalise it.

In sum, the scenario I have presented is reasonable in that it tends toward a progressive narrowing of the options that are advanced in the early stages of the transition by a wide spectrum of left to right, democratic and putatively nondemocratic political forces. And the narrowing occurs around an institutional compromise in the negotiation of which the democratic parties, by a sort of Darwinian selection, increasingly play the central role.

Nevertheless, I have also indicated that the compromise involves sacrifices that go beyond the extremes' original inclination. They are sacrifices which the extremes may hold against the democratic parties for some time to come, thus subjecting reproducibility to a continuous test. Indeed, any extreme progressively drawn by the democratic parties into a series of sacrifices is actually in a more legitimate position for later challenging the final compromise on its own democratic terms: for having "thwarted" democracy or subjected it to exclusive interests and forces, or for threatening its own identity beyond tolerance. It can in other words be said that once the inaugural phase is over, the more serious test for reproducibility will rarely come from the drama of extreme forces still favoring in principle an alternative to democracy. Assuming that they favor it, and at least as long as conditions are normal and steady, this is still of no direct consequence for the way in which the political game will be structured. The serious test will instead come, less dramatically but more ambiguously, from within – as it were – the democratic compromise itself.

Hence the foremost task with which the democratic parties are confronted, given this initial scenario and its later implications, is how to

[17] The scenario of such involution will not be analysed further. The object of the paper is not the failure of democratic inauguration but the costs that may be associated with its success.

alleviate the problem of reproducibility. Everything in the scenario, however, suggests that this cannot be easily done by drastically disregarding the extremes and freezing them out of the democratic compromise. The move would be too risky – the more so the greater the degree that the extremes enjoy popular support and organisational clout – besides being unwarranted by their initial behavior. Thus the democratic parties are likely to opt for a more accommodating and less exclusionary strategy that, while keeping in place the sacrifices to which the extremes have been drawn, will not further limit their ability to survive in some reformed way. This is typically done by making institutional *garantismo* the centerpiece of the democratic compromise.

Garantismo is an approach to constitution-making mainly concerned with making the political market as open and competitive as possible; the aim being not to prejudge or load the future wins or losses of anyone who abides by its easy entry rules. Prejudgment is checked by the very fact of keeping entry requirements to a minimum, as well as by curbing the monopoly of institutions by any force and the monopoly of outcomes by any institution. The reason why extreme forces should prefer this market to a more constrictive one, the nature of whose constrictions they are not sure they can control, is obvious. In fact, *garantismo* may be seen as a strategy which the democratic parties pursue not just to compensate the extremes for previous sacrifices but to induce them to those sacrifices – possibly by dividing them internally on the issue. For example, the prospect of a *garantista* setup may help a reasonable sector of the extreme left to shelve earlier and riskier aspirations to a more "advanced" form of democracy. This still does not mean that the extremes will stop questioning the actual democratic compromise. Exactly because *garantismo* makes losing less dangerous for all, the extremes may still see it as a mixed and ambivalent solution: to the extent that it protects any one extreme it also protects its opposite. But once *garantismo* is in place, questioning the democratic compromise will appear less credible or urgent. So, if there are reasons why the extremes may try to attract out and divide the democratic parties, there are also reasons why *garantismo* may stem if not reverse the trend. From the viewpoint of the democratic parties *garantismo* has the advantage that it makes the reproduction of consent a recurrent, to be sure, but also somewhat more normal activity.

But one direct or indirect cost of *garantismo* is that it sacrifices some of the potentialities of party government – those having to do with the distinctiveness of governing coalitions and with the incisiveness of policy action. To begin first with the latter, *garantismo* tends by its own nature to deemphasise policy activism, as well as forms of institutional engineering that may thwart the operation of an open market. In other words, the emphasis is on the competitiveness of the market, not on its capacity for delivery. Furthermore, there is an incentive for the democratic parties not to commit themselves to any institutional choice or policy reform that may be interpreted as making them lean heavily in the direction of one or the other extreme – i. e., in the direction of "excessive" or "insufficient" democratisation. By holding the centre, as it were, the democratic parties maintain their identity as unquestionably democratic parties, affirm their preeminent interest in the success of the transition, and strengthen their role as the key forces in the transition. In so doing, they also and most importantly intend to strengthen and extend their electoral appeal at a time when, the dictatorship over, society is almost spontaneously mobilised, but political alignments are not yet defined. To repeat, however, all of this carries a cost in governing; the more so as, in a last twist, it may be the extremes themselves that, being left with no other immediate options, will finally insist that the democratic parties adhere strictly to *garantismo* (or will even initiate a demand for it). Thus, even when the democratic parties, by securing their democratic distinctiveness, are returned to government over and over again, it will be a rather limited government that they will preside over. As parties they may be *in* government, but as governments they may have a narrow range of policies on which to act. Party governmentness, to use Richard Katz's term, would be low.[18]

To understand these points in finer detail, let us consider the matter of constitution-making and issues of governance as matters of coalition. *Garantismo*, as the likely outcome of the reasonable scenario I have examined, implies cooperative constitutional coalitions. It may be the democratic parties that set in motion *garantismo*, or as just suggested it may be the extremes or sectors thereof that demand it, or even more likely it may be a bit of both (not even historians, or historians least of all, may agree on the exact interaction). No matter, the end result is a willy-nilly, formal or informal, explicit or implicit, broad and inclusive coalition. And broad constitutional coalitions incorporating, even with different weights, the extremes have a common denominator to agree upon which is minimal indeed: in essence, living together. My remarks above suggest that – at least with some virtue and leadership and a few imponderables – such an agreement once reached should make any one of the following three developments more likely. Either the parties of the new democracy, though continuing to disagree on the optimal terms of the democratic compromise, would keep their disagreement on the backburner; or parties and coalitions advocating a radical and unilateral change in the terms of the democratic compromise would not be voted in; or, when voted in, they would do less than expected about their promises. And this is as it should be for a

[18] I should stress, if it is not clear from previous references to his essay in this volume, that though I do not use Richard Katz's terminology, the problem with which my essay is concerned is more that of party governmentness, than that of partyness of government.

functioning democracy. *That* uncertainty – uncertainty not just about wins and losses but about the rules for wins and losses and the tenure of those rules – does not define democracy. Competition in order to change rules once in government is not what party government is all about.

But the constrictions imposed upon government by the agreement to live together, an agreement broad in its membership but narrow in its terms, are likely to go well beyond the prescriptions against changing rules. Once again, they are constrictions to which governments will be principally held by the coalitional features of that agreement. Central to these features will be a trade-off of great importance to the extremes and to the democratic parties themselves: on one side a partially reformed continuity in the civil and military apparatus of the state, on the other an accentuated parliamentarism revolving around a fully developed party system. Continuity in the apparatus of the state (including possibly but not necessarily the preservation of representative institutions like the monarchy) must be seen first of all as an aspect of national reconciliation of direct importance for the nostalgic right. Kept to a minimum, as our scenario implies, it involves the maintenance of the essential hierarchical and functional structure of that apparatus – in sum the maintenance of its identity – after removing specific features added by the dictatorship and patently incompatible with the democratic order.[19]

To counter continuity, and more central to the pursuit of *garantismo*, there stands the new system of parties. And here is where the problem of governing comes in; for it will not be any system of parties. If it is designed by a broad constitutional coalition to begin with, it is likely to be designed so as to keep access to the political market as open as possible and to prevent monopolistic situations. Chances are, therefore, that access will be regulated by proportional electoral laws, that is by laws that are meant to put no obstacles to the self-generation of political interests and parties. Chances also are that the party system will be placed in the context of accentuated parliamentarism, that is of a system structurally designed to make institutional monopolies more difficult. In fact, reliance on party-based parliamentarism as the centrepiece of *garantismo* may be such that constitution-making, beyond the broad outline of an unconstrained parliamentary system, may amount to a very limited affair. For example, the extreme left (at least that part which expects substantial electoral support),

[19] This may require a limited purge of bureaucratic personnel and the repeal of external decision-making authority violating democratic accountability. Also, reforms may have to be deeper in the case of the judicial system. Continuity may also be seen as a necessity, since changing the apparatus of the state is not easy (even for a dictatorship, let alone a democracy) and since even a democracy must rely on some machinery of government, especially in its inaugural phase. This may explain why a democracy may preserve institutions created by the dictatorship to foster state intervention in the economy.

and the democratic parties perhaps more, may at least initially feel that a new open unrestrained and in sum fully democratic party system is sufficient to circumvent the problem of continuity in the state apparatus. Or the parties may feel that nothing more and better can be done, given the actual political situation. Further, reliance on the simplified solution of accentuated parliamentarism may even lead parties to overlook other and more dispersed forms of *garantismo* that allow competing societal interests more direct entry to a new set of countervailing decisional institutions. Whatever the case, little constitutional attention will be paid to the issue of how to link the old state, as a structure of policy intelligence and implementation, to the new parties. And as long as constitutional efforts remain focussed on implementing parliamentarism, this will have a double effect on governance. First, it will discourage even temporary market supremacy by the government over the opposition. This will be so because parliamentary rules will formally curb the control of any elected majority, however stable, on the policies of parliament and government; but *much more* because any other majority behaviour will be denounced by the opposition as a violation of the collective constitutional agreement and the strict terms for democratic reproducibility. Second, governments will lose coordination with a state apparatus whose continuity and potential or suspected indifference to democratic governance the new party system was supposed to allay. And if such coordination is in any form an ingredient of party government, then party government will suffer on this score as well.

With this, I have fairly exhausted my treatment of the likely implications for governance stemming from a transition to democracy in which, 1) the political extremes cannot be discounted, but 2) the transition nevertheless converges toward a negotiated democratic solution. I wish to insist only on one point having to do with the reason why the constraints upon party governance are likely to be greater than those experienced by democracies that either had, as I will explain later, an "easy" transition from dictatorship or were not born from dictatorship. In my opinion the ultimate reason, the reason that subsumes most of the others, is that the type of "reasonable" transitional scenario I have illustrated involves a process of learning: learning the hard way and in especially delicate and constrictive political conditions what democratic party government is all about, what its upper limits are, what it cannot violate. This in turn is the main reason why I have started my analysis with the scenario above — it best shows my point.[20] Another reason is my belief, which I can only state here, that this

[20] I will discuss later on, but more briefly, a scenario in which some parties are willing to take greater, though not necessarily destructive, risks in the direction of party government. It will show my point *a contrario* — by what the reproduction of consent stands to lose.

scenario is also the most likely one[21] – though it is not likelihood as much as exemplarity that counts. Successor democracies are exemplary and instructive, to return to my introductory theme, exactly because party government must tread particularly difficult waters.

Bearing on this, we must appreciate that, strictly speaking, no amount of *garantismo* can absolutely secure the survival of any specific set of interests against the will of a democratic majority. *Garantismo* can only build an obstacle course on the way to the formation or implementation of that will; it cannot deny its ultimate legality. It is exactly this level of uncertainty that our new democracies find uncomfortable. This does not mean at all that they will dispense with strict institutional arrangements. On the contrary, it means that they will tend to surround them with all sorts of unwritten and stricter cultural-political expectations about their proper use. Any violation of such unwritten rules will be construed as a violation of the democratic bargain, which may strain the reproduction of consent and require a more frequent reassessment of its terms. What therefore differentiates our democracies from, so to speak, more "established" ones are two aspects of the democratic bargain. First, as stated at the beginning of this section, the established democracies will be able to accommodate indifferently to a broader range of institutional arrangements, including those that favour party government. Second and more interesting, having internalised the normative limits to party government, they will be able to afford a freer and more relaxed use of its instruments.

That is, an established democracy with institutional arrangements traditionally intended to favour party government (to exemplify, a two-party system, centralised and strongly organised parties with a distinctive electorate and ideology, executive dominance over parliament) will have no problems putting these arrangements to effective and at the same time legitimate use on behalf of party government. This is so exactly because the expectation is that the use will not violate the upper normative limits of party government. But the expectation is not so much based on the existence of written rules – which in fact may not even exist – as on the implicit and tested certainty that there is no cause for anybody to violate those limits. This in turn may allow the politicians of such a democracy (in particular, the opposition) to place greater confidence upon one fact which the politicians of a new democracy may deem insufficient: namely, that there are at any rate structural disincentives and limits, other than constitutional, to party government *strictu sensu*. These are the limits I have

[21] My claim cannot be proven or disproved by counting cases of democratic transition: they are only unrepresentative instances of a potentially infinite population. As to the possible criticism that my scenario allows for too large a number of variations, I would argue that most variations still revolve around the search for negotiated outcomes and tend to have closely related effects on governance.

in part touched upon in the first paragraphs of this essay and which consist, to recap, of the following: that parties are only parts; that they mediate between complex social formations which have more than an input function into politics and a differentiated state which does not coincide with parties; that they operate in the context of unfolding events which either outstrip their programme or do not lend themselves to competing partisan solutions; that in order to gain marginal votes they must often play down rather than emphasise policy distinctiveness.

Let us finally imagine two democracies – our own new democracy and an "established" one – each with institutional arrangements opposite to the ones above and thereby presumably weakening party government. Let us imagine for instance that both must rely on coalition governments, and both lack constitutional devices giving explicit preeminence to the Executive. It does not take much to surmise that in the established democracy the fact of coalitions *per se* may not turn out to be a serious obstacle to a tolerable version of party government – in sum, to the ability of coalitions to assemble, deliver or adjust if need be a reasonable government programme. It is equally understandable that a government coalition, and its leader in particular, are not bound to interpret the lack of explicit constitutional buttressing of executive powers as a legal or, even more, cultural injunction against enforceable majority rule. There are no political risks – at least no risks for the reproduction of consent – if as a matter of practice that democracy asserts forms of party government which institutional arrangements do not expressly stipulate (and which at any rate are always checked by the other structural disincentives and limits recalled in the previous paragraph). But would our new democracy act the same way? Could it afford to practice party government? Whether or not the appropriate institutions exist, the answer under our scenario remains negative.

What, however, if the initial scenarios had been different? The answer is rather straightforward: since it is always reproducibility that determines whether party government is affordable, and since reproducibility hinges on the presence and role of the extremes, they must be scenarios where the extremes create no problem for the reproduction of interests and thus of consent. I can think of two such scenarios. But I can also think of one scenario where – on the contrary – an early push toward party government, in the absence of the appropriate normative conditions, undermines reproducibility.

The first of these scenarios is self-explanatory. There will be no issue of reproducibility and no obstacle to party government – almost by definition – if the political extremes are initially weak and politically disqualified,[22]

[22] I am aware that these are very gross categories, but I am afraid that finer ones would take us quite afar without greatly improving predictions. Besides, it is not predictions as much as exemplifications that we are pursuing.

and therefore easily discountable. Because the scenario is an easy and indeed not very interesting one, I will not further dwell on it. What deserves understanding is not so much what its outcomes are, so much as what the conditions are that make the extremes weak and politically ineffective.

But let us now suppose that the political extremes, instead of being weak and ineffective, are so prominent that they and not the democratic parties (as in the scenario with which we started) initially hold centre stage in the transition. Ostensibly, the scenario seems to take a turn for the worse. Is party government, in fact democracy itself, eventually possible? The answer is always the same and straightforward: yes, if the extremes, or whichever extreme carries the main burden of the transition, take as their chief task the creation of the institutional conditions for reproducing democratic consent; if in sum they cease to be extremes, except by some external labeling we inertially attach to them. Contrariwise, any early effort to impose and give precedence to party government would backfire, in more ways than if the same efforts had been made by democratic parties. To put it in stronger terms, what I am willing to argue is that scenarios dominated by the "extremes" can and do produce the worst but also the best possible outcome for democracy.

To begin with the latter outcome, let me take the case of what we have labeled the nostalgic right (the reason why I have chosen the right rather than the extreme left will become apparent later). In the scenario dominated by the democratic parties I have presented the behaviour of the nostalgic right as indeed largely nostalgic, if not exactly inimical to democracy: compromising willy-nilly, stalling, blackmailing, and in sum dragging along at best. But this is just one scenario. Some of the remarks I made in the previous section suggest as well that there is no *a priori* reason why the nostalgic right — that is, forces in the coalition that made up the dictatorship — should remain cohesively nostalgic, that the right is not nostalgic by definition and *in toto* but by the structure of opportunities, and that dictatorships can be as expendable as democracies are. It is conceptually quite unwarranted to take the interests of the nostalgic right as fixed and unshakeable when we know that the demise of dictatorial regimes has often been put in motion by secessions within the regime's ruling coalition. And to argue that secessions serve the purpose of saving the old interests begs the question of how such a goal can be achieved *in toto*. Intentions do not count here: strictly speaking, saving old interests through a new regime is an impossibility, since the structures of a regime affect and hence define/redefine the interests served. To say the least, and for reasons that need no restatement, there is no guarantee that old interests be preserved if the new regime happens to be a democracy. To be sure, that is why forces seceding from the dictatorship may wish to arrest the process of liberalisation they have put in motion before it reaches the democratic threshold. But there are circumstances — which is not my task to analyse here[23] – under which those forces may propel liberalisation up to and past the democratic threshold. When this happens, then something else is likely to happen.

If and because it has undertaken the path to democracy, the seceding right (in a way the right more than any other political force) should understand two things about the successful management of transition. First, a new democracy is rarely established by unilateral action. At one point or another, even assuming original unilateral action, pressures for broader founding coalitions will be brought to bear by newly mobilised groups that variously look at the dictatorship as morally abhorrent, economically unviable, politically exhausted, internationally isolated, or just plainly expendable and incidental. Second, of all the forces that may set in motion in the transition to democracy the one that can least disregard the importance of accommodating these newly mobilised groups within the democratic bargain is precisely the right. For one thing, this being almost always a seceding right, it will find it difficult to assert itself over that part of the right that remains nostalgic or undecided, unless it seeks the support of emerging democratic forces. For another and more important, since these forces have good reasons to suspect the motives and the commitment of the seceding right, nothing short of deeds explicitly demonstrating that commitment will buy their support. The most obvious deeds, and possibly the easiest, are politico/institutional: putting no obstacle to the ability of forces that play by the rules to enter the political market, while avoiding institutional arrangements that may be interpreted as stacking outcomes in favor of the right. In sum, once a seceding right embarks not merely on liberalisation but democratisation, the path must be travelled to its political end.[24]

All of this sounds very much like *garantismo*. But the point I wish to make is that – exactly because what is first at stake in the transition is the transfer of consent from dictatorship to democracy – *garantismo* initiated by the right itself has a double advantage over one initiated by forces that always opposed the dictatorship.[25] First, it is a more complete antidote against fears of *continuismo*. Second, and reciprocally, it offers a stronger basis of consent for the new democracy and its new political forces. It allows, in sum, what I have elsewhere called a mutual "forward/backward" legitimation of democratic forces on the one hand, and of reformed forces formerly in the service of the dictatorship on the other (Di Palma, 1980b). And the scope of the constitutional coalition that makes this possible may

[23] Those circumstances have been analysed recently in Schmitter (1980).

[24] A similar scenario would apply to a seceding left initiating the democratisation of a leftist dictatorship (for example, a people's democracy); though I can think of some points of significant difference.

[25] Assuming always, in the latter case, that the right is present and with similar weight. If the political and numerical weight of the right is insignificant or nil the scenario is obviously much easier.

be broad enough to embrace even forces that we would conventionally assign to the extreme left, but find important pay-offs in the collective implementation of *garantismo*.

Finally, the realisation of such a scenario has the ultimate effect of removing normative obstacles to party government. It is exactly broad agreement on the institutional compromise that, by building stronger foundations for the reproduction of interests and consent, should make this last achievement possible. In sum, though *garantismo* as pursued by the democratic parties in the first scenario remains an impediment to party government, here *garantismo* should have the opposite effect: once again, what preliminarily counts in making or breaking party government are not institutions and instrumentalities *per se*, so much as their cultural underpinning and the collective expectations about their proper use.

Besides, the constitutional strategy used by the seceding right should also favor the formation of a party spectrum and party alignments conducive to government competition between left and right coalitions. The seceding right, in order firmly to differentiate itself from the still nostalgic right, will tend to converge toward the more moderate sectors of the forces opposed to the dictatorship. By the same token, its constitutional behaviour will make it easier for the moderate sectors to look at the seceding right as a potential government ally, or may even lead to the formation of parties or federations of parties combining moderate and right-wing forces. On the left, similar incentives toward convergence may operate, since the constitutional behavior of the right should variously weaken the reservations of the extreme left about the terms of the institutional compromise, increase the risks of more dissenting strategies, or divide the extreme left on these issues. None of this means that there will be no real extreme left and no real nostalgic right to resist, oppose, denounce or resent the democratic compromise. But it does mean that the new party spectrum should leave them little political space and leverage — too little for these forces to prevent the rest of the parties from taking a turn at party government.

But what if, instead of the reformed right or the democratic parties, it is the extreme left that takes the prominent lead in the transition; and what if it goes for a more progressive democracy — one that would not be confined to a mere political shell but would place group and class relations on a more "advanced" basis and do away with *continuismo?* Reasons why the extreme left would be persuaded to follow such a scenario are not lacking. The very fact of enjoying an initial lead with respect to the other forces would give the extreme left additional power and drive. It would also give it a sense of potentially expanding authority and support and hence a sense that everything is possible. After all, if the extreme left is in the lead, it must appear to be so, in the initial exhilaration of liberation, because the right (and perhaps not the right alone) is morally, politically and economically bankrupt beyond at least immediate recovery.[26] In fact, under similar initial advantages, even the democratic left may be attracted by the prospects of a more radical democratisation – or may choose or be drawn into a more stable and exclusive coalition with the extreme left.

What would then be the likely implications of this initial scenario for reproducibility and party government? The answer should by now be clear *a contrario* from everything I have said in this section, and I offer it less for demonstration than for completeness. Let us assume that the initial drive by the left will in fact catch the right in disarray and will therefore meet no immediate resistance capable of setting the clock back. The result, as O'Donnell (1980) has described it, will be a process of rapid and purposive democratisation that will go well beyond the strictly political dimension. The process will have three distinctive components of importance for our analysis.

First, it will tend to give first priority to policy content. It will focus on ambitious reform policies affecting socioeconomic relations and institutions as the best strategy to prevent a resurgence of the past as well as to expand and consolidate popular consent. Second, it will tend to soft-pedal a conventionally competitive constitutional framework in favor of politico/institutional arrangements intended to keep in place, monitor and carry forward those reforms. Initially, institutional arrangements should vary considerably as to the locus of monitoring and leadership they prefer – from spontaneous forms of producers' *autogestion* to select local and national partisan or military *juntas* supervising or replacing competitively-elected parliaments and the institutions of the old state. But, in my opinion, fears of reactionary coups and the cumbersomeness of dispersed *autogestion* should sooner or later push the left toward the latter and more guided arrangements (thus making the new regime a borderline case democracy at best). And the push will be stronger if, of the two wings of the left it is the extreme that prevails. Third, in the drive toward policy reforms and constitutional guidance (an approach quite different from *garantismo*), the left is likely to shun political and constitutional coalitions on an equal basis with more moderate sectors of the party spectrum as tactically unnecessary, programmatically stifling and ideologically improper.

Pursuing these three components of "advanced" democracy does mean pursuing some of the behavioural and instrumental conditions of party government: the directness of its policies: the homogeneity of the governing forces selecting them; the constitutional preeminence of these forces over, or at least their circumvention of, the state's implementing apparatus on

[26] In general, it can be said that transitions to democracy almost always place the extreme left or the left as a whole in the position to claim moral and cultural-political superiority. On the contrary, even a seceding right that initiates democratisation must always prove itself.

one side and representative institutions and oppositions on the other. But it also means getting dangerously close, to say the least, to a violation of the normative limits of party government. The left will not look at the constitutional mechanisms it has constructed as mechanisms to be interchangeably used by its adversaries, were they to become the government; it will not see party government as only government by parts, and limited in time; it will not take favorably to uncertainty in institutional outcomes (an uncertainty which reforms were supposed to remove). Even if it settles for a more conventional democratic framework that does not prevent in principle a new majority from coming into government, it will not consider the new majority as being entitled to repeal or alter the reforms it has introduced, since they define the new order. Yet those reforms will have been introduced, by a select majoritiy if any, for the express purpose of stifling the reproduction of conservative interests beyond limits that those interests may find intolerable.

Most prominent among those interests, but not alone, will be the interest of the state apparatus to manage itself internally and capitalism's interest in accumulation. In the intentions of the left, and by its reforms, these interests should be caught in a lopsided zero-sum game which is a far cry from democracy's surplus bargain. But since it is far from likely that, despite the initial advantage of the left, the reforms will be sufficient to make those interests disappear into thin air, the scenario's likely outcome in the short to middle term is the emergence of what O'Donnell (1980) calls a situation of dual power, and naked at that. Let us assume that this polarity will not lead to an abrupt or violent resolution, through destabilising subscenarios that require little fantasy to envison. Even so, government and opposition will continue to compete on issues that touch upon the very structure of the new regime. If then the threatened interests eventually find their way to government, *and* if they revoke what the left has done, it is difficult to predict a long and safe journey for the new democracy — and with it for party government.[27]

III. Conclusions: Judging the Future from the Past?

It is apparent that my scenarios have been constructed by abstracting from concrete cases. Though no case fits perfectly any one scenario, the informed reader will have no difficulty in surmising for instance that the case that

[27] Unless, that is, the new government — aware of the risks of plainly setting back the clock — chooses to negotiate its way through a renewed constitutional process. The process would have to balance a limited step back on reforms with constitutional guarantees that would keep the democratic game open. In essence, it would be a lateral move to a version of the scenario of *garantismo* first discussed in this section.

comes closer to and has inspired the first and most instructive scenario, the one of *garantismo*, is postfascist Italy. West Germany, on the other hand, best fits the "easy" scenario, making the extremes discountable and favoring in that sense party government. Spain and Portugal in the seventies may instead serve to illustrate the two opposite outcomes of transitions initiated by the extremes – the Spanish transition, transforming the extremes into key components of the collective democratic compromise; the Portuguese transition, leading from prematurely installed party government to a crisis of reproducibility and possibly to the lateral more toward *garantismo* indicated in the last footnote.

But it is not the purpose of my essay to discuss concrete cases or degrees of fit.[28] Scenarios are what the word says: plot outlines staged by actors who are called to fill in and improvise. To repeat, their usefulness is in their exemplarity, in their ability to capture and reconstruct deductively dominant trends; it is not in their predicting, fitting or covering all cases. Strictly speaking, scenarios are not predictors of final outcomes: since actors "improvise" at every turn in the plot, and since each improvisation rests on the probability of the previous one, the calculus of final probabilities is elusive in the present state of the art. Neither are they a theoretically barren restatement of actual events, despite their concrete derivation. Though borrowed from reality, scenarios are designed to merge the historical accounts of linear and apparently self-contained sequences into branching-tree developments, and to transform concrete events into contingencies. Thus scenarios are models – not narrative, nor yet theory, but a guide to one. And, as Feit (1969: 157) puts is, "A model is an abstraction. Although it is a translation of real variables into model variables, from which model solutions are generated, these solutions cannot be applied to the real world without another translation."

Another aspect concerning the theoretical status and scope of my scenarios needs clarification. Since they are conceived as branching-tree models of choice, the variables of which are all internal to and shaped by the process of regime transition, they look at transitions as discrete and time-bound rather than even and continuous, and they seek explanations of final regime changes that are contingent rather than structural and probabilistic rather than necessary. They assert, to condense my point, that democracies are made ... in the act of making them. And they assert that variations in democracy, with respect for instance to party government, reflect variations in that act. The approach is eminently sensible (dare I say tautological?) when dealing with the types of transition I have illustrated in the text: visibly abrupt and contentious. But the image of bursts of self-conscious reforms punctuating and interrupting long periods of stasis should not be confined to those transitions.

[28] I have examined concrete cases in Di Palma (1980b; 1983).

The greater incrementalism that may accompany more extended regime changes, their on-again off-again quality, does not subtract from the fact that they too are punctuated by moments of decisions and that, even at greater intervals, one cluster of decisions enters into the probability of the next one. This at least is the way Rustow conceives of democratic inaugurations – making no distinction between countries in terms of length of the transition.[29] And this is why, as suggested in a previous footnote, the logic of scenarios is extendable to all democratic transitions; in fact, it demands extension. Scenarios of compressed transitions give an appealingly efficient and vivid account of the affordability of party government. Yet an account of the fuller variance in democratic governance demands a fuller variance of scenarios.

But instead of branching out I propose to conclude with a speculative "forward" look into an issue regarding the future of party government that my scenarios do not explicitly address. Assuming a western democracy that could not initially afford party government, and assuming that the initial effects are still felt today,[30] how will that democracy cope with today's so-called crisis of party government? The answer is straightforward: not too well, or not as well as other democracies. And the reason is that what is fundamentally at issue in that democracy, then as now, is always the legitimate place of parties in society's *Herrschaftsorganisation*; that is Richard Katz's party governmentness and its viability for the reproduction of competing interests. Seen in their larger environment, political parties – whether in government or opposition – are at best collective legal/legitimate gatekeepers between societal interests and public institutions. It is this collective institutional location straddling agencies of demands and agencies of performance that makes parties the key not only and obviously to party government but also and more broadly to reproducibility and its institutional mechanisms. Hence, whenever that collective location is normatively and factually challenged – as it has been in recent years – it is not only party government but reproducibility itself that is in principle

[29] The first country to which Rustow refers, to illustrate the point that democratic transitions involve a chain of decisions, is in fact England. "Instead of a single decision," he writes, "there may be several. In Britain, as is well-known, the principle of limited government was laid down in the compromise of 1688, cabinet government evolved in the eighteenth century, and suffrage reform was launched as late as 1832". He concludes: "Whether democracy is purchased wholesale as in Sweden in 1907 or on the installment plan as in Britain, it is acquired by a process of conscious decision at least on the part of the top political leadership" (Rustow, 1970:356).

[30] This is a mere assumption. How long inaugural defects last and why, under what conditions they have real consequences, how useful it is to analyse the politics of a given regime in the light of its origins, how new moments of decision affecting governance may come into being past the inaugural phase, are issues in themselves. They are discussed, in a journal issue devoted to the topic, in Di Palma (1980a).

at stake. But the stakes are that much higher in a democracy where the place of parties (and governing parties in particular) in the broader institutional design for reproducibility has been an issue of conflict all along.

Let me take, to exemplify, one aspect of the crisis of party government that, perhaps more than others, touches precisely upon party governmentness and its viability. I am speaking, to put it in trendy language, of the inability of advanced democracies run by competing parties to reconcile welfare with capitalist accumulation. The predicament seems serious. Indeed, the first normative injunction about what parties can and cannot do comes historically from the need to reproduce the interests of capital. In simple words, we are dealing with capitalist democracies and the parties replacing each other in government must consent to this parameter. Thus the initial success of new democracies is based exactly and first on collective consent to the reproduction of capital. But consent means above all consent by the left in exchange, reciprocally, for the protection of its own interests as the left defines them.[31] Hence, when this reciprocal legitimation of capital and labor does not occur or remains uncertain, party government, being unable to guarantee the reproduction of competing interests, becomes less likely or riskier. In turn, a democracy in which the legitimation of capital and labour is still uncertain will be less capable of developing at a later time, if neccessary, new collective answers for new tensions between the two interests. Much has been written recently on neocorporatism as a system of permanent conciliation-cooptation wherever the reproduction of interests through the political market is in crisis. But in our democracy neocorporatism is bound to have a difficult life. Either labour or capital, or both, may look at neocorporatism as a zero-sum game even more lopsided, since it offers no electoral redress, than party government itself.[32] As long as neocorporatism serves only to reduce the general insecurity of its social partners about their future gains and losses, it may prove a viable corrective to the growing uncertainty of partisan mechanisms. But if it is perceived by any one partner as a more effective way through which the others can exact previously unthinkable sacrifices, then the partnership is thereby impeached.[33]

Implicit in what I have just said is the notion that the democracies that are in a better position to rethink party government are to be found exactly among those that have practiced it to everybody's best advantage. Thus in subtle ways, viable neocorporatist arrangements, or any arrangement

[31] That is why new democracies inaugurated by an extreme left, likely to be carried away by its own ambitions and a sense of limitless opportunities, may run the highest risks. Bargaining for mutual survival may not be paramount in its calculus.

[32] Two recent treatments of the topic, focusing on difficult democracies, are Lange (1979); Salvati (1981). For the general argument that neocorporatism may yield the same level of conflict as partisan mechanisms see Maier (1981:54).

[33] Maier (1981:54) makes the almost identical point.

effectively designed to improve reproducibility, do not deny party government but presuppose and recast it. But much of this is stepping into another and quite open topic, and into a new set of scenarios.

Bibliography

DAHL, R. (1970) *After the Revolution?* New Haven, Conn.: Yale University Press.

– (ed.) (1966) *Political Oppositions in Western Democracies.* New Haven, Conn.: Yale University Press.

DI PALMA, G. (1980a) "Da un regime all'altro," 17 *Biblioteca della Liberta* 115.

– (1980b) "Founding Coalitions in Southern Europe: Legitimacy and Hegemony," 15 *Government and Opposition* 162 (Spring).

– (1983) "Italy: Is There a Legacy and Is It Fascist?" in J. H. Herz (ed.), *From Dictatorship to Democracy.* Westport, Conn.: Greenwood Press.

FEIT, A. (1969) "Insurgency in Organizations: A Theoretical Analysis," 14 *General Systems* 157.

FESTINGER, L. (1957) *A Theory of Cognitive Dissonance.* Evanston, Ill.: Row Petersen.

LANGE, P. (1979) "Sindacati, partiti, stato e liberal-corporativismo," 28 *Il Mulino* 943.

MAIER, C. (1981) "'Fictitious Bonds ... of Wealth and Law': On the Theory and Practice of Interest Representation," in S. Berger (ed.), *Organizing Interests in Western Europe.* Cambridge: Cambridge University Press.

O'DONNELL, G. (1980) "Nota Para el Estudio de Procesos de Democratization Politica a Partir del Estado Burocratico-Autoritario." Buenos Aires. (unpublished).

PRZEWORSKI, A. (1980a) "Material Bases of Consent: Economics and Politics in a Hegemonic System," in M. Zeitlin (ed.), *Political Power and Social Theory.* Greenwich: JAI Press.

– (1980b) "Some Problems in the Study of the Transition to Democracy." Presented at the Conference on the Prospects for Democracy: Transitions from Authoritarian Rule. Woodrow Wilson Center, Washington, D.C.

ROSE, R. (1980) *Do Parties Make a Difference?* Chatham, N.J.: Chatham House.

– (1969) "The Variability of Party Government: A Theoretical and Empirical Critique," 17 *Political Studies* 413 (December).

RUSTOW, D. (1970) "Transitions to Democracy," 2 *Comparative Politics* 337 (April).

SALVATI, M. (1981) "May 1968 and the Hot Autumn 1969: The Responses of Two Ruling Classes," in S. Berger (ed.), *Organizing Interests in Western Europe.* Cambridge: Cambridge University Press.

SARTORI, G. (1976) *Parties and party systems.* Cambridge: Cambridge University Press.

SCHMITTER, P. (1980) "Speculations about the Prospective Demise of Authoritarian Regimes and Its Possible Consequences." Presented at the Conference on the Prospects for Democracy: Transitions from Authoritarian Rule. Woodrow Wilson Center, Washington, D.C.

Chapter VII

The Futures of Party Government: A Framework for Analysis

Gordon Smith

Contents

Discussions about the future of party government may prove unsatisfactory for at least three reasons. In the first place, no real agreement may be reached as to what the term 'party government' should be taken to mean. Secondly, it is too easily assumed that party government is faced with a pervading crisis. Thirdly, the examination of future development often lacks a framework which can allow for a systematic analysis and a wide range of variation. These problems are all considered in the following account, less in the expectation that they can be satisfactorily resolved than with the aim of facing some of the difficulties.

I. The Liberal Democratic Context

When referring to 'party government', we generally assume the existence of a competitive party system, implying that the parties are freely formed, that they engage in electoral contests, and that the results of their competition determine the composition of government. In consequence, there is a turnover, rotation or simple alternation of parties in office,[1] and – depending on the extent of the change in the party composition of government – policy changes will be made in the movement from one government to another.

That view of the basis of party government precludes a consideration of single-party regimes, and their exclusion is not arbitrary. Competitive party systems of government have the special feature of being strongly associated with the values of liberal democracy or, perhaps more accurately to be regarded as its working mechanism. It is not difficult to appreciate why the relationship should be so close. Partly, it is a matter of historical experience: it is a fact that liberal democracy has only been maintained in those countries where party competition and party government have become integral features of the political system. Partly also, it is because the values and attributes of liberal democracy – those relating to pluralism, qualified majority rule, limited government and the concomitant theory of checks and balances – are all reflected in the nature and operation of competitive party systems. Above all, the competitive party system institutionalises the freedom of popular choice and the recognition of the rights of opposition which together epitomise the spirit of liberal democracy.

It is clear that liberal democracy and competitive party systems of government have become intimately related, but close as their association is, it does not follow that there has to be a logical and necessary connection between them. Admittedly, the difficulties of visualising a functioning liberal democracy – in the setting and conditions of the modern state – entirely without the contribution of the parties are great, and schemes to that end may appear unrealistic or utopian. It is just as difficult to conceive of a single-party regime successfully upholding the liberal-democratic order, even though one may be able to demonstrate that in principle intra-party democracy could be a complete substitute for inter-party competition.

However, attention given to the difficulties of making liberal democracy work without a competitive party system only deflects the argument from the essential point: that liberal democracy and party government belong to distinctive categories. The precepts of liberal democracy do not solely and automatically point to the parties in a competitive system and to their part in government, and nor can the role taken by the parties be simply and exclusively identified with liberal democracy. Neither conceptually nor institutionally is liberal democracy matched entirely by party government,

[1] It is perhaps better to refer to *potential* turnover, since the system may be fully competitive without changing the party composition of government. Thus Italy throughout the post-war period has experienced only marginal turnover, and in other systems – such as Northern Ireland before the imposition of direct rule – even the 'potential' may be lacking.

and from the other perspective party government serves ends which are only incidentally – perhaps not at all – linked to it. Indeed, under certain conditions the effects of party competition and the outcome of party government may lead to an erosion of liberal democracy.

For two reasons it is important to make the distinction. One is that in discussing the future of party government it is desirable to avoid compounding its particular problems with the more general ones which may affect liberal democracy, those involving the basic values of a society or reflecting weaknesses in the capitalist, socio-economic order with which liberal-democratic systems are identified (MacPherson, 1966). The failure to make the distinction makes it difficult to disentangle the specific problems of party government.

The second reason derives from the need to apply an historical perspective in considering possible future development. From a contemporary standpoint it is, indeed, difficult to visualise liberal democracy without party government. Yet we are also aware that 'party government' did not suddenly happen and that it was itself the product of an evolutionary process – prototypically within the liberal-democratic order, even if for some countries the process was highly compressed. Thus, the movement from parliamentary government to party government can be seen as such an evolution, one not evident in its implications at the time. It may be just as difficult to establish whether party government, in its turn, is undergoing an evolutionary change, but it would be wrong to hold that the fate of liberal democracy is necessarily dependent on the future of party government.

II. Party Government: Category or Continuum?

A competitive party system combines two sets of activities. One set relates to the competitive arena of the parties, the other to their part in governmental decision making. Before discussing the meaning of party government, it is as well to specify what different kinds of activity are involved. The 'competitive arena' refers primarily to the direct relationship between the parties and the electorate, typically although not exclusively maintained by the contesting of elections. But it also refers to the interaction among the parties themselves, as is implied in the idea of a party *system*. The role taken by the parties can be summed up as one of 'socio-political mediation', and their intermediation includes the aggregation of demands, mobilisation, communication and, incidentally, the legitimation of the political system. The second set of activities, the governing orientation, is concerned with the formation and the maintenance of government, the recruitment of governing personnel, the determination of policy and its execution, as well as system legitimation.

This summary of party activity has most of the ingredients that in general terms are associated with party government, even though it neglects the fundamental assumption of the *primacy* of party underlying all the activities which is embodied in the idea of a 'party democracy', rather than just a parliamentary or a representative one. Inevitably, even though the connotation of party government is reasonably unambiguous, there are differences of interpretation: whether the term should be applied to denote a category or whether it is preferable to treat party government as a continuum, ranging from a strong form where all the aspects so far mentioned are well represented to one in which party government only appears as a trace element. The treatment of party government as a category is necessarily much more restrictive, requiring certain specified elements of party activity to be present, a stipulation which can be readily applied to the governing orientation of parties and which lends itself to a constitutional determination. Thus the category of party government may be determined according to the explicit or implicit constitutional rules concerned with the exercise of governing power.

The use of a constitutional 'divide' has the great merit of isolating a distinctive category of party government and separating it from the amorphous area of 'party democracy' which need not have any direct governmental connection. The category of party government thus refers to a particular type of governing system, and on that reckoning we should expect modern systems of parliamentary government to belong firmly in the party government category: they effectively amount to the fusion of party and government. The party or parties in the majority initially form and then sustain the government, they supply the leading personnel, and that personnel proceeds to implement party policy. The fusion of party and government in those ways legitimises the political system, at least for those who support the parties with access to office. Clearly, such a 'model' of party government does not preclude substantial variations in practice, since the ability of the parties to control all aspects of governing cannot be assumed, and an obvious query relates to their ability to implement party policy – whether for instance party policy is supreme and whether non-party agencies can successfully promote rival policies. Moreover, constitutional provisions and practices vary considerably even within the restricted category of party government, so that several dimensions have to be taken into account in making comparisons. (Katz, *supra*: p. 44).

If constitutional forms are taken to be the determining factors controlling the category of party government, the major distinction between parliamentary constitutional forms on the one side and, principally, presidential forms on the other is an apparent consequence. To the extent that a presidential system is based on a separation of powers and the separate election of a relatively independent chief executive, fusion is absent, and the scope for the parties to engage in governing activities may be minimal. On those criteria, the system would not qualify as party government.

The alternative, treating party government as a continuum, can be argued on a number of grounds. In the first place, there may be a disinclination to accept the strictness of a dichotomy based on constitutional rules, since legal forms may obscure political realities, and the categorisation becomes static and unrealistic. Secondly, an exclusive concentration on the governing orientation of the parties makes for a false division between that role and their location in the competitive arena. The distinction is analytically justifiable, but in practice the realms of party action cannot be kept in separate compartments. That is evident in considering how much of government attention is directed towards the competitive arena and how much the latter is used by the parties to obtain a response from government. Thirdly, a sharp division neglects the importance of party influence which may be transmitted officially or informally, maybe just through personal connections, and that influence may be sufficient to qualify as party government, even though on other criteria it is absent.

The attraction of accepting the continuum version of party government is that no political system is excluded as long as a competitive party system is in existence, however much or little the parties have a governing presence, and the problem of demarcation disappears. There is the additional advantage that a continuum allows developments towards party government to be traced over a long period without the artificiality of a constitutional alteration signalling the arrival of party government, and — equally important — any movement away from party government can be similarly followed. The contrast between the two approaches is shown by the attention which the continuum version can give to a situation in which only trace elements of party government are present. That would occur — as one possibility — if the competitive party system was entirely divorced from executive authority. In other words, the parties would operate solely at the electoral level and be powerless in all other respects. There is an approximate example in the party system of Imperial Germany: the German party system developed within a dualistic constitutional system which prevented the parties from enforcing governmental responsibility, deciding government policy, or having a say in the composition of government. Nonetheless, the parties in the Reichstag did enjoy limited legislative and budgetary powers. Governments had to act with the possible reactions of the Reichstag in mind, and the parties were always striving to increase their authority, if for long unavailingly, to win the full powers of parliamentary government and ultimately to control the appointment of the Chancellor. In fact, full party government was granted by the terms of the Parliament Act of 1918, but to take that constitutional alteration by itself neglects the context of development. The same kind of consideration applies to all competitive systems, whether they are moving towards party government or away from it.

The arguments for treating party government as a category or as a continuum are fairly evenly balanced, but the consequences of selecting one or the other immediately affects the range of relevant problems to be taken into account: a categorisation may appear unduly restrictive, whilst a continuum can invite too many factors and slip into the even wider domains of liberal democracy and pluralist society. The present discussion favours the continuum approach on the ground that the scope for possible variation is thereby widened, and that is essential if the total array of 'futures' is to be displayed.

III. 'Threats' and the Functional Trap

The genesis of a debate on the future of party government is inevitably based on evidence of its specific shortcomings, general malaise, or imminent downfall. The symptoms of crisis are variously expressed, affecting party government over the whole spread of its electoral and governing activities (Linz and Stepan, 1978). Yet, as argued here, much of the contemporary evidence is unsatisfactory or inconclusive, pointing to changes in certain variables, but not necessarily affecting the position of party government in the sense of bringing about its displacement. In the background, too, there is the functional mode of thinking which can have the effect of contributing towards a sense of crisis by imputing 'functional loss' to changing electoral and governing patterns.

One such concern is the changing relationship of parties to the electorate, with consequences for the party system and government. The change can be expressed by saying that the parties have lost their integrative ability, particularly their expressive functions, and that has adversely affected party membership, quantitatively and qualitatively. One cause of that loss — to follow Otto Kirchheimer's 'transformation' argument — was that the established parties, in responding to alterations in social structure and outlook, became less ideological in character (Kirchheimer, 1966). If the parties individually lose their integrative ability, the slackening of ties means that the electorate becomes less structured and potentially more volatile in its behaviour. Electoral dealignment, greater volatility, an increase in issue-voting are all factors leading to fluctuating party support and hence to an impression of flux in party systems (Flanagan and Dalton, 1984). That impression is confirmed by the rise of new parties which offer new forms of expressive commitment to sections of the electorate. An implication of the apparent flux is there will be a negative effect on government stability and that the performance of governments will also be weakened.

In the present context, it is impossible to consider all the ramifications of the general line of argument, and the evidence in particular respects is far from conclusive. Thus, to take one central feature, electoral volatility has apparently increased in recent years, but it has been an upward trend rather than a dramatic upsurge (Pedersen, 1983; Maguire, 1983). Yet gross measures of volatility say little about its direction – whether it takes place across the established lines of political and social cleavage, and most importantly whether it is an intra-system volatility or one favouring anti-system forces. If, as the absence of strong anti-system parties indicates as far as Western Europe is concerned, electoral volatility is contained within the pro-system parties, then it cannot be taken as a sign of instability, and if it is largely restricted to intra-bloc movements, then flux itself is more apparent then real (Bartolini and Mair, 1982). However, these questions do not touch upon the most important issue, namely, whether the presumed 'loss' of integrative ability by the parties individually points also to a loss of *system* integration. Indeed, the contrary may be true, and if that were the case then any apparent flux in party systems (Smith, 1979) or a tendency towards governments with shorter life would reflect a changing political style rather than a crisis of party government.

A second contemporary concern is the wide spectrum of behaviour included under the term 'ungovernability' which is seen as a problem especially affecting liberal democracies and thus also a threat to party-based government and its legitimacy. However, the phenomenon of ungovernability does not represent a direct and general attack on the legitimacy of system, but rather a widespread indifference to the authority of government – simple non-compliance, unlawfulness, the pressing of sectional interests regardless of wider consequences. Richard Rose takes 'civic indifference' to be a leading characteristic: 'An indifferent citizen does not need to take up arms against a regime; he simply closes his eyes and ears to what it commands. The apathetic masses may sit out power struggles within the government, and turn the victor's position into a hollow triumph by shutting out a new government behind a wall of indifference.' (Rose, 1979:368).

As much as one may agree that there are numerous indications of a negative response to the claims of government in Western liberal democracies, 'ungovernability' is an unwieldy portmanteau expression which lacks agreed points of reference. It is relevant to draw attention to evidence of industrial conflict, civil strife and disobedience, and to certain forms of lawlessness (Schmitter, 1981; Rose, 1977). But how is it to be decided what symptoms should be included, and how are the various elements to be weighted? How should actions by relatively small sections be matched against the behaviour of the general population?[2] Is there a way of including

[2] The normal pattern of 'unconventional' protest behaviour is that of a minority versus the majority, but the composition of the minority varies from one type of issue to

ultimate expressions of ungovernability — such as revolutionary acts — without swamping the whole index? To what extent should counteracting tendencies be included, in the sense that with the increasing scope of government intervention and regulation there may even be evidence of greater governability? None of these questions denies the possibility that substantial changes in political culture and behaviour have taken place and that in consequence party government may be adversely affected, but they caution against the assumption that a few selected measures can be taken at their face value.

Possibly related to the crisis of ungovernability are the concepts of 'overloaded' and 'overextended' government: the view that governments are increasingly unable to cope with the demands made upon them — that the modern state has been set on a rail of steadily expanding commitments which are open-ended and call for a progressively larger allocation of national resources (Rose, 1980). Competitive party systems are especially affected because the nature of party competition is such that the commitments are not easily shed, and a growing proportion of the electorate has a vested interest in their continuation. The parties are exposed by their competitive stance to assume greater responsibilities, but governments are unable to satisfy mounting demands, so that at some point dissatisfaction with the performance of party goverment is likely to become intense. That portayal of the overextension of party government raises the question of whether the mechanism of commitment only operates in one direction, a ratchet-effect, and whether overload — with the hint of breakdown at some stage — is an ineluctable consequence. The experience of Western Europe during a period of prolonged economic recession has as yet not confirmed the argument, and the prognosis of overload may in part be related to the era of the so-called 'social democratic consensus': the general acceptance by the parties that social amelioration should be secured through the provisions of the welfare state, and that — on the assumption of continuing economic growth — the process of distribution and re-distribution could be continued without threat. Over the past decade it has become evident that the original consensus has worn thin and that party orientations of 'right' and 'left' have regained significance. In other words, the terms of party competition have provided choice regarding the level of state commitments, although it remains to be seen if the choices are real ones and whether the arena of party conflict continues to define the legitimate boundary within which the choices are presented and made.

A fourth kind of threat to party government can be described in terms of 'erosion', referring to the weakening of the party element in government to the benefit of organisations and groups which have either no rep-

another (Barnes et al., 1979). It is only when the 'minorities' coalesce and substantially overlap that the dangers to the existing system become acute.

resentative constituency or one that is based outside that of the parties. Such an erosion can occur on two fronts. One involves the direct penetration of the party by non-party elements, or ones that show a primary allegiance elsewhere, and they can influence government policy and decision making by making use of party channels. The other type of erosion leads to the creation of permanent structures and procedures which by-pass the parties and threaten the position of the representative institutions through which the parties work. Both movements weaken party control, and both differ from 'external' threats in that the process of erosion may be difficult to observe. Certainly, the loss of party control is not a new problem by any means, and part of the difficulty of assessing its real significance at the present time is that it can be too easily assumed that there has been a decline when in fact comparison is being made with an abstract model of undiluted party government or with an idealised past. The argument is, however, that whilst it may be difficult to pin down just how important non-party influences were in the past, present-day tendencies are far less random and derive from the extent of government intervention and the nature of the modern economy. These tendencies are the subject of the various theories of neo-corporatism (Panitch, 1980; Schmitter and Lehmbruch, 1979). What such theories cannot show at all conclusively is whether the loss of party control is irreversible or represents a particular phase of development — a question to be discussed subsequently.

This review of major 'problem areas' of party government could be extended in various ways,[3] but it is sufficient for showing their disparate nature. It is clear that if, firstly, the evidence and implications of each is accepted, and if, secondly, they are all of general application, then party government may be seriously threatened. Yet there are many objections to presenting a widespread crisis syndrome. Even though plenty of illustrations can be cited under one head or another, the incidence of potentially destabilising developments is highly uneven. It is also misleading to aggregate scattered evidence from various countries to assert an apparent general trend which fits none of them, typically, a kind of problem conflation.

A related error is introduced through a reliance on functional terminology. The ways in which parties act in combining the roles of governing and electoral intermediation readily encourages an enumeration of functions which they are seen to fulfil. Yet a functional approach leads to a distortion

[3] Thus Richard Rose (Rose, 1976:372—5) in dealing with the 'obstacles' to party government specifies eight conditions to be met (treating party government in the sense of a category). He concluded that, 'the conditions of party politics in Britain today are not conducive to party government. Only one condition, the choice of government after an election contested on party lines, is unequivocally met.' (1976:412).

if it signifies that a party or a party system primarily exists to 'perform' certain functions. It implies a sense of purpose, set from outside, in the generality of party activity and a kind of overarching system rationality and coherence which we have no grounds for accepting. Emphasis on party functions leads to the treatment of parties and systems as 'building blocks', and their value is judged according to their wider functionality or dysfunctionality. Such a rendering, without overtly being so committed, results in a static view of the political system as between structure and function. Although, for a descriptive account of party behaviour, there is no objection to making use of a functional 'check list', it is important to avoid the functional trap of ascribing problems of party government to a failure in fulfilling certain functions, with the implication that parties should be behaving in a particular way or that a restoration of the *status quo ante* is necessarily the desirable development.

None of these reservations about possible threats to party government should be taken to mean that it has a secure, if flexible, future. The presentation here is concerned to give a much broader account of possibilities, to move the discussion away from particular aspects towards a mapping of a variety of futures. Yet, as will become apparent, the difficulty is that in so doing we may escape specific functional traps only to fall into more capacious ones.

IV. Two Slippery Concepts: Survival and Adaptation

It is evident that if the problems of party government are seen to multiply and intensify, questions are raised about its survival. If its performance were to weaken drastically, then a fundamental crisis is the likely outcome. Yet whilst some types of problem point to the possibility of a sharp rupture, others – relating to the erosion of the party element in government – need not indicate a crisis or breakdown. Instead, the decline in party content, if continued indefinitely, would lead to the gradual supersession of party government in favour of an entirely new form.

This distinction between two modes of replacement – breakdown and supersession – is of basic importance in establishing a framework for analysis. To the extent that the content of party government is not directly bound by factors affecting its performance, in other words that there is the possibility of independent variation, then the range of party government can be surveyed along two dimensions: differing levels of performance combined with varying proportions of party content. Such a framework would thus give a complete array of variations according to two key criteria. On that basis it would then be possible to superimpose a typology of party government, show stages in developmental sequences, besides indicating 'off the map' positions of rupture and supersession. Unfortunately, that attractive vista is somewhat marred by fundamental difficulties in the way of establishing a framework in the first place.

An immediate problem occurs in the treatment of the concept of 'survival' and relating it to the performance of party government. Inevitably, the term invites the interpretation of 'ability to survive', or, put another way, that survival is a 'function', a vital one, to which all others would naturally be subordinated. In consequence, a purposive behaviour is implied for the entity of party government, whereas in reality it is only legitimate to refer to the behaviour of the actors involved, and that may only be contingently directed towards maintaining the institutional abstraction of 'party government' intact. It may be preferable to discard such a slippery concept as survival entirely, but it is less objectionable if used in the neutral sense of 'chances of survival', that is, by making an assessment of the likelihood of breakdown. That assessment in turn requires an evaluation of what minimum level of performance is necessary to prevent a complete collapse. Yet that approach only gives rise to another problem: it is impossible to specify in advance what that level might be. Quite apart from other considerations, it is necessary to render 'performance' in terms of its major components (Eckstein, 1971). If, as assumed here, the fortunes of party government depend on its legitimacy and effectiveness, then the question of 'how much' of each arises, and there is also the problem of the trade-off between them: a surplus on one may compensate for a deficit on the other, making any precise specification of chances impossible. If a 'survival index' were to be composed, it could only be used by making *ex post facto* judgements.

Somewhat similar difficulties apply to the analysis of the second dimension of party government — its extent — in attempting to raise it to the same conceptual level as given by the transfer from performance to survival. Changes in the extent of party government[4] can be seen as resulting from a series of adaptations, and an erosion of party government results from adaptive behaviour. The concept of adaptation is a fundamental one, as is evident from Rosenau's definition: 'The interaction of a political entity's activities and its responses to internal and external demands give rise to daily fluctuations in its essential structures. Keeping these fluctuations in the enduring patterns that comprise a political organism acceptable to its members is what (is) meant by political adaptation, and the practices, efforts and mechanisms that do (or do not) ensure the maintenance of acceptable fluctuations can thus be viewed as the politics of adaptation.' (Rosenau, 1981:3). In the present context, the 'essential structures' and 'enduring

[4] It should be emphasised that the term 'extent of party government' only partially corresponds to the sense of 'partyness of government' as employed by Katz elsewhere in this volume (*supra*: p. 45). The 'extent' of party government subsumes the electoral element as well as partyness in government.

patterns' are those of party government, and the politics of adaptation refers to those factors determining changes in its extent.

An objection to using adaptation as the underlying concept is that it carries the functional implication of systemic preservation and the biological analogy of an organism. As already argued, it is erroneous to treat party government as a self-regarding entity, and the closest approximation is the parties which subscribe to that form of government. For many purposes those parties will identify themselves with party government and its maintenance, but it is the parties – or more accurately the leading groups within them – which are self-regarding, and, as with the question of survival, their concerns and priorities may be different.

Adaptation affecting the extent of party government can take several forms. Partly it will be purposive in the sense that the party actors involved are engaged in an adaptive strategy which would include specific reforms or changes in existing practices or institutions. For the most part however, adaptive behaviour will be 'reflexive', that is, a largely unplanned response to changes in the political system making it impossible to forecast the nature of adaptive reaction (Sjöblom, 1981). The problem of relating cause and effect is particularly acute in analysing adaptation, and allowance has to be made for unintended consequences – serendipity even – which, from the viewpoint of maintaining the extent of party government, could work out better than purposive action which could be misconceived, misdirected, ill-timed and inadequate, whereas a complete lack of adaptive response, in the sense of not making concessions to a changing political environment, riding out the storm, may enhance rather than prejudice party presence.

Whether such concepts as 'survival' and 'adaptation' should be employed at all may reasonably be doubted. Yet they do have a value as long as usage avoids functional/organic implications. Any general assessment of party government must be concerned with these fundamental questions as the basis of more specific studies. It also has to be conceded that we cannot use them in a predictive sense and that only *ex post* judgements can be made with any degree of security – a reservation that applies to most high-level concepts. For the purposes of the present discussion it means that 'futures' can only be seen as a range of possible developments and not in terms of likely outcomes. Finally, even if both 'survival' and 'adaptation' are retained, they can only be used as general signposts: the problem still remains of finding adequate measures for both.

V. An Answer in 'Effectiveness'?

It appears reasonable to hold that the survival or breakdown of party government depends on the effectiveness of its performance. The term 'effectiveness' may be variously interpreted, but a central measure will be its problem-solving capacity or record. A system showing itself to be ineffective will be one with a poor problem-solving record, and its continuing failure will merit perhaps the label of 'immobilism', with the deadlock threatening eventual breakdown. As long as the legitimacy of the system remains high, the collapse may be postponed. Ultimately, however, performance is likely to prove decisive.

The choice of problem-solving capacity does appear to be an eminently suitable approach to the study of the effectiveness of party government and thus of its survival (Sjöblom, 1982). Parties and governments come into being in order to resolve societal problems; an electorate judges a government in part on its record of coming to grips with those problems; political leaders stake their reputations on their ability to do so; governments that have a dismal record will surely succumb, and if successive governments show no improvement the whole system will come under attack.

Yet there are all kinds of difficulty in taking a problem-solving approach to effectiveness. What is to be defined as a problem? Who is in a position to formulate the problem and put it on the political agenda? How is it to be judged whether the correct policy has been adopted? In that respect, can, for instance, a test of 'general acceptability' be applied to find if a satisfactory solution has resulted? What kind of time-scale should be used in making an evaluation? Finally, is the focus on problem 'solving' always satisfactory, or are there other ways of dealing with problems which may show the effectiveness of party government in a somewhat different light?

In posing these questions it is apparent that discussion has to be pitched wider than the narrow sense of party government, since in referring, say, to problem definition, the wide ambit of party activity must be considered. Problem-solving 'capacity' in the strict sense refers to the governing orientation of the parties, but capacity cannot be assessed entirely independently of the ways in which problems are presented in the first place. The parties provide an organic connection, for the more they are able to refine, channel and modify demands, the fewer will be the strains on the capacity of the party-governing system.

Richard Katz, in concentrating more on the party-governing orientation, has outlined four criteria for assessing the problem-solving capacity of party government (Katz, *supra*: pp. 46–47). Firstly, there must be the capacity to ensure that specific policies are implemented. Secondly, there should be the ability to frame policies that will produce the results desired by the policy makers: there should be a coherent means-end relationship. Thirdly, there has to be the ability to choose the 'right' policies. On balance, Katz takes the position that the correct policies are the ones that are perceived to be the best in a retrospective, long-term view. Finally, there is the question of a party's will: is the party prepared (and is it so positioned and structured) to follow the policies through and to countenance the costs?

It is the third test, choosing the 'right' policy which leads to difficulties. Katz supplies the answer of retrospective evaluation, and that view correctly makes judgements about effectiveness a matter of historical record, so that it is impossible to retain the idea of 'survival chances' — we cannot apply chances to a period that is already past: the die has already been cast. But the long-term test is itself open to objections because the longer the time span, the more one has to credit the prescience of the parties (they were 'on the side of history') and their ability to define the totality of the problem in the first place. If the rightness of a policy is restricted to mean that it produces the results desired by the policy makers, then wider problems of interpretation are excluded: it is a closed system. Even so, there is no way of being certain as to whether all or which results were wanted or intended. That applies especially to larger questions of social policy for which the stated or even unstated aims may be to secure greater equality, social amelioration, a less divided society.

There is also an element of artificiality in the restriction of judgement of rightness to the policy makers, because an important test is whether policies are widely perceived as fulfilling the goals. Of course, it would be wrong to put the criterion of 'general acceptability' forward as the sole or ultimate arbiter of policy; nevertheless, from the standpoint of policy makers and if their policies are to stick for any length of time, that must be an important factor in their calculation of desired results. It follows that the greater the cleavages of opinion there are in a society, the less chance there will be of winning general acceptability, and the more difficult it is to specify the 'right' policies in the first place.

That kind of difficulty may be exacerbated by the singular means-end relationship implied by 'problem solving', and there is a sense in which a concentration on this aspect of party government is misplaced. It can be taken for granted that problem solving is the manifest purpose of parties in government, but to accept their pretension at its face value results in a serious distortion of reality, and it may also invite falling into the functional trap by treating problem solving as the given purpose of party government. To appreciate the force of this objection, one has to consider that few political problems admit of a straightforward and 'watertight' solution — in the sense that they do not spill over to other problem areas or do not spark off new problems. Parties are constantly engaged not so much in problem solution as in seeking optimal outcomes to whole groups of problems, re-adjusting priorities, so that even if particular problems are high on the agenda, their original terms will not remain static, and solutions will follow lines different from those intended at the outset.

These considerations point to the fact that governments are pulled several ways at once and that there is seldom a royal road to the solution of specific problems (Pirages, 1976). Instead of taking the strict means-end instrumentality of problem-solving capacity, it is better to use a term which better encapsulates the policy activities of government, and it appears more accurate to refer to the problem-*handling* capacity of party government. If that course is adopted, then solutions to problems appear as *one* of the results of successful handling — but not the only one and not the necessary one.

A variety of strategies is available to governments if solutions are not directly forthcoming or if the costs appear too high (in terms of the solutions required for other problems, in resources, in possible loss of support). A wide range of governmental response is required in the handling of problems — besides the holding response of 'non-decisions' to problems, there are strategies for their redefinition, substitution, dispersal, and even their manipulation, whereby an element of conscious duplicity is involved, hoodwinking the electorate and perhaps the party itself (Schattschneider. 1960).

The operation of the competitive party system also adds to the problem-handling capacity of party government. Party competition encourages the presentation of issues to be resolved, and the prospects and the potential of government alternation continually maintains the promise that solutions can be found. The promise may well prove to be illusory, but that is not the important point: the immediate effect is to direct discontent against the government of the day, not primarily against the institution of party government, at least not in the short run. Thus the system itself is geared to problem handling rather than solution, and the absorption of problems on a system level reinforces the integrative power of the parties.

The effectiveness of party government may be better judged from the perspective of its problem-handling capacity, but it becomes a much more complex matter altogether to reach firm conclusions. In principle at least, it appears feasible to make assessments about problem solving, but problem handling gives no really secure guidelines: it does not lend itself to a clear specification of problems, there is a constant interplay between problems, and all the activities of government serve to obscure what is taking place. Even though there is a temptation to revert to the more precise measure of problem solving, to do so would be to neglect the real process of party government, for that is integral to judgements of its future.

There is a further significant consequence in adopting one approach or the other. If party governments are compared according to their problem-solving capacity (or record), the results may be seriously misleading: a successful/effective party government will counted as one which scores highly on problem solving whilst an ineffective one does not. The latter may be treated as a case of immobilism, a condition seen as a prelude to possible breakdown. Yet once the idea of problem handling is introduced the picture alters considerably: apparent immobilism is compatible with successful problem handling, and the immobilistic features can have a positive value, for under certain conditions immobilism in the short run may be a key to longer-term effectiveness.[5] This positive contribution of immobilism need not be restricted to a late or 'final' stage of party government. On the contrary, apparent immobilism may be an essential precondition for the successful stabilisation of party government in the first place, as the concept of *garantismo* indicates (Di Palma, *supra*: p. 190ff.).

Whilst an emphasis on problem solving leans towards an instrumental evaluation of the political process, successful problem handling may presuppose reserves of goodwill for party government, a high system affect, which can compensate for poor performance in problem solving. It would be wrong to go too far in seeking virtues in immobilism, but it is important to explain why an apparently shaky system of party government is able to survive. To an extent, problem solving and problem handling provide alternative ways to the study of effectiveness, and with the consequence of making it difficult to present that dimension of party government on a single scale. It also makes a simple view of the future appear unconvincing.

VI. Supersession: The Smile of the Cheshire Cat

The adaptation of party government, its changing extent, is related to the dimension of effectiveness, but an alteration in one may lead to higher or lower levels in the other, or there need be no correspondence at all, at least not immediately. Thus a decline in effectiveness may not be accompanied by any change at all in the extent of party government, and such non-adaptation is associated with the idea of immobilism.

A contrast between the two dimensions is evident in the way party government comes to be displaced. The loss of effectiveness leads to breakdown, signifying the sudden end of the regime of party government and its supplantation by a new form. With a decline in the extent of party government, however, its eventual demise might be a gradual affair, perhaps passing almost unnoticed. That decline spans the whole range of party government attributes when seen as a continuum.

At some point along the continuum it would have to be conceded that the label of party government was no longer merited. How that should be

[5] An extreme and telling example of the distinction between problem solving and problem handling is provided by the policies used by the British Government in Northern Ireland over the past fifteen years. No solutions have been found which would be acceptable (in terms of the costs), and long-term 'handling' has been applied; the outcome of successful handling would be that the terms of the original problem could eventually change, then permitting a solution. I am grateful to Peter Mair for the substance of this comment.

decided is another matter. It may seem reasonable to say that as long as *some* elements of party are present, the description of party government should hold. But that view shows an unwarranted bias against other forms any of which may have become predominant. It is the unsettled contest between form and reality. There are parallels here with Bagehot's classic analysis of the English Constitution and the distinction he drew between its dignified and efficient parts (Bagehot, 1963). Bagehot's description of the process by which a once-powerful institution becomes dignified in giving way to a new one, without at the same time being discarded, has weathered well. It is precisely because the old forms are preserved intact that the significance of the new 'efficient secret' may not be generally realised — for Bagehot it was the arrival of the cabinet system of government, but the same kind of formulation could be applied to the movement from parliamentary government to party government. It is as well to remember, too, that Bagehot stressed the value which the dignified aspects of the constitution continued to have for the political system, as an object of regard and a source of legitimacy — principally the monarchy in Bagehot's account — and that contribution is likely to be of critical value if new forms of government are unable to make a claim to legitimacy on their own behalf.

Supersession, in the sense of becoming redundant and giving way to a superior form, accurately conveys the way in which party government might come to be replaced by a new type of regime. Successive adaptations in the direction of supersession could take various paths, none requiring a sharp break with party government, and supersession need not be precisely determinable. Deliberate institutional restructuring, perhaps involving constitutional change, would be the most noticeable in making an explicit transfer of authority. Changes could also occur on a sub-constitutional level, with new organisations and procedures still nominally subordinate to party government, or circumvention might take place, whereby important decisions are taken by bodies over which the parties have little control. Finally, there is the pathway of penetration: non-party influences become paramount within party government, within the structure of government or within the parties themselves. These various developments are not mutually exclusive, and it is likely that supersession would be accomplished by a wide range of erosive action.

The least probable form of adaptation would be one that directly affected the competitive framework of party government. Even at a late stage, elections would be held, parties would campaign, and they would continue to occupy the leading positions of government. But for supersession to have been completed, that would be about all. Strictly speaking, party government would have become vestigial and irrelevant to the real exercise of power, leaving only a legitimising smile to mark its fast-fading presence.

That presentation may appear plausible, but in some ways it is also unrealistic. In particular, it describes a general process of institutional change without advancing any reasons why supersession should occur. It may be the case that party government is affected by a diffuse malaise or immobilism, so that almost by default the decision-making arenas move elsewhere. One might also visualise a process by which new social forces, not permanently containable within the existing structures, gradually adapted party government to their own purposes. Yet such a broad-front erosion is far less likely than one that relates to specific aspects, particular problems and policy areas. In principle, the pressures could effect any sphere of governmental activity — 'national' matters (defence and foreign affairs), social questions, economic policy, to name only a few — and one or more of them may show a weakening of party influence and control. But the spillover-effect from one to another need not be at all large, especially not if the principal actors and interests involved are not closely connected. The result of a sectoral erosion would be to limit and circumscribe the arena of party government, but within the new limits set it would continue to act authoritatively. Such an outcome would mean that a cut-off point was reached well before supersession looked inevitable, and an equilibrium might be maintained indefinitely.

VII. A Symbiotic Relationship?

Theories which in one way or another impinge on the future of party government tend not to foresee radical changes leading to supersession. That has not always been the case, and one only has to recall, say, Burnham's theory of the 'managerial revolution', to appreciate the possibility of complete supersession (Burnham, 1945). Contemporary approaches, however, are less sweeping. That is true, for instance, of Heisler's 'European Polity' model which, as the term implies, is concerned with structures and processes rather than with particular policy areas. The core of that model is based on a presumed switch in emphasis from the input side towards the 'withinputs' of the governmental decision-making system as well as towards the effects of that decision making: '... "withinputs" in general and structurally induced phenomena in particular may be more important influences in determining the contents, timing, form and intensity of outputs (including the patterns of legitimacy through which the outputs will be presented to the political society) than are environmental inputs.' (Heisler, 1974:36). Thus Heisler's account principally sees a change of the way in which party government operates rather than an explicit weakening of the party element of government. There is, however, an important shift in the balance between party-electoral and governing orientations in favour of the latter, as the inputs to the system are weakened and party activity (demand aggregation and mobilisation) become less salient to party government. Instead, the co-optative mode, directed from the governing side, strengthens the alternative link with society by harnessing and co-opting a diversity of interests, as well as using that link to enhance its legitimacy. Whilst the European Polity model avoids presenting a drastic erosion of the foundations of party government, the disjunction appearing between the two orientations of the parties points to a form of supersession affecting the competitive arena, implicitly relegating it to a dignified status.

The European Polity model is of general application in the sense that it is non-specific with regard to the kinds of societal interest that may be co-opted. In that respect it differs from theories of neo-corporatism which largely concentrate on the economic sphere, although it does not appear to be a necessary restriction on their application. However, the fact that neo-corporatist arguments are largely based on the structuring of economic interests underlines the earlier caveat concerning supersession, namely that there need be no overriding pressure to modify party government in non-related policy areas.

Although there are many variations on the neo-corporatist theme — the triangular relationship of organised business interests, trade unions, and the state — Gerhard Lehmbruch's specification of what he terms the 'fully corporatised polity' represents a fair summary of the major characteristics (Lehmbruch, 1982: 5–6):

- Interest organisations are strongly co-opted into governmental decision making.
- Large interest organisations are strongly linked to political parties and take part in policy formation in a sort of functional division of labour.
- Most interest organisations are hierarchically structured, and membership tends to be compulsory.
- Occupational categories are represented by non-competitive organisations enjoying a monopoly.
- Industrial relations are characterised by strong 'concertation' of labour unions and employers' organisations with government.

At least in Lehmbruch's account, advanced neo-corporatist systems do not point to the obsolesence of party government: interest organisations are 'strongly co-opted' into the decision-making process as well as being 'strongly linked' to the parties, but those connections do not necessarily rob the parties of their primacy, and they may be in a much better position to exercise their authotity by coordination and control than if organised interests are excluded from decision making and operate independently. One rendering of the position in a corporatised polity is to postulate an agreed division of labour and a more or less harmonious relationship between party government and organised interests. Indeed, elsewhere Lehmbruch maintained that: 'Neo-Corporatism in general is not conceived as an alternative to parliamentary democracy but instead (as) a sort of symbiosis with the party system which may take varying forms.' (Lehmbruch, 1977).

Yet is that version of a companionable 'living together' entirely convincing? It may be the case that neo-corporatism does not offer a sharp alternative to parliamentary democracy or parliamentary government, but its values are nevertheless deeply opposed to the pluralist ones on which competitive party systems are based. That is at once evident from the terms used to describe the neo-corporatist polity: the hierarchical structuring of interest organisations, compulsory membership, non-competitive organisations enjoying monopoly power, even for that matter the concertation of interests. A symbiotic relationship could only remain secure from disturbing tensions as long as the particular features of the two value systems were kept to separate domains. Yet, in fact, it is precisely their flourishing inter-connectedness which is held to be a leading characteristic of the neo-corporatist polity.

A conclusion that neo-corporatist arrangements within a system of party government do not point to a stable equilibrium means that the possibility of an eventual supersession of party government cannot be ruled out. Alternatively, one can say that the tensions implicit in the opposition of two value systems, pluralism and neo-corporatism, give rise to a dynamic relationship and thus to a continuous process of adaptation in party government — and that could equally well lead away from supersession as towards it.

That line of argument is strengthened in considering the nature of corporatist structures themselves, that is, those aspects which do not directly impinge on party government but refer to the internal ordering and arrangements of interest-group intermediation. Philippe Schmitter has pointed to a number of problems which may adversely affect the practice of neo-corporatism (Schmitter, 1982: 266—77). Thus neo-corporatism may be what he calls a 'fair-weather product', initially stimulated by favourable economic circumstances. If those conditions should change to a period of prolonged stagnation and even decline, then the internal tensions could become acute. Even though Schmitter himself takes the view that corporatist structures are likely to prove more resilient than pluralist ones in adverse conditions, weaknesses are apparent. If neo-corporatism blossoms when there is a secure surplus available for distribution to the participants, the advent of scarcity reveals the conflicts of interest, and the imbalances in the structure of power become apparent. This asymmetry, as Schmitter terms it, is inherent in the nature of the corporatist system; in times of scarcity it makes the distribution of benefits a divisive influence, and 'revolts' can occur on several fronts.

One source of disaffection is the interests which are excluded from or under-represented in the existing system of intermediation; in periods of economic surplus and growth, inequality and inequity will not bear so heavily on them. Another may stem from the membership base of participating organisations, trade unions or business interests; in a period of economic stringency, the leadership has difficulties in enforcing compliance, thus placing strains on the system, geared as it is to managing an elite consensus and avoiding the destabilising effects of membership or mass participation. A third source of revolt can, somewhat paradoxically, be located in those groups which in principle and anyway at the outset stood to gain most from neo-corporatist management. Thus Schmitter points out that they permanently lose their freedom of action — taking the restrictions on the rights of private property as a consequence of the introduction of co-determination as a leading example. The burden of such commitments will not have been evident in the favourable economic climate when they were first established.

None of these negative indications need become decisive for the future of neo-corporatism, but when added to the latent tensions existing between it and party government, there is clearly no convincing reason to accept the idea of a creeping corporatism ousting party government or even that an equilibrium should obtain. Indeed, the way has to be left open for a reversion to party control even where its predominance has been considerably eroded. If neo-corporatism only papers over the cracks of societal cleavage, then we should expect to see a resurrection of party conflict at certain critical junctures, possibly involving a renewal of ideological debate as well. Whatever the eventual outcome for party government might be in those circumstances, just as much uncertainty would surround the future of neo-corporatism.

VIII. Dimensions of Party Government

It is appropriate at this point to draw together the main threads of the discussion so far. Consideration of the two basic concepts, albeit elusive ones, of survival and adaptation led to an examination of effectiveness as a guide to the survival power of party government and the application of the extent of party government as a measure of its adaptation. The assumption has been made that survival and adaptation can be considered separately from one another, so that a loss or gain in effectiveness need not affect the extent of party government, nor need changes in the latter alter effectiveness. Treated in that way, the two dimensions show a range of variations in party government, as represented in Figure 1.

That representation appears to be satisfactory until the problems of assessment are encountered. Thus, as has been argued, if effectiveness is rendered in terms of successful problem solving there are difficulties in establishing criteria for success as there are in definition, and it is by no

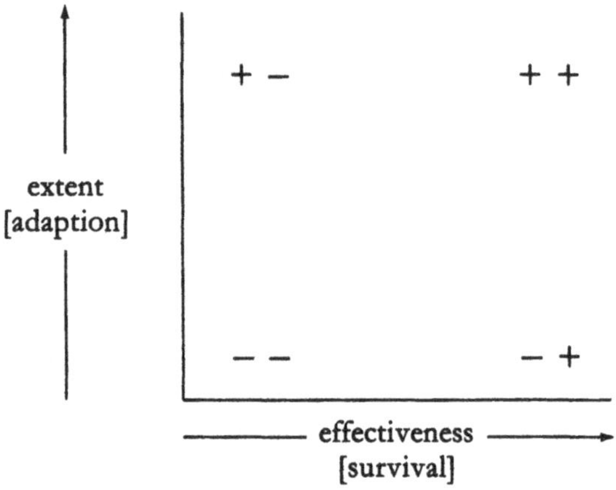

Figure 1. *Dimensions of Party Government*

means certain that solving should be taken as the sole beneficial outcome in meeting problems. Judgements about the extent of party government seem to be less ambiguous, but it is equally hazardous to plump for one central measure. That is not immediately obvious perhaps because of the terminology adopted – the idea of party government as a 'continuum'. Although that usage is helpful in showing the extension of party government beyond the restrictive bounds of a specifically governmental focus, the fact that there are two distinctive facets of party activity involved, governing and electoral, means that a reference to precise 'levels' of party government would be arbitary.

From these objections, it follows that attempts at 'mapping' in the sense of plotting coordinates on the axes of effectiveness and extent would be doubly open to question. If the idea of a 'framework' is to be retained, then the most to be expected is a broad presentation of party government patterns, a preliminary to exact analysis which can properly take into account the variety of sub-permutations which can be applied to particular systems of party government.

It is also evident that the wide degree of variation given by the framework both in terms of effectiveness and extent goes well beyond what could reasonably be encompassed within the appellation of 'party government' and that there is ample room to include its successors. But where? This problem of location has already been raised, namely the difficulty of establishing where supersession can be said to have occurred. Similarly, one would expect party government to be supplanted well before its effectiveness had become negligible, but again it is not feasible to say at what stage supplantation would take place. Moreover, if the aim is to show the patterns of party government and its 'successors', then some specification is required of the major clusters of attributes.

IX. Party Government and its Successors

By making use of the two dimensions of party government as well as incorporating the terminating stages of supersession and supplantation, a number of distinctive 'types' are discernible especially in taking the more extreme positions. As shown in Figure 2, four such clusters emerge combining varying degrees of effectiveness and extent, largely using the descriptions already introduced.

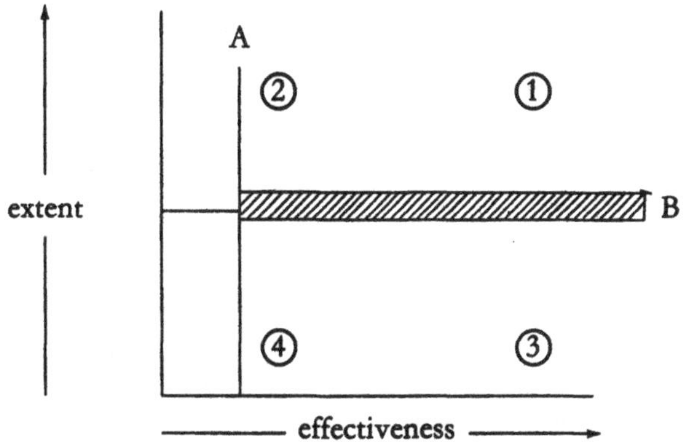

A = line of supplantation
B = zone of supersession

1 = strong party government
2 = immobilist system
3 = super corporatism
4 = corporalist asymmetry

Figure 2. *Party Government and Successor Types*

The line A (= Supplantation) and the zone B (= Supersession) have to be arbitrarily placed, since the extinction of the prevailing form of government might take place anywhere within a range of effectiveness (for supplantation) or extent (for supersession). But a regime would be in jeopardy long before its effectiveness had declined to nil, and the fact that vestiges of party government remain would not point to its continuation in a diluted form. Whilst supplantation can be represented by a single line, denoting the breakdown of party government perhaps through the usurpation of power, supersession involves a zone of transition signifying a probably gradual transformation taking place. Within and astride the line of supplantation and the zone of supersession respectively, the four patterns stand out, whatever particular labels are attached to them.

The grounds for using the term 'strong party government' are self-evident, given the combination of high party presence and effectiveness in government. That is not to say that its strength resides in meeting a narrow set of specifications; on the contrary it has to be treated as a widely elastic category, bearing in mind the permutations of 'extent' and the ambiguities of effectiveness.

Nor does the historical picture confirm a narrow view. Whilst the British form of party and parliamentary government was often held up as a kind of model, in practice few countries followed the example in all particulars. That applies especially to the nature and operation of party systems, whether considered from an electoral or governing viewpoint. The classic, British-type of two-party system has rarely been in evidence elsewhere, and the varieties of multi-partism affect the whole operation of party government, in the manner of socio-political mediation as in the style of coalition decision making. To take one example, the so-called consociational democracies can reproduce the features of strong party government, but in a way which is at variance with an associational view of the political system (Lijphart, 1977).

There is a further way in which the evolution of British party government was atypical, in the early establishment of what has been described as a 'constitutional bureaucracy' (Parris, 1969). Because of its permanence and its ability to serve loyally the government of the day, the bureaucracy compensated for the discontinuities of frequent government alternation. To explain that development, one has to refer to the factors in Britain which facilitated the supremacy of the parties, especially their timing. From its modern beginnings, the British civil service was treated as below the parties, whilst in continental Europe the bureaucracy was above them (Daalder, 1966). The continuing emphasis on political neutrality and subordination to the party in office meant that there has been a successful resistance to the politicisation of the bureaucracy. That British refinement of party government was not followed for a number of reasons of which the terms of early constitutional development was only one, but a general contrary tendency was evident: party politisation of the bureaucracy was seen as a natural extension of party government, even as a necessary condition of party paramountcy.[6] Clearly, there is much room for debate as to whether one mode or the other results in stronger party government — in the sense that the parties have better control over the determination and execution of policy — but it is evident that there can be no one model in this respect (Freddi, *supra*), and it is after all a key area in forming a total assessment of party government for any country.

If there is a central model of strong party government, it is likely to vary from one country to another and to be an amalgam of ideal features and an idealised past — the preservation of a golden age when the parties first won their victories. That may be an unrealistic view and it may also

[6] Thus the secure establishment of the 'party state' in Western Germany can be seen as dependent on party control over the state elites. (Dyson, 1977)

lead to unrealistic expectations of party government, with the consequence that its effectiveness is continually put in question.

Just as it is impossible to work with a single version of strong party government, so must its counterpart in immobilism be treated as a differentiated grouping, even though the particular combination of low effectiveness and high extent of party government is a defining characteristic. A typical immobilist system shows entrenched party-oriented structures incapable of solving basic issues at the same time as they themselves are resistant to change. It is in conditions of prolonged immobilism that demands are made for the overhaul of the existing system, involving drastic reforms of the institutional structure aimed, among other things, at creating a more 'responsible' party system. One type of reform seeks to restore party government to its former, more effective position. The other attempts to secure more effective government, but to do so it requires a diminution of the party element in government. Broadly, the contrast between the two can be expressed by saying that the former represents an adaptation favouring party government, while the latter does not. The point to be emphasised, however, is that the type of adaptation adopted, or at least promoted, helps to distinguish between immobilist systems, since the remedies will be based on a diagnosis of the ills.[7]

Yet one of the qualities of immobilism is that it may prove resistant to both types of reform; adaptive change in either direction may prove impossible to implement because of the deadlock of particular party interests: even though all may concede the desirability of reform in general, one or other will be seen to benefit more from any specific reform. Immobilism thus implies a peculiar 'locking in' of the system, a position that may continue indefinitely. Even here, under conditions of strong immobilism, it is necessary to make a distinction between those systems of party government which fail and those that do not. For the latter, one explanation has already been advanced: there is no single scale of effectiveness, and apparently low effectiveness in the eyes of observers – or even in the judgement of participants – may be based on wrong or at least insufficient criteria. The question then arises as to whether we are truly referring to a case of immobilism or not.

Much more straightforward will appear to be the case of 'failed immobilism', that is, where supplantation has occurred or is seen as an inevitable outcome. The scenario of failure gains in credibility because of the long list of party governments that have failed in the past. But are the precedents properly relevant? There is a vast difference between past and present eras in the degree of 'maturity' attained by party government.

[7] A good example of a preoccupation with institutional reform in an immobilist system is provided by Italy. Stefano Bartolini (Bartolini, 1982) has made an analysis couched in terms similar to those used here.

Failures in the past most frequently occurred in situations where the parties had not yet reached a position of unquestioned supremacy and important sections of the population did not accept the legitimacy of party democracy. A withdrawal of support at a later stage, an alienation from party government, need not be so devastating in its consequence since the parties will have become securely anchored in all parts of the political system. If party government does face the perils of immobilism in the contemporary era, then they should be seen as having a new point of departure, not yet the decay of old age perhaps, but the course taken will not be a simple re-staging of past debacles. Indeed, the meanings of supplantation and overthrow, if they occur, may have to be liberally interpreted in order to allow for a weak form of discontinuity, a short hiatus in party government, a period during which the terms of its re-establishment are decided, rather than making its return impossible. One of the few recent examples of party government failure, the collapse of the Fourth French Republic, fits the description of 'weak discontinuity', and the gradual reassertion of the parties in the Fifth Republic within the new constitutional format is indicative of their resilience.

In concentrating on the strong and the immobilist forms of party government, the much more representative middle ground between them – the area of moderate effectiveness – may appear to lack distinctive features. But it is here possibly that tendencies towards the erosion of party government may be most pronounced. Immobilism is likely to prevent adaptation, and the pressures to adapt will be absent if effectiveness is high. If the middle ground of party government is the norm for most countries, then susceptibility to erosive adaptation is fairly general. But its direction and form are uncertain, and whilst history is littered with examples of outright failure of party government, even though their contemporary relevance may be questioned, the possibility of supersession involves surveying uncharted territory.

Objection may rightly be taken to a portrayal of the succession to party government solely in terms of corporatism, as displayed in Figure 2 above. That procedure has the effect of pre-empting the discussion and shutting out consideration of other erosive forces. Thus, it might be argued, an equally potent source of erosion comes from the attack on the representative elitism inherent in party government and from the demands for a fully participatory democracy. If party government were to adapt to those pressures (rather than being overthrown by them), the picture of supersession would appear radically different from that effected by corporatism, principally in that the policy-making arenas would become widely dispersed as also, presumably, would decision-taking centres and the administrative apparatus of government. All that, of course, in the context of supersession supposes the retention of party government, but increasingly as an empty shell.[8]

[8] Whether it is feasible to think of an 'alternative democracy' arising within the framework of party government is naturally open to doubt. Earlier versions, such as

It has to be conceded that there is no one way of interpreting the nature of supersession. Nonetheless, the grounds for taking neo-corporatism are persuasive. In the first place, the emphasis it puts on economic relationships isolates a basic factor in political development. Secondly, it draws attention to the fact that a pre-occupation with European pluralist traditions neglects the non-pluralistic ones which still persist, even though often submerged (Bendix, 1964; Schmitter, 1974). Corporatism is not a latter-day invention, and it should not be treated simply as an artefact of state intervention: fundamentally it depends on the outlook and structuring of society. Thirdly, as already indicated, corporatism presupposes a coherent set of values and thus a *Weltanschauung* which offers a complete alternative to pluralism.

If the neo-corporatist succession to party government is adopted, a distinction has to be made between the circumstances of the transition to supersession and those of its completion. The 'zone of transition', as shown in Figure 2, may best be equated with the essentials of the 'corporatised polity' as set out by Lehmbruch. That may be acceptable because of Lehmbruch's interpretation of a co-existence obtaining with party government, but the expression should also be used to denote the possibility of continuing transition rather than equilibrium.

Below that zone of transition — that is, when supersession has indubitably taken place — the corporatised polity will have given way to an even stronger form for which the new title of 'super corporatism' may be appropriate, with its ineffective, asymmetrical counterpart appearing alongside. Whereas the corporatised polity must leave open the question of whether party government is still a reality, no doubts need exist about super corporatism. Admittedly, the residues of party government could be present, but the balance would have finally shifted in favour of the corporatist mode. A resolution of the tensions might occur through the corporatist polity itself surmounting a critical juncture, perhaps a crisis of asymmetry. But for the consolidation of super corporatism it would be necessary to evolve procedures and institutions which minimised the danger of the crisis recurring. To do so, super corporatism might have to extend its scope well beyond the economic and related spheres and move into the explicitly political realm. In turn, that would require super corporatism to supply a general direction and authority, and ultimately it would have to acquire a legitimacy of its own to replace that of party government.

What the basis of corporate legitimacy would be is an imponderable. There are two contrasting possibilities. One is that it would somehow latch

anarcho-syndicalism or even guild socialism, have to be seen as more-or-less abrupt departures rather than as co-existing forms. Much more difficult to assess is the compatibility of the new alternative politics with party government. To the extent that it seeks a transformation of party democracy, then — as possibly the case of the Greens in West Germany — it faces the problems of succumbing to the 'parliamentary embrace'.

on to the doctrines of the corporate state in justification. Even though neo-corporatist tendencies in modern, industrialised societies have no ideological thrust of their own and no connection with the advocates of the corporate state, there is nevertheless a potential correspondence between the structural implications of neo-corporatism and the organic view of society. The harmony is underlined by the incompatibility of both with the pluralist model.

The other possibility is that super corporatism would come to display a democratic potential. That may seem unlikely, but one has to consider the terms on which supersession came about, namely, the gradual erosion of party government. It could be the case that even though party government was losing its hold, the new form would have to adjust to the old conceptions if it were to become widely acceptable.[9] Moreover, the imbalances of corporatist asymmetry might have to be overcome by making quasi-democratic concessions. If development were on those lines, a fully 'incorporated' regime could conceivably become a pale imitation of party government. The circle would then have almost turned in full.

Such a view of a successor to party government inevitably raises questions. Could super corporatism acquire a legitimacy in its own right? Would such a system provide adequate political leadership? Could corporatist attempts to implant democratic practices be sustained? Finally, could corporatist values be transformed into pluralist ones? The inclination must be to answer these questions negatively. It is one thing to argue that there can be a co-existence between neo-corporatism and party government, together with the values on which competitive party systems are based, but quite another to see corporatism as being able to absorb those values into its own.[10] The negative judgement is that supersession — if it followed

[9] It is doubtful in this respect whether conventional and now largely discarded forms of functional representation would prove suitable. One possibility of democratic development within a neo-corporatist arrangement could take the form of the control of the 'wage-earner funds' in Sweden, based on the Meidner proposals for collective capital formation. (Meidner, 1978) As implemented by the Swedish Social Democrats, the wage-earner funds are administered regionally, and the regional boards — on which the trade unions are strongly represented — would at least in part be subject to popular election.

[10] How one finally judges the ability of corporatism to absorb liberal-democratic values depends to a large extent on the choice of the primary corporatist model, whether that of liberal/societal corporatism or the state/authoritarian version. Thus Martin argues that the latter lacks the essential characteristic of 'a genuine bargaining relationship' and further that, '... the affinity between the two corporatisms is, in a decisive sense, slighter than the affinity between liberal corporatism and pluralism.' (Martin, 1983:102) In the present context — the discussion of super corporatism — it would be wrong to extrapolate any 'affinity' in existing circumstances to a situation in which corporatist arrangements had a specific and dominant political role.

the corporatist path – necessarily entails not only the loss of party government, but also a fundamental reorientation in the structure and values of the societies affected.

X. Conclusion

A discussion of the nature of super corporatism is remote from current concerns and realities. For that reason it may be objected that an examination of the future of party government and its possible successors invites all kinds of unsupported speculation. Although that is a valid criticism, the case for deliberately taking a wide canvas to sketch possible development is not thereby weakened: it is important to treat party government in context, within an array of other types and with linkages to them, not just as a self-contained and discrete entity. Nor in taking that approach does it necessarily imply either that the supposed problems of party government point to a looming crisis or that developments have to lead away from party towards some other directing agency. It is true that the preceding account has at times been couched in those terms for the convenience of advancing the arguments, but the reversibility of change and the need to avoid over-simple interpretations have been stressed.

Yet the basic difficulty that has had to be faced throughout this presentation is whether or not a broad framework can be soundly constructed. There may be no entirely satisfactory solution, for the more generously the total picture is envisaged, the more diffuse are the concepts that have to be employed. In turn that gives rise to all the consequent difficulties of attempting to translate them into lower-level equivalents. Even if that is satisfactorily accomplished, formidable problems arise in seeking to make the more specific measures operational and to give them an unambiguous rendering. Those hazards have become apparent in the preceding account: the initial choice of the rarefied concepts of survival and adaptation, the attempt to reduce them to the more manageable ones of effectiveness and extent, the ensuing problems of interpretation, the need to tread warily in nearing such matters as supplantation and supersession.

It is unlikely that completely acceptable solutions have been found at any stage of this analysis, and indeed that could be the outcome of any similar enterprise. Yet on some such basis the effort to see party government in a wider perspective has to be made if its future is to be discussed sensibly at all.

Bibliography

BAGEHOT, W. (1963) *The English Constitution*. London: Fontana, (Originally published in 1867).

BARNES, S., M. KAASE et al. (1979) *Political Action in Five Western Democracies*. Beverly Hill and London: Sage Publications.

BARTOLINI, S. (1982) "The Politics of Institutional Reform in Italy," 5 *West European Politics* 203 (July).

BARTOLINI, S. and P. MAIR (1982) "Report on a New Framework for the Analysis of Changes in Western European Party Systems." Paper presented at ECPR Joint Sessions, Aarhus (April).

BENDIX, R. (1964) *Nation-Building and Citizenship*. New York: Wiley.

BURNHAM, J. (1945) *The Managerial Revolution*. London: Penguin Books.

DAALDER, H. (1966) "Parties, Elites and Political Development in Western Europe," in J. La Palombara and M. Weiner (eds.), *Political Parties and Political Development in Western Europe*. Princeton, N.J.: Princeton University Press.

DYSON, K. (1977) *Party, State and Bureaucracy in Western Germany*. London: Sage Publications.

ECKSTEIN, H. (1971) *The Evaluation of Political Performance: Problems and Dimensions*. Beverly Hills and London: Sage Publications.

FLANAGAN, S. and R. DALTON (1984), "Parties under Stress: Realignment and Dealignment in Advanced Industrial Societies," 7 *West European Politics* 1 (January).

HEISLER, M. (1974) (ed.), *Politics in Europe: Structures and Processes in Some Post-Industrial Societies*. New York: David McKay.

KIRCHHEIMER, O. (1966), "The Transformation of the Western European Party Systems," in J. La Palombara and M. Weiner (eds.), *Political Parties and Political Development*. Princeton, N.J.: Princeton University Press.

LEHMBRUCH, G. (1977) "Liberal Corporatism and Party Government," 10 *Comparative Political Studies* 91 (April).

– (1982) in G. Lehmbruch and P. Schmitter (eds.), *Patterns of Corporatist Policy Making*. Beverly Hill and London: Sage Publications.

LIJPHART, A. (1977) *Democracy in Plural Societies*. New Haven: Yale University Press.

LINZ, J. and A. STEPAN (eds.) (1978) *The Breakdown of Democratic Regimes*. Baltimore: Johns Hopkins University Press.

MACPHERSON, C. (1966) *The Real World of Democracy*. London: Oxford University Press.

MAGUIRE, M. (1983) "Is There Still Persistence? Electoral Change in Western Europe, 1948–1979," in H. Daalder and P. Mair (eds.), *Western European Party Systems: Continuity and Change*. Beverly Hills and London: Sage Publications.

MARTIN, R. (1983) "Pluralism and the New Corporatism," 31 *Political Studies* 86.

MEIDNER, R. (1978) *Employee Investment Funds: An Approach to Collective Capital Formation*. London: Allen and Unwin.

PANITCH, L. (1980) "Recent Theorisations of Corporatism: Reflections on a Growth Industry," 31 *British Journal of Sociology*.

PARRIS, H. (1969) *Constitutional Bureaucracy*. London: Allen and Unwin.

PEDERSEN, M. (1983) "Changing Patterns of Electoral Volatility in European Party Systems, 1948–1977: Explorations in Explanation," in H. Daalder and P. Mair (eds.), *Western European Party Systems: Continuity and Change*. London: Sage Publications.

PIRAGES, D. (1976) *Managing Political Conflict*. London: Nelson.

ROSE, R. (ed.) (1980) *Challenge to Governance: Studies in Overloaded Politics*. Beverly Hills and London: Sage Publications.

Rose, R. (1976) *The Problem of Party Government.* London: Penguin Books.
– (1977) *Governing and Ungovernability: A Sceptical Inquiry.* Glasgow: University of Strathclyde.
– (1979) "Ungovernability; Is There Fire Behind the Smoke?" 27 *Political Studies.*
Rosenau, J. (1981) *The Study of Political Adaptation.* London: Frances Pinter.
Schattschneider, E. (1960) *The Semi-Sovereign People: A Realist's View of Democracy.* New York: Holt, Rinehart and Winston.
Schmitter, P. (1974) "Still the Century of Corporatism?" 36 *Review of Politics* 85.
– (1981) "Interest Intermediation and Regime Governability in Contemporary Western Europe and North America," in S. Berger (ed.), *Organizing Interests in Western Europe.* Cambridge: Cambridge University Press.
– (1982) "Reflections on Where the Theory of Neo-Corporatism Has Gone and Where the Praxis of Neo-Corporatism May Be Going," in G. Lehmbruch and P. Schmitter (eds.), *Patterns of Corporatist Policy Making.* Beverly Hills and London: Sage Publications.
Schmitter, P. and G. Lehmbruch (eds.) (1979) *Trends Towards Corporatist Intermediation.* Beverly Hills and London: Sage Publications.
Sjöblom, G. (1981) "Notes on the Notion of Party Adaptation." Presented at ECPR Joint Sessions, Lancaster (April).
– (1982) "'Problems' and 'Problem Solutions' in Politics." Presented at ECPR Joint Sessions, Aarhus (April).
Smith, G. (1979) "Western European Party Systems: On the Trail of Typology," 2 *West European Politics* 128 (January).

Name Index

Subject Index

Bei Fragen zur Produktsicherheit wenden Sie sich bitte an:
If you have any questions regarding product safety,
please contact:

Walter de Gruyter GmbH
Genthiner Straße 13
10785 Berlin
productsafety@degruyterbrill.com